THE
BEST
AMERICAN
POETRY
1991

◊ ◊ ◊

OTHER VOLUMES IN THIS SERIES

THE
BEST
AMERICAN
POETRY
1991

◊   ◊   ◊

Mark Strand, Editor

David Lehman, Series Editor

COLLIER BOOKS

MACMILLAN PUBLISHING COMPANY

NEW YORK

MAXWELL MACMILLAN CANADA

TORONTO

MAXWELL MACMILLAN INTERNATIONAL

NEW YORK • OXFORD • SINGAPORE • SYDNEY

Collier Books
Macmillan Publishing Company
866 Third Avenue
New York, NY 10022

Maxwell Macmillan Canada, Inc.
1200 Eglinton Avenue East
Suite 200
Don Mills, Ontario M3C 3N1

Macmillan Publishing Company is part
of the Maxwell Communication Group of Companies.

ISBN 0-02-069844-5

ISSN 0-1040-5763

Macmillan books are available at special discounts for bulk purchases
for sales promotions, premiums, fund-raising, or educational use.
For details, contact:
Special Sales Director
Macmillan Publishing Company
866 Third Avenue
New York, NY 10022

First Collier Books Edition 1991

10 9 8 7 6 5 4

Printed in the United States of America

CONTENTS

David Lehman was born in New York City in 1948. He has pub-
lished two collections of poetry, *Operation Memory* (1990), and *An
Alternative to Speech* (1986), both from Princeton University Press.
His other books include *Signs of the Times: Deconstruction and the
Fall of Paul de Man* (Poseidon Press, 1991) and *The Perfect Murder*
(The Free Press, 1989). He has received fellowships from the
Guggenheim Foundation, the Ingram Merrill Foundation, and the
National Endowment for the Arts. In 1990 he received an award
in literature from the American Academy and Institute of Arts and
Letters.

FOREWORD

by David Lehman

◊   ◊   ◊

Conventional wisdom has it that most of the poetry written in an era is fated to be minor. In the cosmic view of things, this proposition seems self-evident. Judged by the standards of Shakespeare and Milton, how many contemporaries will strike future generations as major? Critics, whose job it is to make discriminations, are not the only ones who put poets in their place. The poets themselves do it unconsciously. It may help motivate us—some of us anyway—to adopt Hemingway's metaphor and imagine that we are getting into the ring with Rilke when we write our next poem. Reading, however, as lovers of poetry rather than as pugnacious aspirants to personal greatness, we are bound to be less severe in our judgment, more generous with our hearts. Reading for the pure pleasure of it, we find abundance.

Tracking the poetry published in the United States in any one year is an instructive experience. The first time you do it, you might begin with a cool skepticism. You can't imagine coming across seventy-five poems worthy of acclaim. What you realize soon enough is that it's a difficult task just to keep up with what's out there—there is so much of it, and so much of it is good. One constant in this anthology series is that each of the four guest editors to date has admired more works than could be included in even a capacious volume. The hardest part in the making of this book occurs in those late December days when five or ten or fifteen poems must finally be dropped from an ever-burgeoning manuscript. For the editors, the thrill of discovery may be the most pleasurable part of the enterprise. Thirty-six of the poets represented in *The Best American Poetry 1991* have appeared in none of the three previous volumes, eclectic though these were. A mere handful of names have turned up four years running.

Our rules are considerably less complicated than those that govern the writing of sestinas. Each year a distinguished poet, acting as guest editor, makes the selections from periodicals published in the preceding calendar year. No volume will contain fewer than fifty or more than seventy-five poems, and three poems are the maximum for an individual poet in any given year. The series editor assists the guest editor, in part by scanning magazines and making recommendations. Translations are ineligible; otherwise there are no restrictions as to form, subject matter, style, or idiom—and every reason to rejoice in the diversity that seems inevitably to emerge.

The reader of these pages will find sonnets and songs, elegies, verse essays, dramatic monologues, narratives. The subjects range from nature (woods and gardens, flowers and leaves) to second nature (myths, dreams, memories). The settings include a hospital ward, a beauty parlor, a playground, a lunch counter, the Metropolitan Opera, a country fair. Seemingly by accident some titles appear to pair off. A number of poems treat sexual themes with sensitivity and candor; two are entitled "Desire." Two poems that have "evidence" in their titles are narratives of an investigative character. Of the two sets of haiku, one is oriented in the traditional direction while the other features pop icons from the Hollywood hills. We have an acrostic, a cento, a villanelle, a self-described "entertainment," and an ad hoc form whose only rule is that each line must consist of five words. We also have a poem entitled "Cigarettes" by a poet named Ash.

Mark Strand, my choice to edit this year's anthology, is an experienced anthologist who put together an influential selection of *Contemporary American Poets* two decades ago. *The Best American Poetry* is designed to reflect the taste and values of the guest editor, and it is a pleasure to work with someone as definite in his judgments as is Mr. Strand. Moreover, he is highly respected by poets who transcend the usual sectarian boundaries, and he happens to be writing the finest poetry of his life. In 1990 he published *The Continuous Life*, a brilliant book. He was also appointed the nation's poet laureate, proving that not every government decision affecting the arts is wrong.

Mr. Strand and I decided to enforce very strictly the rule limiting eligibility to poems that appeared in magazines in the year 1990. This seems a good place to salute those magazines—and the editors who are the unsung heroes and heroines of American letters. With sadness I note the passing of *The Yale Review* and with gladness the rumor that the administration of that university has reconsidered its decision to jettison the venerable journal, an exemplary model of a literary quarterly.

Another campus-based periodical, *Mississippi Review*, wrote to a number of poets recently asking us to comment on the allegation that contemporary poetry lacks "vision." It occurred to me that there may be some unwritten rule of lit-crit discourse that presumes an invisible but highly questionable link between the pulse of poetry on the one side and the agents of presidential power on the other. Seven or eight years ago, when the New Formalism was new, I remember seeing it smeared as "Reaganetics." Now, evidently, all of contemporary poetry has been accused of being Bush League—a victim of that "vision thing." On the face of it, the knock is absurd. Read the poems in this book in good faith and then tell me that our poets lack a power of vision commensurate with their mastery of invention and craft.

But discussion of the "vision thing" may produce some good if it causes us to take stock of our first premises and reexamine our practice in the light of our principles. W. H. Auden remarked that a young poet who liked tinkering with words had a better chance of getting somewhere than a young poet who wrote because he or she had something to say. I think that's true. But something further needs to be said. If verse without some kind of formal restraint is like playing tennis without a net, poetry that is short on statement conjures up an image out of the movie *Blow-Up*: tennis without the ball. The work on display in *The Best American Poetry 1991* demonstrates that an athletic metaphor is often very much to the point. These are poems of dexterity, speed, and power; of lyric grace under imaginative pressure.

Mark Strand was born of American parents in Prince Edward Island, Canada, in 1934. Educated at Antioch College, he received advanced degrees from Yale and the University of Iowa. His books of poetry include *Sleeping with One Eye Open* (1964), *Reasons for Moving* (1968), *Darker* (1970), *The Story of Our Lives* (1973), and *The Late Hour* (1978). A volume of his *Selected Poems* was published by Atheneum in 1980 and was reissued last year by Knopf along with his latest collection, *The Continuous Life*. He has also published short stories, translations from the Spanish and the Portuguese, and a study of the painter William Bailey, and he is working on a monograph on Edward Hopper. A recent recipient of a MacArthur Fellowship, Mark Strand teaches at the University of Utah and lives with his wife and son in Salt Lake City. In 1990 he became the fourth poet laureate of the United States.

INTRODUCTION

by Mark Strand

◇   ◇   ◇

1.

It is 1957. I am home on vacation from art school, sitting across from my mother in the living room. We are talking about my future. My mother feels I have picked a difficult profession. I will have to struggle in obscurity, and it may be years and years before I am recognized; even then there is no guarantee that I will be able to make a living or support a family. She thinks it would be wiser for me to become a lawyer or a doctor. It is then that I tell her that although I have just begun art school, I am actually more interested in poetry. "But then you'll *never* be able to earn a living," she says. My mother is concerned that I shall suffer needlessly. I tell her that the pleasures to be gotten from poetry far exceed those that come with wealth or stability. I offer to read her some of my favorite poems by Wallace Stevens. I begin "The Idea of Order at Key West." In a few minutes my mother's eyes are closed and her head leans to one side. She is asleep in her chair.

2.

I do not intend to make fun of my mother. Her failure to respond as I had wished was actually the failing of most people. Hearing poems read, like reading them, is different from other encounters with language. Nothing else we read prepares us for poetry. My mother was a reader of novels and books of general nonfiction. Her responses to what she read were, I believe, knowing and well articulated. But how is poetry different from what she was used to? The difference that comes to mind first is that the context of a poem is likely to be only the poet's voice—a voice speaking to no one in particular and unsupported by a situation or situations brought about by the words or actions of others, as in a work of fiction. A sense of itself is what the poem sponsors, and not a sense of the world. It invents itself; its own necessity or urgency, its tone, its mixture of meaning and sound, are in the poet's voice. It is in such isolation that it engenders its authority. A novel, if it is to be believed, must share characteristics with the world we live in. Its people must act in ways we recognize as human, and do so in places and with objects that seem believable. We are better prepared for reading fiction because most of what it tells us is already known. In a poem, most of what is said is neither known nor unknown. The world of things or the world of experience that may have given rise to the poem usually fades into the background. It is as if the poem were replacing that world as a way of establishing its own primacy, oddly asserting itself over the world.

What is known in a poem is its language, that is, the words it uses. Yet those words seem different in a poem. Even the most familiar will seem strange. In a poem, each word, being equally important, exists in absolute focus, having a weight it rarely achieves in fiction. (Some notable exceptions can be found in the works of Joyce, Beckett, and Virginia Woolf.) Words in a novel are subordinate to broad slices of action or characterization that push the plot forward. In a poem, they *are* the action. That is why poems establish themselves right away—in a line or two—and why experienced readers of poetry can tell immediately if the poem they are reading possesses any authority. On the other hand, it would be hard to know much about a novel on the basis of its first sentence. We usually give it a dozen or so pages to earn its right to our attention. And, paradoxically, it has our attention when its language has all but disappeared into the events it generated. We are much more comfortable reading a novel when we don't feel distracted by its language. What we want while reading a novel is to get on with it. A poem works the opposite way. It encourages slowness, urges us to savor each word. It is in poetry that the power of language is most palpably felt. But in a culture that favors speed reading along with fast food, ten-second news bites, and other abbreviated forms of ingestion, who wants something that encourages a slowdown?

3.

The reading of nonfiction is no greater help than the reading of fiction in preparing one for poetry. Both my parents were avid readers of nonfiction, pursuing information not just for enlightenment but to feel in control of a world they had little say in. Their need for certainty was proportional to their sense of doubt. If one had facts—or what passed for facts—at one's fingertips, one could not only banish uncertainty but also entertain the illusion that one lived in a fixed and static universe, in a world that was passive and predictable and from which mystery was exiled. No wonder poetry was not something my parents found themselves reading for pleasure. It was the enemy. It would only remystify the world for them, cloud certainties with ambiguity, challenge their appetite for the sort of security that knowledge brings. For readers like my parents, poetry's flirtations with erasure, contingency, even nonsense, are tough to take. And what may be still tougher to take is that poetry, in its figurativeness, its rhythms, endorses a state of verbal suspension. Poetry is language performing at its most beguiling and seductive while being, at the same time, elusive, even seeming to mock one's desire for reduction, for plain and available order. It is not just that various meanings are preferable to a single dominant meaning; it may be that something beyond "meaning" is being communicated, something that originated not with the poet but in the first dim light of language, in some period of "beforeness." It may be, therefore, that reading poetry is often a search for the unknown, something that lies at the heart of experience but cannot be pointed out or described without being altered or diminished—something that nevertheless can be contained so that is it not so terrifying. It is not knowledge, at least not as I conceive knowledge, but rather some occasion for belief, some reason for assent, some avowal of being. It is not knowledge because it is never revealed. It is mysterious or opaque, and even as it invites the reader, it wards him off. This unknown can make him uncomfortable, force him to do things that would make it seem less strange;

and this usually means inventing a context in which to set it, something that counteracts the disembodiedness of the poem. As I have suggested, it may have to do with the origin of the poem—out of what dark habitation it emerged. The contexts we construct in our own defense may shed some light, may even explain parts or features of the poem, but they will never replace it in the wholeness of its utterance. Despite its power to enchant, the poem will always resist all but partial meanings.

4.

It could be that my mother, on that day in 1957, sensed this and felt that she was safer within the confines of her own darkness than within that supplied by Wallace Stevens. But not all poems try to remind us of the dark or the unknown at the heart of our experience. Some try not to, choosing to speak of what is known, of common experiences in which our humanness is most powerfully felt, experiences that we share with those who lived hundreds of years ago. It is a difficult task—to speak through the poetic and linguistic conventions of a particular time about that which seems not to have changed. Each poem must, to a certain extent, speak for itself, for its own newness—its ties to and distortions of the conventions of the moment. It must make us believe that what we are reading belongs to us even though we know that what it tells us is really old. This is a form of deception that makes it possible for poetry to escape the commonplace. It is when the conventions of another time, which have been worked and reworked, are used again that we have banality—those worn-out, sentimental verses, say, that are the stuff of Hallmark cards. And yet, it is precisely through those conventions that we recognize poetry to be poetry. By using old figures, recombining them, altering them slightly, by using meters, by reemploying rhyme schemes and stanzaic patterns, fitting them to contemporary speech, its syntax, its idioms, poems pay homage to the poems that preceded them. And this is something that someone unfamiliar with poetry may not know, and on hearing or reading a poem will not catch. This is the secret life of poetry. It is always paying homage to the past, extending a tradition into the present. My mother, who was not a reader of poetry, could not possibly have been aware of this other life of the poem.

5.

It is 1965. My mother has died. My first book of poems has been published. My father, who, like my mother, has never been a reader of poems, reads my book. I am moved. The image of my father pondering what I have written fills me with unutterable joy. He wants to talk to me about the poems, but it is hard for him to begin. Finally, he starts. He finds some of the poems confusing and would like me to clarify them. He finds others perfectly clear and is eager to let me know how much they mean to him. The ones that mean most are those that speak for his sense of loss following my mother's death. They seem to tell him what he knows but cannot say. Their power is almost magical. They tell him in so many words what he is feeling. They put him in touch with himself. He can read my poems—and I should say that they might have been anyone's poems—and be in possession of his loss instead of being possessed by it.

The way poetry has of setting our internal houses in order, of formalizing emotion difficult to articulate, is one of the reasons we still depend on it in moments of crisis and during those times when it is important that we know in so many words what we are going through. I am thinking of funerals in particular, but the same is true of marriages and birthdays. Without poetry we would have either silence or banality, the former leaving us to our own inadequate devices for experiencing illumination, the latter cheapening with generalization what we wished to have for ourselves alone, turning our experience into impoverishment, our sense of ourselves into embarrassment. Had my father lived longer, he might have become a reader of poetry. He had found a need for it—not just a need for my poetry but for the language of poetry, the special ways in which it makes sense. And now, even though it is years later, I sometimes think, when I am writing well, that my father would be pleased, and I think, too, that could she hear those lines, my mother would awaken from her brief nap and give me her approval.

THE
BEST
AMERICAN
POETRY
1991

◇ ◇ ◇

The Voice From Paxos

◇   ◇   ◇

Early in the first century, sometime during
the increasingly destructive reign of Tiberius,
a ship was making its way slowly up
the western coast of Greece for Italy.
Having just finished dinner, many of the passengers
were strolling around on deck, enjoying
another cup of wine, admiring the sunset
or the dark shoulders of Paxos, a small island of olive groves
that for a brief time separated the vessel
from the forbidding limestone headlands of Epirus.
The wind lessened, then ceased altogether.
The ship drifted. The trees near the shoreline
grew larger as they disappeared.
Suddenly a voice erupted from them, calling
the name of the Egyptian helmsman, unknown to all
but a few on board. "Thamus!" it shouted, and again,
"Thamus!" When it called a third time Thamus answered,
and the voice, louder still, as if in pain
or anger, no one afterward could figure out, now said,
"When you pass near Palodes let them know
the great god Pan is dead!"
Passengers and crew alike, puzzled
and suspicious, started arguing
about the significance of what they'd just heard,
some sure the voice should be obeyed,
some certain it was crazy to get involved
in what was clearly none of their business.

If he had a good wind, Thamus decided,
he'd sail past Palodes as usual,
but if he were becalmed, as they'd been a few minutes earlier,
he'd do the voice's bidding. Next morning
off Palodes, the sea was a breathless mirror.
He stepped to the rail, leaned out, and repeated the words exactly.
There was a rush of wind, and from the hazy coastline
came the sound of countless people crying out—
the sound a crowd makes when an acrobat slips fatally
from her partner's grasp, the sound of any multitude
unable to escape what it must recognize.

from *The New York Review of Books*

Evidence: From a Reporter's Notebook

◇ ◇ ◇

1

The city tosses and turns on the third rail
as the intern slams the clipboard on the desk.
He says, "We aren't finished with her yet."
"But Doc," I say, "maybe she's finished with you."
Schmoozing with an edge is what I call this.
He doesn't want the bruise of the six o'clock news
to blue-blacken his name by association.
He just wants someday to escape to a clinic
attached to a golf course
and drive his balls out
into the green bay it overlooks,
while back here, we all cook
in the same old grease
gone rancid from ceaseless poverty and crime.
"If I had a dime," he says, "if I had a dime . . ."
Then his voice trails off
and he stands and tries to swim
through the forty-foot waves
of three whole days and nights without sleep,
but each time, he's thrown back
on the hospital beach,
along with the dirty syringes, gauze,
and those who've drowned

in the contaminated water of their lives.
I say, "You know the hymn that goes,
'Some poor drowning, dying seaman
you may rescue, you may save'?"
"No," he shrugs, "it's more Charles Ives to me,
discord and disharmony
to go with all the inhumanity
that welcomes me each night
with open jaws and glistening teeth.
The victim, if she is one, is down the hall
and on the right. And this time, Maggie,
try to leave the way you came.
Don't make promises, or false claims of justice.
Let the lame stay lame,
don't set them dancing across the floor
in their own blood before they realize it."
"And what?" I say. "Go too far? But Doctor,
they're already there,
along with you and me, we need them,
they feed our superiority complexes.
You don't do Temple, I don't do Church,
but we've got faith, we're missionaries,
in search of some religion, some congregation
to place us in context,
even if it's someone else's.
And she *will* dance, as you and I will
and the TV viewers too,
to the fascinatin' rhythm of vaginal rape
and sodomization with a foreign object.
Hand me my tap shoes. I can't wait."

2

"You some reporter, right?" she says.
"It was a white man did this.
Said it is to show you niggers
who climbed from back of bus

to sit with us.
You nigger bitch, you get what you deserve,
and then he twist my arm behind me.
See the scratches, the splotches.
He drags me through some bushes and I got cuts.
You see 'em. You do.
He bit me too."
She tears at her skirt
and raises her knee, so I can see
high up her inner thigh,
too high, almost to knotted hair where underwear
of shiny fabric, nylon, I guess, begins.
"And when he finished with me," she says,
"he spit between my legs and rub it in."
I have learned not to wince
when such details are given;
still, I feel a slight
tightening of stomach muscles
before I make myself unclench
and do the true reporter thing,
which is to be the victim,
to relive with her again, again,
until it is my own night of degradation,
my own graduation from the shit to shit.
"Go on," she says, "write it down or somethin',
tape it, film it.
We got to hit him hard, hurt him. OK?"
"We will," I say, my smile in place now
like my hair, my friendship a brand-new dress
I wear until I wear it out or down,
but even as I take her hand extended to me,
so that we are banded together
in her stormy weather,
both without raincoats, umbrellas,
I flash on the report just read—
questionable rape, no tears, no bleeding there
or in the other place,
and bites that could be self-inflicted.

"Dirty sonofabitch," I say,
"is this United States of Revenge, or what?
We've got everything we need, got television,
and I have got your story
before the competition."

3

Six straight days, she's front-page news.
She makes guest appearances by dozens.
Everybody's cousin wants their piece
of tender meat,
but I've already eaten there
and I'm still hungry.
I'm suffocating too and I need air,
I need a long vacation from myself
and from my protégée
in all the ways manipulation pays,
when you play off the outrage
and the sympathy of others.
And she's a natural, she was born to do it,
should have her own byline in *New York Times*,
and I should have a Watergate,
should get my chance for Pulitzer glory,
but even Woodward faded like a paper rose
once he got his story.
I mean, you've got to know when to let it ride
and let it go, or else you wind up
some side show in Hackensack, or Tupelo.
You see, I couldn't prove that she was lying
and I couldn't prove she wasn't,
but that doesn't mean I abandoned her.
I swear the story led me somewhere else,
to the truth,
whatever that is, an excuse, I know, but valid.
Reality is a fruit salad anyway.
You take one bite, another, all those flavors,

which one is right?
She chose the role of victim
and for a while, I went along,
until tonight, when I look out
my window over Central Park
and think of other women whimpering
and bleeding in the darkness,
an infinity of suffering and abuse
to choose my next big winner from.
What I do, I take my own advice.
I whip my horse across the finish line
before I shoot it.
I step over her body
while the black sun rises behind me,
smoking like an old pistol.
The unofficial rules of this game
are that once found out,
you aim your tear-stained face into the camera.
You make your disgrace, your shame, work for you.
They don't burn bitches anymore,
they greet them at the back door with corsages
and slide them out the front into a reed basket
to float down the Nile, repentance,
into the arms of all us Little Egypts.
Welcome back.

4

My latest eyewitness news report,
focused on false accusations,
took as a prime example
my own delectable sample of the sport.
Even Warhol would have been proud,
would have remained in awe
long enough to list her name in his diaries,
might have understood her appetite,
have gained insight into her need,

though even her staunchest supporters
cannot explain away all contradictions,
all claims of violation that don't add up.
But really, if they only knew, in spite of that,
the lens through which we view the truth
is often cracked and filthy with the facts.
It could have happened. That is the bridge
that links the world of Kafka to us still,
the black pearl in pig's mouth
that won't be blasted out no matter what we do,
that finds us both on Oprah
or on Donahue, facing the packed pews
of the damned and the saved,
to send our innocence,
our guilt, across the crowded airwaves
to be filtered through
the ultimate democracy of TV,
which equalizes everything it sees
and freezes us to the screen between commercials
for movies of the week and shaving cream,
each show a rehearsal for the afternoon
when with a cry
she spreads her chocolate thighs
while I kneel down to look,
but still I find no evidence
of racist's or even boyfriend's semen.
I press my fingers hard against her,
then hold them up before the audience,
wet only with the thick spit of my betrayal.

from *Pequod*

DICK ALLEN

Talking with Poets

◊ ◊ ◊

Gossip is most of it, a barrier of thorns and small berries
Cultivated to disguise a wall,
False entrances and gates with shallow courtyards behind them,
And sometimes a few gypsies slowly dancing in firelight
Or swinging pails as they take a path down through the forest
To an old mossy well. Small heaps of masks,
And costumes with puffy sleeves or threadbare blouses
Lie beside the moat, are rummaged through
As often as not. But the poets seldom talk
Of forays they've taken; although they are always riding
In and out, mounting or dismounting, holding
The traces, wiping their brows and calling
For strong drink and friends, their verbal reports
Are sketchy, reluctant. No, they would rather laugh
Than speak of high rooms and the maiden's cot,
Books on stone shelves, what shackled prisoners
They may have been shown. . . . Yet if all this sounds
Too romantic, consider the cop coming home
To his house in the suburbs, how he pretends
There are no city streets until he walks their shadows;
Or the bored-to-death businessman,
The void he plunges daily, rising out of it
Like a circling, wounded hawk, blood under his nails
And in his throat, seeking Lethe
In television comedies or children's homework grades;
Or the doctor who vanishes
Into a nightmare of tumors, splintered bones,

The cardiographic line of a dead horizon,
CAT scans and mottled skin, before she finds herself
Whispering for the mercy of an airplane above layered clouds,
Flirtation, oblivion. . . . Still, if only the poets
Would cease in their talk of grants and reputation,
Reviews, or lack of them, readings, teaching loads,
Editors and enjambment, then on an autumn evening
When the wall is a looming thing of masonry,
Bulwarks and turrets, and a king walks by himself
Under limpid banners, how I would love to hear
(for I have read their books, and like you marveled),
Of the way they find Blue Sailors by a country road,
Wander in Sibelius, or how they've taught their lines
To study a landscape starting with morning sunlight
Coasting the grass. Talking with poets,
I could be enthralled by cries of Russian wolves,
The smell of vanilla flavoring in an open brown bottle,
What happens when they look at statesmen's eyes—
If only they were not so distrustful, so afraid, so exhausted,
So bent on saving themselves for the perfect man or woman
Who will listen to their voices in another time
More living to them now than these roses, these open palms.

from *The Hudson Review*

Bookmaking

◇ ◇ ◇

Words, let water from an unseen infinite Ocean
Come into this place as energy for the dying
and even the dead.

Rumi

At the Pierpont Morgan I go up and down
    the glass cases of the East Room,
studying bindings, toolings, papercutting,
    as if by learning your craft,
I will know you in the books exposed before me,
    the thick seams clasping
the packets together the way your hand will
    fold around my forearm,
your urgent fingers whitening my skin
    as if to bind us in a certain moment
of knowing; the pearled vellum lucent
    as lovemaking, the leather covers
pockmarked in a scarred masculine pattern
    as if we undressed hastily
and your jacket's rough tweed pressed
    against my leg as you bore down,
parting me, the way I've seen you take
    a book in both hands, parting
its thick wedge of pages to the exact passage
    you want me to read.
I go slowly over each display, accustoming myself
    to this new way of looking

at books: gold leaf, embossed crescents, Dove's bindings,
       Zaehendorf's aquamarine fancies:
I read each legend card carefully
       as if to know you better
without the distraction of your body
       beside my body,
the vocabulary of your craft still odd on my tongue
       like the taste of you at first,
an uncertain pleasure, the self posed between
       its celibate single-mindedness
and its being cracked open with the creaking give
       of a new binding in a book you've made.
I study them now—books I've known, abstractly,
       books we've both loved with a passion
almost of the body: *Leaves of Grass, The Marriage
       of Heaven and Hell, To the Lighthouse,*
changed utterly as I pass by, taking each one in,
       marveling. Now they have become objects:
physical shapes: the filigreed leaves closed
       into solid gold, the leather tooled
into splendid, intricate beds of flowers,
       the embossed medallion like the spiral
swirl of an ear the finger pleasures
       to follow. Now they have become
texts, tomes, volumes—books I would touch
       were they not encased in their carefully
monitored boxes for the generations to come.
       Now the words become flesh,
your body, my body, side by side in my small twin bed.
       I lean over, closer, clouding the glass
with my frank breath, wanting you,
       the idea of you no longer enough
to hold me until the next time we meet,
       the body keen to the hunger you have awakened.
I lean forward for the righting touch
       of the physical world: the dark warm
wood of the case gleaming with polish.
       Now, I am knowing my body,

late into its fourth decade in the passionate way
    you have known it: the great seam
of the spine centered in the jacket of the shoulders,
    the ligaments tooled on the plates
of the clavicles, the legible bones of the wrists
    and the ankles. And my breath comes
quickly for time seems suddenly short
    for all the knowing of the body
of the world, the touching all the body of the world,
    and the handing down to the generations to come
the world's body loved by our passionate arts.

from *Green Mountains Review*

JOHN ASH

Cigarettes

◇ ◇ ◇

Problems of translation are, perhaps, not so great
between languages, as between different versions
of the same language. Why, for example, does
"fag" mean homosexual in America, when,
in England, it means cigarette? Does this imply
that those who first observed the phenomenon
of smoking in the New World were homosexual?
This would cause some consternation on Columbus Day,
and, in all likelihood, the assumption is unjustified,
since Columbus and his crew were not English-speakers.
Yet, if we dismiss the idea of happy crowds of
homosexual Spanish or Italian mariners
returning to Europe with cigarettes in hand,
eager to introduce this new pleasure to their lovers,
we should perhaps concede that there is some connection
between the two ideas. It was Oscar Wilde, after all,
who described smoking as "the perfect pleasure, because"—
he opined—"it always leaves one unsatisfied."
It is clear from this that he was thinking of sexual pleasure,
of the working-class youths with whom he so recklessly dined
in fashionable restaurants of the eighteen nineties.
A cigarette is like a passion in that it is inhaled deeply
and seems to fill all the empty spaces of the body,
until, of course, it burns down, and is put out amid
the shells of pistachio nuts, or whatever trash
may be at hand, and the passion may leave traces
that in time will grow malignant: he who has taken pleasure

may die many years after in the room of an anonymous
hotel or hospital, under the blank gaze of a washstand,
a bad painting or an empty vase, having forgotten entirely
the moment that announced the commencement
of his dying. And perhaps he will not understand:
it is another false translation, like someone stumbling over
the word for cigarette in a new and intolerable language.

from *Mudfish*

Of Dreams and Dreaming

◇   ◇   ◇

Tell me more about that long street. Actually we're overextended;
time is running out. While still all things to all people we
are no longer swimming in the pool left by the sunrise. No, a
forest has resumed the strict narration. One puts gloves on
to ward off something. What is it? And living by a chair
so close to a thermometer no one can count it is business,
that is, it can't be put aside, and coming out to your guests,
to warn them, is the recreational side we love, that, and all
things, all producers of silence that let this hay
into the tunnel and came out the far side of sleep. Really,
your life is so fascinating. I don't get it. Neither do I—
I mean I was originally the fencing instructor here.
Now my head gets buried in the flour
of reading this translucent page as a vacuum mounts,
and so off to bed. Really it's too bad, though not calculated,
and can never be—Everests of tiny snow crystals would
have to be accounted for first, and that's not likely.

Meanwhile we live in the paperweight of swirling blizzards
and little toy buses painted vermilion like the sky
when it rises up reasonably to our defense in the half-hour
after sunrise or before sunset and likes to, it likes
the idea of museums. Then so much of us is fetched away.
Often you think you can see or even smell some part of it
before it too is put away, used and put away. But then these
so recent nights would be part of the elaborate past, that old
contraption, the one we were never sure about—

It is lively still, playing to packed houses.
What must the present-day analysts think, the ones who husk it
for what that's worth, then come to play games with us
as a consequence of their own dangerous behavior.
It was night over a mountain that seemed to be there, readily
and so useful we threw ourselves on the ground dank with animal
emotions and choked-out expletives: December first! The cocksucker
hasn't been around lately we see through gaps in the dead
or is it dormant vegetation. One of us has to go the whole way now:
shall we draw straws? Don't be ridiculous but don't look
either in the direction of the walrus, the caves of the sea
hold us, though we appear to you here on this simple street
asking so little. The third time it happened I thought I was seeing
it in a new light. Then the follow-up call came. Did I want it
delivered with the sheaves of my imagination, those other ones,
and if so what would I do with these lesions marking the enchanter's
space if he is off somewhere, bold song
if ever I sang one? Though this night I shall untune
the most insistent, entrenched breaths of purpose just so I say you
can come to me, an attack like those told of in time to
an insane purpose that is what we call history; then it will be no
            nearer
to a resolution, by God, I have to cry out if this mess is what is
left at my doorstep. In the future we'll
have no time for backbiting conversations like this one.
Differences will be put aside. Aye, and rainbows too, slugs
of narrative even the best of which could follow to what ends
in wild weeds, here at the wind. An' if my daughter
bring it over to you there'll be no less use for a mouse
found in your castle and turned out into blind day, the passion
some think comes at night. And we're all over you.

Suddenly it was my time. I don't know whither the watchman
vanished. He told us of the night, then vanished.
The stars are purring in the little Mississippi runoff of the
pure, bulging sky. Ours to consider, no doubt. And what if when
            we pay
it off, in full, it still runs toward us, too badgered to think

to mention what other tales might have been in store, only the last
    men
took them away. These were never seen again. My toothache is
    subsiding
but I won't I guess be the ultimate one, the who-by-definition-saves
what one is after, cornflower that obliges us by never appearing
in the sole instant it is wanted, but is somewhere behind that house,
no, that other one. Besides, when in doubt you can strike a match.

from *Grand Street*

Great Stone Face

◇   ◇   ◇

Perhaps something ought to be said about how deadpan
It all is, your experience as it is called, although
It seems you are its, really, rather than vice versa;
How for all your convulsive sobbing, laughter and pity,
It never sheds a tear or tips a wink, never betrays
Even the merest flicker of amusement.
It's hard making your mind up without any hints,
And someone should say something about how you feel
You are never quite getting the point, about how
Every time the bucket plunges deeper down the well
To haul up the subtle something glittering there,
A pause for thought arrives to cancel understanding,
Make nonsense of your efforts at an accurate account.
Of course, it's just such uncertainty that makes us
What we are, just this tremendous reserve in things
That leads us to expect an object of our curiosity
And sets us sifting the air of spring afternoons
In search of whatever it could be that brings
The astonishing crocus to life beneath our feet
And splashes forsythia about in fauvist strokes.
The distance it all keeps is what keeps you looking
(Through language, through landscape's irregular grammar)
For what it is that enthralls you so, what it is
That draws you forth to shiver like the flowering leaves,
And that will someday put you down, an exhausted thing,
Will cast you back upon some inscrutable conclusion,

Letting you drop out of a vast indifference, out
Of some private dissatisfaction, releasing you
One day in an uneasy response all its own.

from *Partisan Review*

JOSEPH BRODSKY

In Memory of My Father: Australia

◊ ◊ ◊

You arose—I dreamt so last night—and left for
Australia. The voice, with a triple echo,
ebbed and flowed, complaining about climate,
grime, that the deal with the flat is stymied,
pity it's not downtown, though near the ocean,
no elevator but the bathtub's indeed an option,
ankles keep swelling. "Looks like I've lost my slippers"
came through rapt yet clear via satellite.
And at once the receiver burst into howling "*Adelaida! Adelaida!*"—
into rattling and crackling, as if a shutter,
ripped off its hinges, were pounding the wall with inhuman power.

Still, better this than the silky powder
canned by the crematorium, than the voucher—
better these snatches of voice, this patchwork
monologue of a recluse trying to play a genie

for the first time since you formed a cloud above a chimney.

from *The New Yorker*

21

GERALD BURNS

Double Sonnet for Mickey

◊　◊　◊

In *Kiss Me Deadly* Cloris Leachman asks Mike Hammer in the car
　　Do
you read poetry? He doesn't even answer but just looks at her. The
　　plot
may be said to turn on a book of Christina Rossetti poems but to
me it is that pause, a careless sneer on Meeker's face as he not
only does not answer but sees no reason to get mad. She has no
　　right
to ask the question in the first place of a tough guy whose hair,
just longer than a brush cut, is stiffened by something bryllish that
　　might
ten years before have been brilliantine and he marine rather than air
force straight, chin tending to plumpness suggesting a tight military
　　collar
forsworn. His girlfriend whose chin likewise etcetera gets evidence
　　on johns
in ways not admirable. On the walls of his hideous apartment are
　　camera cases, statues and two-dollar
framed people, everyone's limbs pointlessly extended, plasticman
　　fixed for a decade in bronze,
none of this inadvertent. She asked him knowing he would look at
　　her as if a bad
smell in the car were hers and she, producing it, would know he
　　knew she had.
That look is not eternal. It is a product of the late fifties like *Bucket
　　of Blood,* rude look

at art, snapshot of The Thinker with your sweetheart on his lap and
      I prefer

another photo of one of its castings blown half apart by terrorists
      who took

monument for establishment, ecriture for prefecture (how do you
      deface an Anselm Kiefer,

already glued up with straw and so on?) It's probably the locution,
      a Rodin

that maddened them, one of an oeuvre, thing valued as one of a
      series of makings

but then it's also celebritous, like the Sphinx now falling to bits,
      another endangered Man

as Hammer is, in the film made because there first were novels
      about his undertakings

but then one doesn't recognize a Hammer from sketchiest drawing
      or collage

the way a sphinx or thinker's fair game for cartoon or cover art. A
      taste for him is more

like going to the fights, choosing to smell of something that goes
      with Gillette, massages

a jaw wider than its forehead and thinks of kicking in a green door

behind which shuttered Experience waits, twirling a trilby, trying
      on a smile

above the angled shoulders built up from folded gauze we thought,
      then, a masculine style.

from *Temblor*

A Whippoorwill in the Woods

◇ ◇ ◇

Night after night, it was very nearly enough,
they said, to drive you crazy: a whippoorwill
in the woods repeating itself like the stuck groove
of an LP with a defect, and no way possible
      of turning the thing off.

And night after night, they said, in the insomniac
small hours the whipsawing voice of obsession
would have come in closer, the way a sick
thing does when it's done for—or maybe the reason
      was nothing more melodramatic

than a night-flying congregation of moths, lured in
in their turn by house-glow, the strange heat
of it—imagine the nebular dangerousness, if one
were a moth, the dark pockmarked with beaks, the great
      dim shapes, the bright extinction—

if moths are indeed, after all, what a whippoorwill
favors. Who knows? Anyhow, from one point of view
insects are to be seen as an ailment, moths above all:
the filmed-over, innumerable nodes of spun-out tissue
      untidying the trees, the larval

spew of such hairy hordes, one wonders what use
they can be other than as a guarantee no bird
goes hungry. We're like that. The webbiness,
the gregariousness of the many are what we can't abide.
          We single out for notice

above all what's disjunct, the way birds are,
with their unhooked-up, cheekily anarchic
dartings and flashings, their uncalled-for color—
the indelible look of the rose-breasted grosbeak
          an aunt of mine, a noticer

of such things before the noticing had or needed
a name, drew my five-year-old attention up to, in
the green deeps of a maple. She never married,
believed her cat had learned to leave birds alone,
          and for years, node after node,

by lingering degrees she made way within for
what wasn't so much a thing as it was a system,
a webwork of error that throve until it killed her.
What is health? We must all die sometime.
          Whatever it is, out there

in the woods, that begins to seem like
a species of madness, we survive as we can:
the hooked-up, the humdrum, the brief, tragic
wonder of being at all. The whippoorwill out in
          the woods, for me, brought back

as by a relay, from a place at such a distance
no recollection now in place could reach so far,
the memory of a memory she told me of once:
of how her father, my grandfather, by whatever
          now unfathomable happenstance,

carried her (she might have been five) into the breathing night.
"Listen!" she said he'd said. "Did you hear it?
That was a whippoorwill." And she (and I) never forgot.

from *Boulevard*

Blue Lonely Dreams

◊ ◊ ◊

Hi Roy. Hope all is well;
just wanted to drop a line
to let you know we miss you.
Down here, sand is falling,
and it is slack and spare,
pleading in a whisper
that sweeps the leaves
into the drainage gutter,
and shrieks in a slow winded high note
that is not falsetto, but a voice
truly able to hit this note.

How goes the opera, upstairs?
Is it as good as touring the country
and singing for strangers
who care for you and your music?
Now the ghostly words
in the ghostly librettos
are ghosts themselves,
disguised as snowflakes
and floating in the air like a raft on the bayou,
distilled before reaching the ground.

We had tickets for the original
February date at The Beacon.
I had read an article about your induction
into The Rock and Roll Hall of Fame,

and was pleased to learn
that we were both born on April 23rd.
On the day of the concert,
the doctor said they would have to operate
on my mother's lung cancer.
She stayed with us that night,
insisting that we go to see you play.
I didn't know how I was going to get through it,
but I knew it would be best for everyone if we went.
When we reached the theater, the marquee read:
TONIGHT'S SHOW CANCELLED. I couldn't believe it:
the immediate feeling was one of voodoo,
or magic, or a shared faith.
It was like being forgiven
for a mistake you were allowed to make,
but hadn't made. The ushers at the door
told us that your throat was sore;
the voice you had loved from the first time
you heard it; the passion you had balanced
with a preacher man's stance.

On March 10th, two days
before the rescheduled concert,
my mother was given a clean bill of health.
Radiation treatments and chemotherapy
would not be needed.
The show you did on Saturday night
was another answered prayer,
and served as a reminder
why other prayers are better left unanswered.
By then, we considered you a good friend.
Who could grasp what depths
your voice was coming from?
It was as familiar and otherly
as a lone tree on a huge, rolling plain.
The walls of The Beacon were swaying,
and the red and white notes were birds
lifted into the cerulean air.

And here you are today,
on the cover of the new issue of *Rolling Stone*:
black glasses, black shirt and black hair.
Nice of you to drop by on this,
our last day at 51 West 68th Street.
I was just writing you a letter,
and was going to close by complaining
about how traumatic moving is.
By this time tomorrow,
we'll be living downtown.
I just finished reading your last interview.
Life's a bitch, but it's funny, ain't it?
I mean, with The Traveling Wilburys' collaboration,
and a new album of your own
set for February release,
along with a planned tour to support it,
and you up and die.

I guess no matter how many times it comes,
success is always a little too early or too late.
But in your wisdom, and in the short, full range
of your emotional wilderness,
you looked at it differently:
one must continue to do what one must do,
though meaning and purpose might seem to vanish
20,000 Leagues Under the Sea.
Time barks, the rooster crows,
and both beliefs resurface
with nothing having changed
and everything further revealed.

I've got a lot to learn
about taking things in stride,
but as you said, I'm not alone anymore,
only terribly lonely.
Once again, thanks for stopping by.
If there's anything we can do for you,
just holler. If I get the chance,

and wind up upstairs some day,
I look forward to hearing you sing
"Blue Lonely Dreams," that quintessential song
you spoke about writing in the interview.

Take care, Roy, be well. I hope the girl
who is coming to pack the cartons
is mysterious and beautiful.
After all, death is out there somewhere,
squaring its shoulders, dancing the bolero
and growling like a tiger
lying among the reeds;
but too much has happened already,
and though not enough is never more,
an image can ease the pain.
I feel more for the stray kitten at the doorstep
than I fear death. The pitch of the wind ripping
through the reeds is a crescendo rising
interminably above the previous crescendo.
At the window, the sunshine is making the leaves shine.
The doorbell breaks my concentration,
and I open the door and all my hopes are realized.
On a day when it feels good to be alive
in an apartment that will be empty tomorrow,
and already in thought, was once ours,
the girl says she's not allergic to dust
as I sneeze and rejoice in the bloodstained minutes
that fall upon the white ocean,
that sink below the blue sea.

from *The Paris Review*

ALFRED CORN

Infernal Regions and the Invisible Girl

◇   ◇   ◇

Frances Milton Trollope, the mother of the novelist, arrived in America with three of her children on Christmas Eve in 1827. She settled in Cincinnati, where, eventually, she built a "Bazaar." It was an emporium for fancy goods, the upper stories reserved for social and cultural events. On her return to England, Mrs. Trollope completed Domestic Manners of the Americans, *published in 1832 to acclaim in England and opprobrium in America. Mary Russell Mitford, novelist and dramatist, author of* Our Village, *was a friend and literary sponsor. The following conversation takes place between them at Harrow, after Mrs. Trollope's return, a time when it's possible to imagine her practicing aloud for her book.*

Had I the tenth part of your great descriptive
Powers, my dear Miss Mitford. . . . I do not,
Yet I am writing very diligently.
Three years' atrocious discommodity:
The nearest thing of course is Dante, nor
Do you imagine I mean the *Paradiso*.
Lasciar ogni speranza. . . . Yes, precisely.
I felt that I had come to River Styx:
Miasmal waters of the Mississippi,
And crocodiles, the horror, the horror of them!
How one pitied the wretched woodcutter
Who lives in their society on the shore,

Selling fuel to passing steamboats, half
Dead from hunger, burning with ague, whisky
His single remedy and sole distraction. . . .
At first the town of Cincinnati seemed
A different prospect, built of brick and stone—
The site is truly splendid, hills and slopes
That overlook the beautiful Ohio.
Even so, I ought to have foreseen
An outpost in the American wilds, not forty
Years old, could hardly produce amenities
Comparable to those of Bath or Malvern.
Its citizens are far outnumbered by
Their roving pigs, who swarm the streets and act
As unpaid rubbish carters, for there are
No others to perform that service. Of course,
Like most new towns, it's based on commerce, not
On ancient feudal privilege and custom.
Still, I maintain that manners cost us nothing,
That a gentlewoman travelling
With her children and no husband there
To assist her might in reason hope to have
Kindly treatment from all but crocodiles.
As she was English she could count on nothing
Of the sort! How they loathe their mother
Country and all its works! Fanatical
Patriotism. . . . Also, I was female,
Therefore had broken hallowed rules of conduct
Merely by refusing to stay at home.
A seven-fold shield of insignificance
Guards American womanhood from the least
Stain of independent activity.
The Yankee disposes; his wife and chattels obey.
He also chews tobacco, and he spits
Whether provoked or not—Miss Mitford, we
Laugh, but it is revolting, you can't conceive—
And then, a *total* lack of probity
Where interest is concerned, which might, believe me,
Set canny Yorkshire at defiance. Money

Tops the range of Yankee aspiration.
My wish to show them other modes of life
Overrode natural caution. Would they
Ever have attained the realms where I
Proposed to take them? Ah, it cost me dearly
To leave my marvelous Bazaar so soon
After building it. A charming resort,
Egypto-Graeco-Moresco-Gothic, the style—
Byronic, one might say, or like the Regent's
Pavilion. Commerce on the street level,
And all of painting, music, and poetry
I could arrange for on the floors above:
A slow ascent to Heaven, as in Dante.
In fact, they had their own *Inferno*—surely
I mentioned meeting a Frenchman named Dorfeuille?
Disheartened, but very nice. His Western Museum
Had not done well. Geology and fossils,
Though most instructive, brought few visitors.
Some novelties and freaks of nature fared
Little better. No, his greatest triumph
Was our "Infernal Regions," devised with help
From a young sculptor—Hiram Powers, very
Gifted. The figures, formed, alas, in wax,
Were nonetheless extremely fine. Ha-*ha*,
They gave the spectators a terrible fright,
And that experience was much enjoyed.
Hell is the core of their religious faith,
You see. I heard a three-hour Baptist sermon
On the dread topic, worse by far than our
Infernal Regions. "Revivals," so they're called,
Provide the summer entertainment, and—
I shan't forbear to say—are vile occasions
Indeed, a base infection of irreligion.
It shall be called a heinous libel, yet
I tell you that young *ladies* put themselves
In fits of madness—answering the divine
Afflatus (they believe). They rush headlong
To the great altar, fling themselves to earth,

——

33

And then the groans, the tears, the flailing limbs,
The shrieked and inarticulate confessions—
More than one young person's neck I saw
Encircled by a reverend arm, as he bent
Forward and whispered like the toad at Eve's
Ear. . . . A shocking spectacle, but then
Infernality's the key to Yankee
Affective life, for it reminds them of home;
And anyone who had the skill to give
Visible form to such imaginations
Was sure to draw the multitudes. These thoughts
I represented to Monsieur Dorfeuille.
I made his fortune! Not my own, I fear.
The difficulties were immense, children
Ill, my dear husband far away, unable
To comfort. . . . That second year I too was stricken.
Nine weeks I could not leave my room. The novels
Of Mr. Cooper occupied my hours—
You've read them? I never closed my eyes but saw
Myriads of bloody scalps afloat in my dreams. . . .
Red Indians crept about with noiseless tread;
Forests blazed; whichever way I fled
A keen eye and a long rifle were sure
To be on my trail. . . . But I eluded them
And have survived. Ah, here's my son! Henry,
Come and greet our guest. He was my mainstay
In America, Miss Mitford. And—
Shall I tell this? Of course I shall. You see,
"Infernal Regions" was not the first tableau
That I devised for our good friend's Museum.
The old Egyptian Mysteries have always
Held a fascination for me, thus
I wondered whether we might not set up
A secret oracle in a magic chamber. . . .
But not for gawking eyes. Instead, the voice
Of a girl, invisible but near at hand
To answer any question posed (provided
It was proper, of course). They came in droves

To consult this prodigy, and some believed.
Her answers came in Latin, French, and Greek,
Striking wonder into the hearts of all—
Much as the poet reverses his sacred Muse.
No, Miss Mitford, the oracle was not
Myself, I speak no Greek nor Latin, only
A little French. It was my boy, my Henry.
He was so young his treble voice could be
Mistaken for a girl's. Concealed in the gloom
Of the Magic Chamber, he replied to all
Their questions—very sagely, may I say.
Advice in Greek was listened to with hushed
Respect, however little understood.
They hearkened to *invisibility*—
A source of truth not readily confuted—
But never once to me! Perhaps, when I
Myself have put on invisibility,
Speaking to them from print on page, they shall?

from *Poetry*

Desire

◊   ◊   ◊

A woman in my class wrote that she is sick
of men wanting her body and when she reads
her poem out loud the other women all nod
and even some of the men lower their eyes

and look abashed as if ready to unscrew
their cocks and pound down their own dumb heads
with these innocent sausages of flesh, and none
would think of confessing his hunger

or admit how desire can ring like a constant
low note in the brain or grant how the sight
of a beautiful woman can make him groan
on those first spring days when the parkas

have been packed away and the bodies are staring
at the bodies and the eyes stare at the ground;
and there was a man I knew who even at ninety
swore that his desire had never diminished.

Is this simply the wish to procreate, the world
telling the cock to eat faster, while the cock
yearns for that moment when it forgets its loneliness
and the world flares up in an explosion of light?

Why have men been taught to feel ashamed
of their desire, as if each were a criminal
out on parole, a desperado with a long record
of muggings, rapes, such conduct as excludes

each one from all but the worst company,
and never to be trusted, no never to be trusted?
Why must men pretend to be indifferent as if each
were a happy eunuch engaged in spiritual thoughts?

But it's the glances that I like, the quick ones,
the unguarded ones, like a hand snatching a pie
from a window ledge and the feet pounding away;
eyes fastening on a leg, a breast, the curve

of a buttock, as the pulse takes an extra thunk
and the cock, that toothless worm, stirs in its sleep,
and fat possibility swaggers into the world
like a big spender entering a bar. And sometimes

the woman glances back. Oh, to disappear
in a tangle of fabric and flesh as the cock
sniffs out its little cave, and the body hungers
for closure, for the completion of the circle,

as if each of us were born only half a body
and we spend our lives searching for the rest.
What good does it do to deny desire, to chain
the cock to the leg and scrawl a black X

across its bald head, to hold out a hand
for each passing woman to slap? Better
to be bad and unrepentant, better to celebrate
each difference, not to be cruel or gluttonous

or overbearing, but full of hope and self-forgiving.
The flesh yearns to converse with other flesh.
Each pore loves to linger over its particular story.
Let these seconds not be full of self-recrimination

and apology. What is desire but the wish for some
relief from the self, the prisoner let out
into a small square of sunlight with a single
red flower and a bird crossing the sky, to lean back

against the bricks with the legs outstretched,
to feel the sun warming the brow, before returning
to one's mortal cage, steel doors slamming
in the cell block, steel bolts sliding shut?

from *Antæus*

Bringing It Down

◇　◇　◇

The man watched
    and though he was accustomed
        to what he saw

it struck him he was looking
    at a sky
        that could hold a jet

and no longer a god.
    And against decency,
        for reasons

he didn't want to know,
    he began to bring
        that jet down,

the plane getting larger
    as it descended
        out of control,

a fire in the fuselage,
    then the few lives
        he'd help save.

The man simply wanted to feel
    at ease, that's all.
        That's how he thought:

first some wildness, then
   a healing ease.
      He wanted one person

he'd brought down
   to be whole,
      smiling up at him,

her seatbelt still on.
   He brought on
      the dark clouds.

From where he stood
   he brought them
      from the west

and the noise began.
   What harm
      in a little more damage?

He brought the wind, the hail.
   There weren't enough
      rewards in this world,

he felt, for the things
   he imagined,
      but didn't do.

The man went inside.
   He had some
      unanswered letters

on his desk. One he'd never
   answer because it was
      too detailed and thoughtful,

full of a love he couldn't match.
  He'd save no lives,
    he thought.

Even if he rummaged
  through the wreckage, everyone
    would be too far gone.

He put the letter in a box
  of letters, the box
    he expected to astound him

when he was old. The lost, the dead
  would speak to him then.
    He'd make sure of that.

from *The Georgia Review*

CAROLYN FORCHÉ

The Recording Angel

◊   ◊   ◊

I

Memory insists she stood there, neither able to go forward nor back, and in that
Unanimous night, time slowed, in light pulsing through ash, light of which the coat was made, light of their brick houses
In matter's choreography of light, time slowed, then reversed until memory held her, neither able to go forward nor back
They were alone where once hundreds of thousands lived

Doves, or rather their wings heard above the roof and the linens floating
Above a comic wedding in which corpses exchange vows. (A grand funeral celebration. Everyone has died at once.)
Walking home always, always on this same blue road, cold through the black and white trees.
Unless the film were reversed, she wouldn't reach the house, as she doesn't in her memory, or in her dream
Often she hears him calling out, half her name, his own, behind her in a room until she turns
Standing forever, where often she hears him calling out

He is there, hidden in the blue winter fields and the burnt acreage of summer
As if, in reflecting the ruins, the river were filming what their city had been

42

And *had it not been for this* lines up behind *if it weren't for that*, until
the past is something of a regiment
Yet look back down the row of marching faces one sees one face
Before the shelling, these balconies were for geraniums and children
The slate roofs for morning
Market flowers in a jar, a string of tied garlic, and a voice moving
off as if fearing itself
Under the lepered trees a white siren of light searches
Under the lepered trees a white siren of sun

II

A row of cabanas with white towels near restorative waters—this
place, where once it was possible to be cured
A town of vacant summer houses
Mists burning the slightest lapse of sea
The child has gone to the window filled with desire, the glass light
passing through its hand
There are tide tables by which the sea had been predictable, as were
the heavens
As sickness chose from among us we grew fewer
There were jetty lights where there was no jetty
What the rain forests had been became our difficult breath

At the moment when the snow geese lifted, thousands at once after
days of crying in the wetlands
At once they lifted in a single ascent, acres of wind in their
wingbones
Wetlands of morning light in their lift
Moving as one over the continent, as a white front, one in their
radiance, in their crying, a cloud of desire
The child plays with his dead telephone. The father blows a kiss.
The child laughs
The fire of his few years is carried toward the child on a cake
The child can't help himself. Would each day be like this?
Hours on film yet only a moment of normal life

And the geese, rising and falling in the rain on a surf of black hands,
    sheets of rain and geese invisible or gone
Someone was supposed to have come
Waves turning black with the beach weed called dead men's hands
The sea strikes a bottle against a rock

III

The photographs were found at first by mistake in the drawer. After
    that I went to them often
She was standing on her toes in a silk *yukata*, her arms raised,
    wearing a girl's white socks and near her feet a vase of calla
    lilies
Otherwise she wore nothing
And in this one, her long hair is gathered into a white towel
Or tied back not to interfere
She had been wounded by so many men, abused by them
From behind in a silk *yukata*, then like this
One morning they were gone and I searched his belongings for them
    like a madwoman
In every direction, melted railyards, felled telegraph poles
For two months to find some trace of her
Footsteps on the floor above. More birds. It might have been less
    painful had it not been for the photographs
And beyond the paper walls, the red maple
Shirt in the wind of what the past meant
The fresh claw of a swastika on Rue Boulard
A man walking until he can no longer be seen
"Don't say I was there. Always say I was never there."

IV

The child asks about earth
The earth is a school. It is a waiting room, a foyer giving onto
    emptiness. It is for desires, small but beautifully done
The earth is wrapped in weather, and the weather in risen words

The child is awake, singing to himself, speaking in a language
      ending with the word *night*
Unaware of the sea entering, of the eternal dunes burying
Wooden matchsticks in a cup
The meaning of an object or its lack
Their preoccupation with suitcases and their contents
God returns to the world from within and the past
Is circular, like consequence
The earth tentative, blue: a fire wrapped in cold water
A sudden gust of yellow tickets, a cold blue rail and some boat lights
The barrier dunes, blue asters, the parabolic dunes, and wind
The children have returned to the beach, this time a boy and a girl
      hurrying toward then away from the water
He is wearing a red jacket and it is not important, the jacket
The child asks if fish have tongues. The other laughs, giving white
      tissues to the dog
A white sail tied over the bay's mouth muffles the sea
On the water's map, little x's: a cross-stitched sampler of cries for
      help
And yet every lost one has been seen, mornings in winter, and at
      night
When the fishermen have cast their nets one too many times
They surface, the lost, drawing great hillocks of breath
We on the shore no longer vanish when the beacon strokes us
The child's boat plies the water in imitation of boats
Years they sought her, whose crew left on the water a sad Welsh
      hymn
Voices from a ketch lit by candles
Days pass and nothing occurs, nights pass, nights, and life continues
      in its passing
We must try then to send a message ending with the word *night*

V

A river that later caught fire
A stone with its own list of names
Nothing that worked once can be tried again

That's what he told me. I didn't know
At night I found myself in a pasture of refuse
When the city vanished, they were carried on black mats from one
place to another with no one to answer them
Vultures watching from the white trees
A portable safe found stuffed with charred paper
An incense burner fused to its black prayer
In the city's perfect emanation of light
We lost every alternate route
We were there, ill there, in the birthplace of humanity
In the last of the world's open cities, rain begins
The china cups are cleared from the chiming tables
A garden of black silk blooms
Forget the fish, the bottle, the bath towels stiffening on the grate
Sleeveless pajamas, skirts of fire and flowers
A girl's face turned toward a cup of water with no mouth
Hello child, hang your coat here. This is what she said after so many
years. This was all she said

VI

It was an island wrapped in white fog, Angel Island, a wingless rock,
a way station
Now it isn't possible to go farther, paper-thin and floating
Each small act of defiance a force
There would be blank winds in the debris and palm carnage in the
half-life
Our faces are there
Mine bears the mark of your palm, yours the marks of gelignite
A bar of light touches the floor of a house long since torn down
Where the walls were, silence was
The playing cards you clipped to a window fan
To imitate the sound of helicopters all those nights
So as to return to the ruins of a wished-for life

Even the sign warning us away implied an obligation to go on
A bottle, a red bandana, a yellow bucket of bones behind the gate
We find a shovel near all of this
And as these were the final months, a radio

Their flesh like fallen snow
Leaf shadows burnt into a post
Burns of bamboo on bamboo canes
These ruins are to the future what the past is to us

VII

Someone has written FUCK with dogshit on the walls of Simone's
    atelier
A pall of exhaust over Paris
The woman with the shaved head seen twice in different
    arrondissements
And on Rue Victor Considérant, a boy with a white toy M-16
The days marched shouldering their little events
Tiny birds on the dining tables flew from spoon to bowl
As far as anyone knew, no one drowned
The hotel is no longer there
We were its final guests

A stone wall, white roses, birds and the whine of bright aerial
    antennas
Every window casement an empty portrait: radiant, formless,
    ancestral
In which he longs for her, whomever, her white bed
The remote possibility of another life
To look in the windows of that little place expecting someone
The two of us, the child, the two blue boats and the brown
The child comes into the room and leaves, comes and leaves

I loved her, he said, she was the woman of my life. Her blank eyes,
    her _____, this is what he loved
She sliced the photographs from their frames, chose what to bring
    with us, said
"Look what they've done to the windows! To my life."
You are a child, you think only of love, in whose other arms you
    will find refuge
The man walks on, blank and without veering. Where there are
    objects, he walks over rather than around them
The knife rises in her hand as she wipes her eyes
Comment vivre sans inconnu devant soi?
He departed with great pledges of love and went back to his life
    never to call her again

VIII

Dear L, I thought I knew what I was doing
On the island, a fuselage of wrecked plane, a wing in sharp
    vegetation
A radar dish filled with pumpkin plants
The blue wash of a cratered road
One thinks: The way back under cover of darkness
But as sickness chose from among us, we grew fewer
And so as not to appear in uniform he walked in his underwear
Through the village as if he were only strolling the asylum grounds

One morning slides aqua into the next, the night beach lit and tired
GRÈVE painted on the wall but what *grève*? Nothing to strike for here.
    Better pay? Better pay for what? Everybody in this no-name
    village is *chômeur*
It means they would carry your shit for you from your ass to the pit
    if they were paid
They plant flowers in cracker cans on the porch stair. They plant
    hibiscus in their wrecked cars
When you are talking about stupidity, only the military knows the
    meaning of the word *infinite*

Always he travels without maps as it is better to become lost than
    spend time thinking about the road
He drinks holy water, then pours some into a bottle in case he needs
    it again
Perhaps you have seen one of them?
A familiar man or woman, maimed, or a beggar who appears in
    several places at once
Why now and in such numbers?
If there are two doors, then only one gives onto normal life
Here, in this open field, that can never be a field again

IX

It isn't necessary to explain
The dead girl was thought to be with child, until it was discovered
    that her belly had already been cut open
And a man's head placed where the child would have been
The tanks dug ladders in the earth no one was able to climb
In every war someone puts a cigarette in the corpse's mouth
And the corpse
The corpse is never mentioned
In the hours before his empty body was found
It was this, this life that he longed for, this that he wrote of desiring,
Yet this life leaves out everything for which he lived

Hundreds of small clay heads discovered while planting coffee
A telescope through which it was possible to watch a fly crawling
    the neighbor's roof tiles
The last-minute journey to the border for no reason, the secret house
    where sports trophies were kept
That weren't sports trophies
Someone is trying to kill me, he said. He was always saying this.
Oranges turning to glass on the trees, a field strewn with them
In his knapsack a bar of soap, a towel the size of a dinner napkin
A map of the world he has not opened that will one day correspond
    to the world

In the spring, lilacs and mud roads, and later blossoming wind
Then the drone of beetles in high grass as if the grass were droning
He said a tongue doesn't have bones, he said tit for tat
Like a sack filled then emptied then filled
He was thin yes, but when he walked past it was not as if a human
    being had passed
And always he thought: This is it, the end of the world. God is
    coming
You were first in my thoughts, a chimera, first, then in the whisper
    of a sack's progress over the earth you were speaking:
We doubt we exist. We doubt with certain wisdom the world
Such pains as you took to convert a bedroom into a fire-base
Where an angry God, spilled blood itself, lives

X

Having taken these white rooms for a season, I imagine that it
    might be possible to recover
For an hour each afternoon I vow to sit in meditative expectancy
The light far on the rock promontory reaches Paris, where an old
    man's hand reaches out of the Seine, his wristwatch brilliant
    enough to catch the eye of a boat captain
There are times when the child seems not yet to have crossed into
    the world, despite having entered a body
Memory a wind passing through the blood trees within us
Someone was supposed to have come
He wrote: I tore open your letter and licked the envelope's seal for
    any lingering trace of you

In the worst of centuries, a merely difficult week, nothing, nothing,
    then from nothing, something
I noticed it today while walking to the pharmacy, where they were
    already selling woolen underwear
The market was closed. Monday. There were dead flowers for sale.
    Dead marigolds. Hydrangea. Peony.
Smoke rose in a perfect line from the roof
Then it wasn't possible to go farther

Everything seemed intentionally placed where it was, even the
    garbage bins
The children marched, holding their booklets
Peach leaves slipped earthward. Wind filled the souvenir shops
Doves painted white on the stopped wind
Making up a sort of game

Lamps in fog. Light fingering the canals.
And now, the defenselessness for which there is no cure
But it is a matter of shared history, or, as it were, we lived the same
    lie
Why lie? Why not life, as you intended?
I have the memory of a child in the southern slums, lifting the lid of
    an abandoned toilet
The child on my back, however was it kept from singing?
And falling back toward night
It was as if someone not alive were watching
Slowly, that is, over time, itself a barrier
And just then the doves rose and battered the wind
Where a notebook was kept once during a visit
*"This is my cap. This is my coat. Here's my shaving gear in its linen
    sack."*

from *Antæus*

ALICE FULTON

The Fractal Lanes

◊   ◊   ◊

Being menial, how can we let vastnesses strike through
Our fastened nerves, or see—being the ordered smallnesses
We are—the whole spill, squeeze, and boiling without
Losing heart, mind, or being
Insinuated—hugged or struck into the unwanted
Northless utmosts, the Southless balconies between
Gables of dust, rotundas of sun? Can it be our comfort's

Derived from our dumbness? It's good to know there are infinite
Exponents within the arrays we've made, that our laws block less
Visible more spectral evidence. Maybe a little
Equity—currently scarved in subterfuge—some
Linchpin—circumspect, magnetic—is yet to be
Opened and made cogent. Practice makes
Pattern. Repeat a thing till the *again*
Sculpts presence. It's some world when

The power leavening each cell's so variously
Hushed that we can't see or hear it. The thrill's in thinking it
Exists as latent prism: the red, yellow, and blue

Rays within a spun concolorous white wheel, the phrases
Interwoven down the left side of some poems, which might stay
Ghostly and unknown till pointed out. Though we base the stars'
Hermetic chemistry upon the light they hurl,
The earth's so close our measures blur. We go by lakes

And rumblings from the core. To think the ground we glide on then
Reside in holds more oxygen than the air! It makes our dying
Meager, too evident for credit—that unreckoned—breadth.

from *The Yale Review*

LOUISE GLÜCK

Celestial Music

◇ ◇ ◇

I have a friend who still believes in heaven.
Not a stupid person, yet with all she knows, she literally talks
     to god,
she thinks someone listens in heaven.
On earth, she's unusually competent.
Brave, too, able to face unpleasantness.

We found a caterpillar dying in the dirt, greedy ants crawling
     over it.
I'm always moved by weakness, by disaster, always eager to
     oppose vitality.
But timid, also, quick to shut my eyes.
Whereas my friend was able to watch, to let events play out
according to nature. For my sake, she intervened,
brushing a few ants off the torn thing, and set it down across
     the road.

My friend says I shut my eyes to god, that nothing else
     explains
my aversion to reality. She says I'm like the child who buries
     her head in the pillow
so as not to see, the child who tells herself
that light causes sadness—
My friend is like the mother. Patient, urging me
to wake up an adult like herself, a courageous person—

In my dreams, my friend reproaches me. We're walking
on the same road, except it's winter now;
she's telling me that when you love the world you hear celestial
    music:
look up, she says. When I look up, nothing.
Only clouds, snow, a white business in the trees
like brides leaping to a great height—
Then I'm afraid for her; I see her
caught in a net deliberately cast over the earth—

In reality, we sit by the side of the road, watching the sun set;
from time to time, the silence pierced by a birdcall.
It's this moment we're both trying to explain, the fact
that we're at ease with death, with solitude.
My friend draws a circle in the dirt; inside, the caterpillar
    doesn't move.
She's always trying to make something whole, something
    beautiful, an image
capable of life apart from her.
We're very quiet. It's peaceful sitting here, not speaking, the
    composition
fixed, the road turning suddenly dark, the air
going cool, here and there the rocks shining and glittering—
it's this stillness that we both love.
The love of form is a love of endings.

from *New Letters*

The Phase After History

◇ ◇ ◇

1.

Then two juncoes trapped in the house this morning.
  The house like a head with nothing inside.
The voice says: come in.
  The voice always whispering *come in, come.*
Stuck on its one track.
  As if there were only one track.

Only one way in.
  Only one *in.*
The house like a head with nothing inside.
  A table in the white room.
Scissors on the table.
  Two juncoes flying desperately around the
room of the house like a head
  (with nothing inside)
the voice-over keeping on (come in, *in*),
  them fizzing around the diagram that makes no

  sense—garden of upstairs and downstairs—wilderness
of materialized
  meaning.
Home.

Like this piece of paper,
yes take this piece of paper,
    the map of the house like a head with
whatever inside—two birds—

    and on it all my efforts to get the *house* out of their
way—
    to make detail withdraw its hot hand,
its competing naturalness.
    Then I open the two doors to make a draft,
(here),
    meaning by that an imbalance

    for them to find and ride—
the inaudible hiss, justice, washing through,
    the white sentence that comes alive to
rectify imbalance—
    —give me a minute.
In the meantime

    they fly into the panes of glass: bright light,
silently they throw themselves into its law: bright light,
    they float past dreamed-up onto the screen
called 7 am, nesting season, black blurry terms,
    the thwacking of their
heads onto resistant
    surfaces.
Then one escapes,

sucked out by the doorful of sky,
    the insanity—*elsewhere*—
so that—give me a second—
    I no longer remember it—
and the other one vanishes though into here, upstairs,
    the voice still hissing under the track *in in*,

the voice still hissing over the track.
　　　What you do now is wait
for the sound of wings to be heard
　　　somewhere in the house
—the *peep* as of glass bottles clinking,
　　　the lisp of a left-open book read by breeze,
or a hand going in to the pile of dead leaves—

(as where there is no *in*, therefore)
　　　(as where—give me a minute—someone laughs upstairs
but it's really wings
　　　rustling up there
on the cold current called history
　　　which means of course it's late and I've
got things

to do).
　　　How late is it: for instance, is this a sign?
Two birds then one: is it a meaning?
　　　I start with the attic, moving down.
Once I find it in the guest-
　　　bedroom but can't
catch it in time,
　　　talking to it all along, hissing: stay there, don't

move—absolutely no
　　　story—sure there is a sound I could make with my throat
and its cupful of wind that could transmit
　　　meaning. *Still* I say sharply as I move toward it, hands out—
High-pitched the sound it makes with its throat,
　　　low and too tender the sound it makes with its

　　　body—against the walls now,
down.
　　　Which America is it in?
Which America are we in here?
　　　Is there an America comprised wholly
of its waiting and my waiting and all forms of the thing

even the green's—
    a large uncut fabric floating above the soil—
a place of *attention*?
    The voice says wait. Taking a lot of words.
The voice always says wait.
    The sentence like a tongue
in a higher mouth

    to make the other utterance, the inaudible one,
possible,
    the sentence in its hole, its cavity
of listening,
    flapping, half-dead on the wing, through the
hollow indoors,
    the house like a head
with nothing inside
    except this breeze,
shall we keep going?
    Where is it, in the century clicking by?
Where, in the America that *exists*?
    This castle hath a pleasant seat,

the air nimbly recommends itself,
    the guest approves
by his beloved mansionry
    that heaven's breath smells wooingly here.

2.

    The police came and got Stuart, brought him to
Psych Hospital.
    The face on him the face he'd tried to cut off.
Starting at the edge where the hair is fastened.
    Down behind the ear.
As if to lift it off and give it back. Easy. Something
    gelatinous,
an exterior
    destroyed by mismanagement.

Nonetheless it stayed on.
    You suffer and find the outline, the right
seam (what the suffering is for)—
    you find *where it comes off:* why can't it come off?
The police brought him to Admitting and he can
    be found there.

Who would have imagined a face
    could be so full of blood.

Later he can be found in a room on 4.
    He looks up when you walk in but not at yours.
Hope is something which lies flat against the wall,
    a bad paint job, peeling in spots.
Some people move by in the hallway,

    some are referred elsewhere or they
wait.
    There is a transaction going on up ahead, a commotion.
Shelley is screaming about the princess.
    There is a draft here but between two unseen
openings.
    And there is the western God afraid His face would come off
into our eyes
    so that we have to wait in the cleft
rock—remember?—
    His hand still down on it we're waiting for Him to
go by,

    the back of Him is hope, remember,
the off-white wall,
    the thing-in-us-which-is-a-kind-of-fire fluttering
as we wait in here
    for His hand to lift off,
the thing-in-us-which-is-a-kind-of-air
    getting coated with waiting, with the cold satinfinish,

the thing-which-trails-behind (I dare do all that may
    become a man,
who dares do more is none)
    getting coated, thickly. Oh screw thy story to the
sticking place—
    When he looks up

    because he has had the electric shock,
and maybe even the insulin shock we're not sure,
    the face is gone.
It's hiding somewhere in here now.
    I look and there's no listening in it, foggy place.
We called him the little twinkler
    says his mother at the commitment hearing,

because he was the happiest.
    The blood in the upstairs of the duplex getting cold.
Then we have to get the car unimpounded.
    Send the keys to his parents.
Do they want the car?
    His wrists tied down to the side of the bed.
And the face on that shouldn't come off.
    The face on that mustn't come off.
Scars all round it along the hairline under the
    chin.
Later he had to take the whole body off

to get to the face.
    But me in there while he was still breathing,
both of us waiting to hear something rustle
    and get to it
before it rammed its lights out
    aiming for the brightest spot, the only clue.

Because it is the face
    which must be taken off—
the forward-pointing of it, history?,
        that we be returned to the faceless
attention,
        the waiting and waiting for the telling sound.
Am I alone here?
        Did it get out when the other one did
and I miss it?
        Tomorrow and tomorrow and tomorrow.
The head empty, yes,

        but on it the face, the idea of principal witness,
the long corridor behind it—
        a garden at one end and a garden at
the other—
        the spot of the face
on the expanse of the body,
        the spot on the emptiness (tomorrow and tomorrow),
the spot pointing
        into every direction, looking, trying to find
corners—

(and all along the cloth of Being fluttering)
        (and all along the cloth, the sleep—
before the beginning, before the itch—)
        How I would get it back
sitting here on the second floor landing,
        one flight above me one flight below,
listening for the one notch
        on the listening which isn't me

listening—
        Sleep, sleep, but on it the dream of reason, eyed,
pointing forward, tapering for entry,
        the *look* with its meeting place at

vanishing point, blade honed for
        quick entry,
etcetera, glance, glance again,
        (make my keen knife see not the
wound it makes)—
        So that you 1) must kill the King—yes—
2) must let her change, change—until you lose her,
        the creature made of nets,

        whose eyes are closed,
whose left hand is raised
        (now now now now hisses the voice)
(her hair made of sentences) and
        3) something new come in but
what? listening.
        Is the house empty?
Is the emptiness housed?
        Where is America here from the landing, my face on

my knees, eyes closed to hear
        further?
Lady M. is the intermediary phase.
        God help us.
Unsexed unmanned.
        Her open hand like a verb slowly descending onto the free,
her open hand fluttering all round her face now,
        trying to still her gaze, to snag it on

those white hands waving and diving
        in the water that is not there.

from *The Paris Review*

The Consolation of Boethius

◊ ◊ ◊

I dreamt my love was lost, uncomforted.
He lay alone in Pavia, eclipsed
by fortune, by the catastrophic tides
of men, by Caesar's imminent collapse,

so long forgotten, left so long to grieve,
his body was its own sarcophagus,
the deep, impenetrable cell his grave.
Nothing moved but wind through starlit grass.

Insensibly, as mist across a marsh,
I came to weep with him and called his name,
my fingers swimming through a dreamer's mesh
too weak to drum his deafened tympanum.

Between the bars of summer moonlight, domed
like Saul on the Damascus Road, sheared
of custom, shorn of sense, my love lay damned,
despair his brutal, bloodless vanquisher.

His shadow seemed a white-haired Senator
who calmly bends above the bath he's drawn,
his last campaign a test of temperature
where courage and the taste of salt will drown,

who drops his tunic from his sword-scarred flanks,
the royal purple marbling with rose.
A cockroach jousting with a blot of ink
defiles his final parchment as it dries.

I saw his face search out the Pleiades,
his sockets guttering a prayer, for hope,
for consolation. When the spirit dies
before the flesh, it sheds a haunted shape.

His voice, beginning as a murdered oath,
refused to void the carnage he surveyed,
and suddenly it swelled to challenge death,
a trumpet on the pass at Roncevaux.

I heard him rail, "Give over, heart, and howl!
She will not come again. I site the shell
of heaven's ear, in every shaft I hurl
Sophia—thousands do not dent the shield.

I wept in fever once until she came.
Her kisses quenched my burning heart, she prayed,
and with her tender lips' viaticum,
I lived, and wrote, the ghost of her reply.

But now indenture's thumbscrew, loved of saints,
a host of fiends and frenzies, undisguised,
collude and so beguile me from my sense,
the great circumference of the world is squeezed

into the skull I hold in both my hands.
My first and last companions, grief and rage,
defeated, dwindle down to candle ends
in hammered sconces Faith, the kitchen drudge,

forgot to douse. They blink contentedly
beside the crawling tankard and the crumbs.
Such little lamps to stay a constant law.
Too small to light the hardwood of my crimes.

Such tiny stars, extinguishing like snow
that flecks a dead love's hair. Twin sparks I place
midship. Two lanthorns that can't guide me now.
White noons that trespass on my darker peace.

Desire sighs upon the wicks, it fans
exhaustion, feathers up in hope, ascends
in fervent wingbeats toward the rafters, finds
the scaffolded cathedral of my hands—

Sophia, Virgin, Sister, intercede!
You said ill fortune draws a man to God
with grappling hooks, but God has turned aside
and left me barbed and dangling at the gate.

I've wished for everything on earth and failed.
All writing burns. My words won't come again.
But I would give all language up to feel
small comfort from the rustle of your gown.

This fractured rooftree frets, the brightness stirs,
not with the suspiration of my prayer
but my breathless unbelief—those stars
are paper fixed in vaults of priories

that sparkle in the zodiac by day
but die by night, a mockery of stars.
Oh God, I haven't got the heart to die,
or travel heavenward on golden stairs.

I've lifted up my eyes and cannot see—
Sophia, where's salvation? What's my crown?"
He read the silence of the earth and sky,
and died, because he did not know I'd come.

from *The Paris Review*

The Afterlife

◇ ◇ ◇

in memory of Howard Moss

THE LIGHT DRESS

But now a year has passed and we can think of it calmly;
you are already in a white dress.

Olga, in *Three Sisters*

Out of a brown-paper cocoon
let a pale dress be wrestled
into resurrection from winter's long wrap.
Blanched in buttermilk and lemon,

moth wing fed by laundress through mangle,
let the white dress dangle in the afterlife
clothes pegs lift from the earth below.
Let it fall from starch's grace

and bleach under the full-blown moon
that last year sharpened its scythe
until a final sliver cut into cloud
over the ghost of an orchard

where each blossom opened farther,
a powdery mouthful of water
quenching the petals that withered around it.
Let the hand-stitched lawn lie sprawled,

a last patch of that snow holding,
dear life, where sleep cleaves to shade.
Though ground warms enough to be broken again,
on this the youngest's name day

let her shrug off the year's crepe.
In a dressing room somewhere backstage
shared with the blue, the black gowns
of the two cast as her sisters

let an actress shed her own clothes
for the white dress, calling up the first
of the words put to her mouth in the play
of a life borrowed against another.

A SNAPSHOT

> *Life will get the better of you.*
> Vershinin, in *Three Sisters*

The schoolmaster's forgotten the present
he already gave his sister-in-law:
here's his little history of the school,

another copy. She can't recall
how that window or this ceiling
would be spoken of in Italian;

and the song about an oak tree by the sea,
with a green *blank*, then *something* gold,
haunts his wife, who hums again the part she knows.

The doctor's noted down a cure
for baldness, then scratched it out.
Just before lunch they had their photograph taken,

a new leaf for the album to press
under its gathering dust.
Who is the one whose face lies in shadow?

THE WINGS

From battlement to keep,
the ice palace wept itself a moat.
No more would mummers skate away the chill,
their breath fog the ballroom's blue cave,

nor ice candles dipped in kerosene be set aflame.
A hand that coolly checked a brow for fever
would dissolve its imprint into those walls
of water held together by water. Downstream,

starched nurse navigating from bedside to bed,
the first floe charted toward reopened sea,
past an iceboat about to reverse engines homeward.
A warmed column of air filled with the cries

of heavy gray birds guiding one another higher
until the only cranes left in the province
stalked a folding Japanese screen
carved next to a bed with linens of ice

whose pillows melted, tear into tear.
Feet in a pond where before they'd waded
in icicles' stubble, the birds held, breathless,
the hush a taxidermist would labor to catch,

stretching a skin he's tanned
over gauze-dressed plaster, faded feathers dyed
to mimic the transient tinge of the living.
Then the glass eyes.

THE NEXT ACT

Between vistas painted into vastness
onstage and the cramped quarters off,
a young soldier girds for a last scene

before his brigade moves out,
the thirty-nine words assigned him to deliver
waiting final polish under his breath.

A shallow sigh mists an untarnished buckle
he buffs by rote with a heavy sleeve.
"Goodbye, echo." "Goodbye, trees."

THE AFTERLIFE OF THINGS

Into the disguise of everyday
the actors pass, improbable

as angels and as invisible,
while here lies the mustache

that distinguished a baron
from a colonel, and his spirit gum.

Whalebones corset a wasp waist,
a pigeon breast of unrehearsed air.

One stained wing of a collar
flaps free of its limp shirt.

On the dressing-room floor
powder to gray the hair

has come to grief—O be the man
strolling without overcoat

a foreign city only an ocean away,
every dog and soap bearing the smell

of civilization, not home:
how distant the dead, just out of reach.

The earth turns dustier
than you would remember.

from *The New Yorker*

LINDA GREGERSON

Safe

◇ ◇ ◇

K.M.S. 1948–1986

The tendons sewn together and the small bones
    healed, that your hand
    might close on a pencil again

or hold a cup. The delicate muscles made
    whole again,
    to lift your eyelid and govern your smile,

and the nerves new-laid in their tracks.
    The broken
    point of the kitchen knife—and here

let the surgeon be gentle—removed and the skull
    knit closed
    and the blood lifted out of the carpet and washed

from the stairs. And the nineteen-year-old burglar returned
    to the cradle or
    his mother's arms—he must have been harmless

once, even he, who is not sorry, had
    nothing
    to lose, and will never be harmless again.

*   *   *

Emma is learning to wield her own spoon—
        silver for abundance,
    though it seldom finds her mouth as yet.

She hates to be fed, would rather starve,
        but loves
    to steer the precarious course herself.

Silver for pride, then, or luck of the sort
        some children
    are born with, omitting

the manifold slippage
        that separates
    privilege and weal. Luck in this popular figure

is three parts silver anyway,
        that the child
    not succumb to crack in the schoolyard,

rats in the hall, the clever fence with a
        shopping list,
    bad plumbing, bad food, and hatred-on-a-staircase

with a knife in hand and dim designs
        on jewelry
    or a VCR. The spoon was superfluity—

the best part of your paycheck for a child
        you haven't lived
    to see. Friend, her cheek is fresh as hope

of paradise. And every passing minute in the hours
        of light
    and the hours of darkness, in the fever

of pneumonia or the ignorant sweet wash
          of health,
     the miraculous breath

moves into her lungs and, stitch
          by mortal
     stitch, moves out.

                    *   *   *

When the paramedics came at last, my friend
          .apologized:
     she must have hit her head, she thought,

she'd just take a minute to mop up the mess
          by the phone.
     Her broken hands, for which

the flaw in memory had provided no such
          alibi,
     her broken hands had kept him two or

three times from her face.
          And later
     when the anesthesiologist had

launched her on his good green gas
          and launched her,
     as they do sometimes, a shade too fast,

she slipped the bonds of recall altogether.
          Safe
     as houses. You know what a house is for the likes

of us: down payment on the nursing home,
          our four-square
     pledge to be debtors of conscience, if debtors

in conscience may not look too closely
　　　　where credit's
　　refused. Our piece of the here for here-

after, which shows us diminished regard
　　　　and just
　　such a face as fear has made:

one night a woman came home to her house
　　　　and locked its useless
　　locks, and buttoned her nightdress and read

for a while, and slept till she was wakened.

　　　from *The Atlantic Monthly*

ALLEN GROSSMAN

The Ether Dome
(An Entertainment)

◇   ◇   ◇

"I'm going to foreign parts, brother."
"Foreign parts?"
"To America."
"America?"
Svidrigaylov took out a revolver and cocked it.
Achilles raised his eyebrow.
"Vot now, this is not the place for jokes!"
"Why shouldn't it be the place?"
"Because it isn't."
*"Well, brother, it doesn't matter. It's a good place. . . . If you
are asked, say I said I was off to America."*
He lifted the revolver to his right temple.

Crime and Punishment

1. O WONDROUS UNIVERSE!

O wondrous universe! O beautiful one!
Never more ocean, the work of God,
Nor nepenthe, nor mandragora, nor vapors of hemp!
Never more the moon, a man of stone,
Never more earth, pastor of the dead!
And the sun—that clumsy arsonist—has fled
The burning factories of the dawn
(A double agent with an absolute device,

Ambiguous instructions and a suspicious limp)
Who was at noon, according to police reports,
Far to the south—out of this ice. —But you
And I are growing old. . . . It is Autumn
In America. And there is a body
On the path in the Public Garden.

Someone
Has stopped to think beneath a monument,
As if it were the last chance of the mind
Before the Millennium. Thus, at the end of life,
The philosophers of pain must bid, "Farewell!"
To all the countries of the world with their dying breath,
Or *in extremis* sigh: "What has been concluded
That we may conclude with regard to it?"—
Unless a poet tells the story ("Let us begin!").
Then, they all sit down beside their shadows on
The ground, like weary shepherds in a pastoral.
"Tell us," they insist, "what happened to *you*?"
And for a moment, "Farewell!" hangs like a moon
Not yet risen below the horizon
Of all the countries of the world—until
The song and the echoes of the song are done.

2. I FELL IN LOVE.

I fell in love with a woman at a party,
In Cambridge, Massachusetts, thirty years ago.
It was one of the other hours, and one
Of the other loves—when Love has something in mind
She will not suffer us not to know. Therefore,
In a room to which I never can return,
Suddenly I saw the Lady of Pain
Who rules the Ether Dome. Her name is Asenath,
As full of memories as wind and rain.
She had gray eyes, and appeared to be surrounded
By children and animals. I knew from the start

She was a woman who preferred to live near water.
"How does it feel to be the beautiful one?"
I thought, "Is it a kind of happiness?" But she said,
"Come!" Then I followed the children and animals
Under the blue firmament of the Ether Dome,
Her kingdom. She showed me a table there laid out
In knives—a table, and a bed. To the left,
A god in plaster, Apollo Belvedere, expressing ease.
To the right, an Egyptian mummy with uncovered eyes,
Black hair, and her teeth still in her head.
On the bed lay the body of a man, or a woman,
A *body* in any case—the sad Miami of a soul:
Suffering and death in a beautiful place
Near water, unconscious, subject to the Law.
Two men in aprons worked with bloody knives
At a prominent cyst in the lower jaw.
Both wore dark suits, and shirts laundered in France.
There was an odor in the air like moly crushed
Or the oblivion of a long romance:
"Here first," she said, "under this azure dome
Anesthesia was devised (by ether in a sponge)
Producing insensibility to pain.
Knowledge of that discovery spread from
This room to all the countries of the world,
And a new era for surgery began. . . ."
Her voice, memorious as wind and rain.

3. WHAT DO I LOVE?

Philosophers of pain, what do I love?
What does love *intend* by this mysterious
Pastoral that prolongs "Farewell!" and adorns
The end of a grave thought with the carnality of rhyme:
Apollo of the charming scrotum, his arrow gone elsewhere;
An everlasting mummy with vanity of teeth and hair;
Two men in black with knives mending a jaw;
An odor in the air, uncanny, arousing awe?

I loved the traffic of the waters in her voice,
The great whales in it, the weeds and horns,
The children on her bosom—like infants at the shore
Of a warm sea. Love wanted me to know
The Lady of Pain in the time of the other hours,
The beautiful one with storm-gray eyes, the blind
Pastor of animals in the Millennium
(*Nostra effige*), who said to me, "Be true
To the poet's word! Work hard! Restore the gods!
And die in your time. This is my tomb. Love
Intends another odor and another room
In which the human image dwells serene
Among the things of stone—witness to the universe—
The greatest poet—flesh and bone—(she paused)—
And send your shirts to France if you want them clean."

4. Someone Lies on a Path.

Someone lies on a path in the Public Garden
(The dream-body moves, the real is still
And makes no motion), drunk or lost in sleep
Beneath a monument without a name—the last
Chance of the mind before the Millennium.
The heavy engine of the unseen moon
Hammers at the sill of night—"Farewell!", "Farewell!"—
Like a freight train on a grade, running late,
Raising up the cold stone of the moon's light
Above the horizon of all the countries of the world.
The paths of the Public Garden are chill and dry.
The philosophers of pain are dead, their shadows gone.
The song and the echoes of the song are done.
Far off a woman or a man, with jaw intact,
Is barking like a dog at the dilation
Of the lunar dawn—the petition of a nation!
—And Apollo descends on America
Out of a barren mountain of the moon
(A pinnacle, in fact, of fiery snow).

Terrible is the bang of the arrows in his quiver,
Terrible is the twang of his silver bow:
The one arrow of age with a ragged edge
That cannot be withdrawn, and a second arrow,
Tipped with the leaf of the elm, the aspen, or the beech
(No metal harder) that flies with a cry,
Like the sparrow, of the sorrow of children;
And another arrow which is sorrow
For the children's sorrow. In the shadows of ships
I saw Apollo kneel on the moon-gray sedge,
Among the mice at the Atlantic shore, and shower
Arrow after arrow, as the mind delivers wounds
(A beautiful god at work by the light of the moon)
Upon the bodies of the men, women, mules and battle hounds.
And all cry out, or bark, or bray, "Let us begin!"
Among the dying circulate two men in black;
And ever do the fires of the dead burn thick
Lighting the room, like a world that is seen
From without, at night, by a philosophic wanderer,
Wherein the beautiful one prepares her bed.

5. BY SUCH A LIGHT AS THIS.

By such a light as this, in such a room,
We all of us shall read the book of pain
Backward, toward the beginning, a thousand years,
Sleeping or waking—all of us—the same.
Thirty years ago—or more—when I was young
I read, all day, the book as it was written,
And then, by night, page after page of the same
Book in dreams—a student of the other hours:
Iam redit et virgo, "Now returns the maid!"
And the song we sing a little higher;
Redeunt Saturnia regna, "Now the Millennium!"
In the sleep of the beautiful one.
Between the first encounter as in a dream,
An unfeathered arrow, arrow of metal unknown

(The glance of Asenath, Lady of Pain,
The queen, seeing and being seen—in lace),
And the consummation, there intervene ten thousand
Snowless winters, and death without renown,
(A love, in fact, like any other in a college town)
Wherein a million worlds die and are born,
And all the peoples and the blaze of the face.
Between the assignation and the interview
Expands the time of a long life—my own—
Some dim hilarity—(incongruous,
In any case)—of the conscious soul—
With no clear aim, like an autumnal rain,
The death-in-life of Cambridge pastoral.
It comes to this: the body on a path
Discoursing, drunk or lost in thought ("*Tityre tu*"),
By moonlight to Asenath, the Queen—
A body thrown, as it were, beneath a monument
To be the ultimate inquisitor
Of sentiment before our other hours dawn
And the fires of Millennium are sown.

6. WHERE IS THE SUN TODAY?

Where is the sun today? Where has he gone?
Far to the South—the sad Miami of the soul—
He is in Opa-Locka at the Old King Cole Motel
(These days a coronary hospital)
Feeding the manatees in the canal.
He watches at his ease the fires to the North,
Limps to and fro, concerns himself with "truth,"
Tries verses, as he says, a little doggerel
Devised in tribute to the great McGonagall:
"Now Old King Cole was a merry old soul
And a merry old soul was he (tweedle dee)
He called for his pipe and he called for his bowl
And the truth in poetry (twee tweedle dee
Tweedle dee). But his motel beside the sea

Is the gate of hell. Love moved its maker
But couldn't pay the bill. I am not dead,
Says the McGonagall." With this and other
Poetic Gems he entertains the Pelikans.
To him the manatees reply—without remorse:
"There are a million suns like you in the universe,
Each with an absolute device, ambiguous
Instructions, and also a suspicious limp,
Signifying impotence—and the 'consolations' of hemp.
Look! Look to the sea. A lady there
(A million suns, or more, shine down on her
And every one is a "McGonagall,"
That is to say, a poet without a soul)
Is walking on the sand among her animals.
The children entertain her with their laughter
(The beautiful one, *en grande toilette*, our mother)
Which is why she prefers to live near water."
—Northward the factories are flaming in the dark.
But here in Opa-Locka beside the pool
Two men, fastidious in black despite the weather,
One with a sponge, the other with a knife,
Open and close the gates of hell all summer
And the sun who feeds us, a clumsy fool
With an absolute device—the natural man
Wanted (in any case) by the police—
Watches the Millennium come on and the new life.

7. ABOVE THE PAGES.

Above the pages. . . . Above the table in the room
Where these pages lie . . . a lady hovers and peers
Down, as if to say, what new thing is this
Since I died—what new thing has he done
In the last hour before dawn, when the wind
Falls and then hauls round on shore. The day dawns.
And the wind rises, again, bringing odors
Of the salt sea and the seaweed. A lady hovers

And peers, "What new thing?"—The children are gone
From her bosom and the animals from the shadow
Of her knees. Alone in her death and cold,
She gathers her laces against the sea wind,
Turns, and looks down at the writing of her child
(She knows what she likes, dead or alive).
It is as if the universe turned back
(The greatest poet, in fact the only one),
Stopped on the long walk of her enduring habit
From life to death in the morning twilight
Across a shadowed room toward the high windows
Which open on the gardens and the sea,
And read the pastoral of our misery to the end,
The actual work at night of the left hand.
But I sleep on into the light of day
(A philosophic wanderer among the things of stone
Interrogating the lunar pastorals of Millennium,
"What do I love? What does Love intend?")
With the cold barrel of a loaded gun
(First light, out of the fatal oceans of the night, under wind,
Empty of everything but origin and end,
Or light fallen at noon that detonates upon the ice,
The absolute device of the Autumnal sun)
In my right hand pointed toward my head
Where is, where dwells the lady Asenath—
The mind! Kill her, the Lady of Pain in me.
Kill me, the body at the end of a cold path.
And if anyone ask you, then, any god
Or any philosopher, or any shadow
"What has he done in the night?", "Where has he gone?",
"What does he know?" say only I have gone to America,
America by moonlight, the beautiful one,
America by the light of the sun.

8. ALL THINGS VISIBLE AND INVISIBLE.

All things visible or invisible, visible and invisible,
All things before and all things after this time,
Angels and women and men, angels or women and men,
And the visage of their being that shows itself
In war, and the other that shows itself in the Millennium,
Come to the light. We walk, together, through America
(She is wearing—as demanded by the fashion—
Un chapeau cloche in honour of Wallis Simpson,
And carries in her arms a baby with a tiny face
Bundled against the cold and weary of circumcision)
In the new life. "Behold" (I say) "the ruined factories
Of the dawn, the fires now thin, pale and dying
In a rising light (the dying of dying)—and the pyres,
The corpse fires of Apollo's making, and the grave
Person of Egypt, vain of hair and eyes.
The monument presents the angel Metatron,
The angel of the face, the beautiful one,
A tall woman, or a man with turbaned head—."
"I was in heaven," said Asenath, "when Enoch died,
And saw and heard. The *ofanim*, the *seraphim*, the *cherubim*,
All those who move the throne of God and the ministering
Spirits whose substance is consuming fire,
At a remove of six hundred and fifty million
And three hundred parasangs, noticed the presence
Of a human being and exclaimed, 'Whence the odor of one
Born of woman—a grain of incense that perfumes
The universe visible and invisible, and disquiets all things:
The one object of desire (the rest is loss,
Or cosmos) equal to the mind's desire
Of an object, light of the fire by which
The philosophic wanderer at night
(The body on the path that has no motion)
First catches sight of America
Under the moon, and reads the name of the nation?' "
The monument is inscribed on the south side,
"Neither shall there be any more pain,"

And on the west, "First proved to the world Oct., 1846."
"This also cometh of the Lord of Hosts"
Is written on the north, and on the east
The rest is darkened by unseasonable rain. . . .
Walking with mother in the new life
I have explained these and other matters.
Whether she has understood, or not, it is now done.
("There is no angel of the face without a kiss,
No face at all," she says, "unless you make it up, *du fard*.")
Let McGonagall, the sun, clean up the park.
Let the sea cows make their moan and drown.
Pay me, philosophers, throw me a bone.
Shadows, tell me what passes current in the dark.

9. A FULGUROUS FLASH!

A fulgurous flash! *Le remède dans le mal.*
The angry similitude of a thought
(Killing and quickening, leaving him well taught)
Made him awake, as if the light had kissed
His head and left the room, saying nothing,
Never to return. The whole night he had been alone,
God knows where. But at least he had made up
His mind; and the swallow sang to him of Fate
Like Mrs. Simpson in the bath with Edward VIII:
"Here come," she whispers, "the Regulators of the World.
Here come War, Poetry, Law, Religion—
And with some luck (and skill) the duke's erection."
There is an odor in the air of things brought from afar,
Sandalwood, cinnamon, jute, urine, tar,
And Metatron, the angel of the face,
The human form of everything—the Mind
That wrestled with Jacob at the ford of Jabbok
And instructed him in triumph after our kind.
("This night," she said, "no enchantment prevails.")
Metatron is Master of the Work, a youth
With hair (as the Americans say) slicked off the face.

No veils, philosophers, nothing to conclude—
A boy who walked with god and then was not. . . .
Everything has an angel in charge of it;
And when they sing in chorus there rise in the Ether Dome
The iron bells of the ancient tower of Kublai Khan,
O wondrous universe! Then the Millennium
And the purification of women after eight days
And the drowning in the river called Dinur
Of angels who did not sing punctually at the right hour.
And there will be no more sea and no more
Seafaring. And the Mind whom I so deeply love,
The poem of every man or woman who has ever lived,
Will be seen (O beautiful one!) like a moon
In eclipse over America—Lady of Pain—
Hanging in the empty firmament, a bare flat place;
And the moon will turn once more in the vacant
Universe of love, and wipe the tears
Forever from his eyes and smooth his face. . . .
"Kiss me," she says, "or I'll tear your heart out."
And pastor earth will sing to him and all the countries
Of the world build up his monument because
He answers, with confidence, like a man
In a well-made suit, "My lords and lordly shadows,
And you, fastidious masters of the knife, killing and quickening,
And you, drugged singers of the doggerel of life,
Inscribe it on the east side of the stone:
This happened to me!" And then—*for her*—"TAKE THIS KISS."
And in a flash the hieroglyph is written and erased
(Thus waking thought appears and disappears at dawn
On the great streams of the universe
By an absolute device defaced, or lost
Like dew at the same hour brightening the air
Which the sun draws upward and devours)—: "ONLY THIS IS."
—And now the song and the echoes of the song are done.

10. "YOU MUST KNOW EVERYTHING."

Once more we are alone, among the bathers,
On the shore of the sky. And time is hunting us,
Insectivorous time, and there is only infinite space.
No sun, no moon, no dome, no doom, no door,
Only the obscure pathways of a thought
Lead us again and yet again to this shore
Where are traces of fire. Listen! The shepherds
Are whispering in the dark, the weary shepherds
Of the pastoral strayed far from the meadow
Of their common song, by night, into this shadow.
But I say to you, I have done this entertainment
For a reason: in time there will come a time
Whether then you will be sitting on the ground
Or standing against a wall, alone then
Or in company, that the man or woman
Always to your left, but mostly unseen,
Will suddenly come clear and say to you,
"Now it is your turn to sing, here is the instrument."
And then, my dear, you must know everything.

from *Western Humanities Review*

THOM GUNN

The Beautician

◇   ◇   ◇

She, a beautician, came to see her friend
Inside the morgue, when she had had her cry.
She found the body dumped there all awry,
Not as she thought right for a person's end,
Left sideways like that on one arm and thigh.

In their familiarity with the dead
It was as if the men had not been kind
With her old friend, whose hair she was assigned
To fix and shape. She did not speak; instead
She gave her task a concentrated mind.

She did find in it some thin satisfaction
That she could use her tenderness as skill
To make her poor dead friend's hair beautiful
—As if she shaped an epitaph by her action,
She thought—being a beautician after all.

from *Ploughshares*

89

Tubes

◇ ◇ ◇

1.

"Up, down, good, bad," said
the man with the tubes
up his nose, "there's lots
of variety . . .
However, notions
of balance between
extremes of fortune
are *stupid*—or at
best unobservant."
He watched as the nurse
fed pellets into
the green nozzle that
stuck from his side. "Mm,"
said the man, "Good. Yum.
(Next time more basil . . .)
When a long-desired
baby is born, what
joy! More happiness
than we find in sex,
more than we take in
success, revenge, or
wealth. But should the same
infant die, would you
measure the horror

on the same rule? Grief
weighs down the seesaw;
joy cannot budge it."

2.

"When I was nineteen,
I told a thirty-
year-old man what a
fool I had been at
sixteen. Listening,
he looked crestfallen:
'We were always,' he
said glancing down, 'a
fool three years ago.' "

3.

The man with the tubes
up his nostrils spoke
carefully: "I don't
regret what I did,
but that I claimed I
did the opposite.
If I was faithless
or treacherous and
cowardly, there was
much to fear—but I
regret that I called
myself loyal, brave,
and honorable."

4.

"We are all dying
of something, always,
but our degrees of
awareness differ,"
he said offering
the vein of her choice
to the young woman
with many test tubes.
"We die of habits,
deplorable ones
like merely living:
finally fatal."

5.

"Of all illusions,"
said the man with the
tubes up his nostrils,
IVs, catheter,
and feeding nozzle,
"the silliest one
was hardest to lose.
For years I supposed
that after climbing
exhaustedly up
with pitons and ropes,
I would arrive at
last on the plateau
of *Walking-level-*
forever-among-
low-blueberries-and-
moss-with-red-blossoms,
or the other one
of *Lolling-in-sun-*
looking-down-at-old-

valleys-I-started-
from. Of course, of course:
A continual
climbing is the one
form of arrival
we ever come to—
unless we suppose
that the wished-for height
and house of desire
is tubes up the nose."

from *Boulevard*

Garden

◇ ◇ ◇

I poked my finger in the dirt and put the seed,
and Satan clapped me on one shoulderblade and said,
Most righteous! though of course no one was there.
A crow flew out of the buttock of a thunderhead.
No rain for weeks. I carried water by the doublebucket
under the dereliction of great fleets of cloud.
My shankbones swashed through species of brown grass.
Which time, the seed grew, flowered, and bore fruit,
a fact so biblical I walked between the rows of corn,
green walls to either side, strode forth like Moses
after the exit sign began to flash. And Satan came
again by twilight in the body of a coon, and said,
Ah! hissing from his throat, upreared on hind legs,
black lips curled back from the pointed teeth, and smiling
vanished into the touch-me-nots, the flowers even
while the light failed orange as minute live coals.

from *The Atlantic Monthly*

Who We Are

◇   ◇   ◇

On a morning like this one, when the mist is lit from within,
a silvery light without center that envelops you so that you breathe
light in the air and you can't even see to the mailbox, it's then
you feel cut off from time, dangling in space suspended: Where
in this silvery glow are the deeds, the chants, the annals, the tales
of the Founders of Cities, the Heroes who saved us from past
allegorical monsters, historical perils, from real dangers imagined
and imaginary dangers made real by being
predicted after the fact by poet and oracle? It was
these—the strophes that told how Grandfather's own great-grandfather,
with only his own shrewd courage and motherwit, broke
the back of the wind and manacled wrists of the waves,
by guise and disguise outwitting the one-eyed warrior-shaman
who led the horde that surrounded our palisade (Remember
how his captive Raven leapt on the enemy's head, black
wings blindfolding the chieftain's eye while the great beak croaked
its doomward prophecy, routing
all terrified outlanders!)—it was these,
as we coped each day with a new raw dawn, a further
spilling of the sun in the roiling sea, that made us aware
of who we are and in that knowing
felt resurgent the ancient strengths of night and early day. Nothing
there was in our world that denied us this: The brickwork city,
the wooden sills, the clay roof tiles, the gables, steeples, the pewter
mugs, stoneware jugs, the cobbled streets, toward evening
the reaching shadows, all, all were what they were, none threatened
the clock with a sundial's obsolescence where the garden fountain

is perpetually lit by light that has no need to heed
where our tiny sun and insignificant speck of moon may chance
to float in their cubit of space around this dustfleck
we do our dreams on. Now, if we could see
through the globuled light like a featureless movie screen
with only the projector's bulb intensified before the flicker
of coming attractions disturbs and distorts the blazing white
monochrome of its purity, we could find
what denies us this. Denies
by the hum and clatter that rise not with the wind nor fall as the
        wind fades,
denies by the clutter of junked vehicles encircling earth in rings
parodic of those other planets' moons, denies by thrusting,
        swollen shadow
of mushroom clouds that billow above the wind and drop their
        wizard's curses
on distant pasturage, on heads of newborn babes. Denies
the place of our space, denies the time
of our time gone before, expanse of time
stretching as a prairie on which the first covered wagon had but
        traveled
the first few leagues while ahead there beckoned
undulant plain, the rumbling bison herds, a vivid sky
streaked with circling hawk and eagle, now shrunken out of mind
behind the gilded arches of our miracle miles, our
car lots, parking lots, developed lots, the neon arms
arching over asphalt so that night shall never fall.
The fourteen screens in the show window all are tuned
to the same minuscule mannikin in unison enacting
the same holdup firing the same shot driving the getaway car in
        wild evasion
of the same pursuit crashing the same barrier amid the same
crescendo of squealing tires and the same
interruptions announcing the virtues of the same
floor cleanser. Now
will your lines recall
our vanished world as far behind us now as
Achilles' vengeance was and the heaped dead and blackened stumps

of Troy's walls fallen in twilight were to those Achaean towns
that required a blind man's lyre to keep them from forgetting,
or will your lines take shape from the shapelessness around you,
the jointed facts devoid of nature where our hive
pursues and still pursues our ends
unknown while the stars still hold their posts in beleaguered
        constellations,
and still the planets swing in accustomed arcs around us and
        the earth,
ignorant of our quick profits and brief pleasures, as before
drinks rain, hoards its green force through seasons of ice, of
        deprivation
till it feed roots again, offers its annual bounty to the fecund,
        the lucky
fields of daisies, the woodchuck in the bank, the treetop cicada
who, living in time's terrain and in the rhythms
of space, of space and time know nothing.

                    from *Grand Street*

JOHN HOLLANDER

The See-Saw

◊ ◊ ◊

Of the remedies acting primarily on the body, the see-saw especially has proved efficacious, especially with raving lunatics. The see-saw movement induces giddiness in the patient and loosens his fixed idea.

> G.W.F. Hegel, Zusatz to section 408 of the
> *Encyclopedia of the Philosophical Sciences*
> (trans. A. V. Miller)

Margery daw.
And up she went as I went down
And up she went and then I saw
The hair between her legs was brown.

Hold the handle with just your thumbs
And flap your fingers. Smile and frown
And giggle and sigh . . . we know what comes
Up must come down.

Up! and the end of the tip of me thrills:
Now I see over
The playground fence to the lovely hills,
The shadowy dales, the meadows of clover.

Down! and I bump . . . a hardened cough . . .
Against the place where I have a tail
(Do I have a tail? If I do, then they'll
Cut it all off.)

Mechanical Operations of
The Spirit oscillate between
The high of hate, the low of love,
As we have seen;

As we have sawn
So shall we rip, this way and that
Way, up and down, and my peace has gone
Off to war in a funny hat.

Two bolts on the handle dream of me
Like eyes (those very eyes I see
Saw something dirty they did to you,
Margery Doo)

A fulcrum with an idée fixe
(Hear how it creaks!)
Won't be shaken, *Balance is all*.
I'm unbalanced, a head-shaped ball.

Margery Dall:
I'd fill her up but my thing's too small,
She'd fill me down with her legs apart.
Every stopper gives me a start.

Here I come and she goes there,
Each of us President of the Air,
Slave of the Ground.
It's square that makes the world go round.

Toes just touch the ground, she and I,
Gravel and sky,
Balanced now in the midst of flight
Listen for yesterday, wait for night.

Something bad back-and-forth was there
Under Grandmother's rocking chair,
With his hanging weights and his swinging cock,
Grandfather Clock

Punishes Pa,
Ravishes Ma, and ticks the tock
Of now and then and the Time they mock.
Und ich bin hier und Margery da.

And she goes low and I go high
By an inexorable law:
See me be born? I saw Margery die,
Margery Daw.

See saw.

My wooden slope can't get to sleep,
The peaks are sunken, the moon down deep,
The desert damp and the sea sere
Margery Dear
I'm here there, and you're there here.
Margery Day,
Sold her old bed to lie on straw
To die on straw on the Days of Awe;
Margery Daw on the Days of Play
Goes up and down in the same old way

Und ich bin hier und Margery da
Tra la la la.

Out and down and up and back,
All comes on now faster and faster
When will I rest? and when will Jack
"Have a new master?"

I watch the light by which I see
Saw away at my wooden head,
Living or dead?
I haven't been told and I'll never be.

Who is it calls us home from play?
That nurse of darkness with Nothing to say.
One last up and down. And then
Never again.

from *The New Republic*

Desire

◊ ◊ ◊

*It is this stale language, closed
by the immense pressure of all
the men who do not speak it,
that he must continue to use.*
Roland Barthes

Five inches from
such eyes
snow the size

of a sentence
falls, shudders down
like light.

Then the light
king fades,
and poetry's corpse

on the sofa sits,
swelling toward
the door.

Clouds in transit
feather brains,
operatic with desire

yet temporal on
the whole,
like gasoline

and fire.
"Containably romantic,"
the eye strides

toward desire.
It wants to coincide
with incidental

things, making
distance rare.
Exchange or

substitution
makes metaphor
aesthetic crime

in realism's mind,
painting "real
if nonexistent"

landscapes in
the man.
Containing words

and other clutter,
the body's packed
in lime

beneath the author's
house.
Synthesis is

its merit,
the unity in
scatter

coming on
like trucks,
though meaning

shits on that.
Thought ought not
resemble

that which it
endorse?
Rupture loves

the difference.
On the other hand,
intimate conviction

leads to
certain actions
final as

the night.
I can touch
you now

in sequences
of light
and words record

this urge,
but Chinese students
burn the train

and history knows
the difference,
swaying like

a train.
Tyrants' shadows
in its windows

strike a blow
on poetry's nose,
as if the future

might remember
"accident's practical
connotations."

The night
is blind
with tyrants.

from *O.blēk*

Second Nature

◊ ◊ ◊

In the dream you are living in Akron again,
Your parents' basement, a temporary refuge
For close to thirty years, first from the heat,
Then from anyone, and now from the past.

The television upstairs surrounds you like rain
Falling steadily, each burst of applause a deluge
That drowns out the music and the muffled beat
Of voices onscreen and off. You fall asleep fast

And dream that you are living in Akron again
But a few blocks away, on Pershing Avenue,
Where you have just woken up and don't know why

Until you hear the scratch on the screen of rain
Falling ten years before from a sky still blue
As if to frame yet another way of saying goodbye.

from *The New Yorker*

RICHARD HOWARD

What Word Did the Greeks Have for It?

◇ ◇ ◇

Tendered by Professor Ames, tidings from
  the universe—or at least
from the university (Plato claims
  there is the same difference
between learned and unlearned men as
  between living and dead ones)—

such oracles always come to us clad
  like this in the apparel
of poppycock, and by way of a gloss
  my knowing colleague had scrawled
"yesterday's newspaper is old news, but so
  is today's newspaper—thus:"

Dear Abby, my friend and I are having
  a difference of opinion.
He insists that Damon and Pythias
  were both homosexuals,
I say they were straight. Can you check this out
  and let us know?—Bewildered.

Forestalling Abby, I must first record
  my delight that the two of you
are having a difference—good thinking!

Our disregard of unity
is every bit as significant as
    our exhibition of it;

provided you differ . . . Precedent compels
    me to ask: What is "straight"?
The danger lies in being persuaded
    before understanding. Let me
instance, *a contrario*, the occasion
    when Gladstone, being informed

a canon of Windsor soon to be made
    a bishop was a bugger,
only remarked, "In an experience
    of fifty years I have learned
that the pagan qualities you refer to
    are frequently possessed by

men of immense erudition, the most
    absolute integrity,
and the deepest religious convictions."
    It *is* bewildering. Myself
I have noticed that when most of us say
    "his heart is in the right place"

we locate that heart rather lower down
    than we care to acknowledge,
and on inspection, the lump in the throat
    is really in the trousers.
Larkin is right: what counts is not to be
    different from other people

but from yourself. There is more repression
    in heaven and earth than is
dreamed of in most psychoanalysis.
    As for that pair in Plutarch,
their devotion seems to have excited
    suspicion even among

the ancients, the same alarm set off by
     Jesus—laying down your life
for another, for all others, appears
     just as suspect as getting laid
by your best buddy. You might tell your "friend,"
     Bewildered, who sounds so sure

of his categories, this much from me:
     the class of men he discerns
is a social, not a biological
     entity. Our genes contain
no instructions as to who is and who
     is not homosexual;

nor do laws of survival require that
     distinctions be made between
the world of the straight and some other world.
     Those whose natures have kept them
at a distance from the community
     cannot appear undefiled

among you without a lurid aureole,
     looking stranger than they are;
they do not need defending—your contempt
     cannot hurt them, they are dark
and love will find them anywhere; nor do
     they need encouragement, for

if they would remain authentic, they must
     live only off themselves, hence
cannot be "helped" without being harmed first.
     Charity begins at home,
but how far does it spread? Where will it all
     end? *Shift, shift, fellatio,*

as Hamlet might have satisfied *his* friend's
     curiosity back then.
These days we cannot let the matter rest:

Did Franz? Was Walt? Would Vincent? . . .
With a sigh, the unconsenting spirits
flee to the welcoming shades.

from *The Threepenny Review*

The Woods

◊   ◊   ◊

In this summer month, two separate men were lost
in the local woods. Can woods be local?
Is there more than one wood? It is unlikely.
Though there are two kinds of woods, visible, and not.

The first man was feeble-minded. Left
his goodwill party, saw something, heard
something, went to it. They found his body
later, after something found it first.

Fright, or starvation; or exposure. Woods
which are close and secret, practice exposure.
If he heard the cries, the dogs, the cries,
why didn't he answer? Why didn't they hear him?

Anyway, the second man was strong-
minded as another; knew woods, went in alone.
They say: Never go in alone. But even in visible
woods, is that persuasive? They are interesting.

Even in high sun they offer such levels
of shade—the tops of their tallest trees just stir
in the biggest wind. They are dark green to black
according to whether the light is sun or moon.

The second man was never found at all.
Never. So people began to say he came out
elsewhere, into sunlight or moonlight, for his own
purposes. But could the woods make him vanish?

The difference is, the visible wood stays put,
though it stirs and acts within itself. It is bounded.
The invisible wood stretches, arrives, and is there.
Going in alone is inevitable, unfortunately.

Also, dogs are forbidden, and silence enforced.
There is supposed to be a treasure, or witch, at the center.
But which, cannot be known, short of encounter.
And those lost who return—and there are some—

cannot find the dictionary word to tell
how it went. If it's the treasure, they usually stay;
and if it's the witch, they can stay too,
and she will send out a Doppelgänger instead.

Another difference is that fewer are lost,
even temporarily, in the visible wood.
And another yet, that those broken or careless few
who are, are usually found; and found in time.

from *Ploughshares*

Body and Soul

◇ ◇ ◇

1. HOTEL

If there was something one of them held back,
It was too inadvertent or too small
To matter to the other, after all.

Afterwards they were quiet, and lay apart,
And heard the beating of the city's heart,
Meaning the sirens and the streetcries, meaning,
At dawn, the whispery great streetsweeper cleaning
The things of night up, almost silently.

And all was as it had been and would be.

2. RAIN

Some bright umbrella, suddenly blowing free,
Escapes across the carhoods dangerously.
And we run after—
                    only to be lost
Somewhere along the avenues, long avenues
Toward evening pierced with rain; or down a mews
Whose very cobblestones the young Hart Crane
Once rinsed with a golden urine mixed with rain.

3. Street Musician

A cold evening. The saxophonist shivers
Inside his doorway and ignores the givers
Who pause to drop their small change in his hat.
High now or proud, he leans back out of that
And lifts his horn in some old bluesy riff
His fingers just do get through, being stiff—
Yet so sincere, so naked that it hurts.
Punk teens, in pink hairspikes and torn T-shirts,
Drift past; a horsecop towers above the cars;
And office lights wink on in place of stars.

Silence of cities suddenly and the snow
Turning to rain and back again to snow . . .

from *Antæus*

Elegy

◊   ◊   ◊

Light on the table so capable of leaving.
Jackal of noise drifting through these rooms, scent of heat.

Think of that day you took me to the eye doctor's,
His blurry office, the shining medical charts.

What did I see when he placed a picture of a fly before me?
I saw it fly, become what it claimed to be.

Tonight, unobserved, blackness lifts you out of your grave in Florida,
Atom by atom, and translates you back through its sieve.

But I still think of you lying in the ground in street clothes,
Flowers rocketing past you through the black horizon of soil

Until they burst into blooms in the outer space which was your life.
Close my well-repaired eyes, open my unrepaired heart,

And I can feel your fingers trembling under the earth
As you try to catch them. Think, instead, of that day.

We took the ferry home.
The bent wire of a seagull's leg stirred the silence

And then an unruly alphabet of birds clamored behind the boat,
Kite of speech mimicking the air.

Your expression said let the birds have their reasons,
Let their beautiful resemblances mean less than their lives.

from *The New Yorker*

ROBERT KELLY

A Flower For The New Year

◇ ◇ ◇

At first I couldn't remember the name
of the vine-borne flower that climbs
so scraggly up the south wall of my porch,
I see it now, bare and crazy-looking, like a hank
of twine a cat got tired of bothering,
and that every spring you coax so carefully
into a few meager gorgeous deep purple blossoms,

but that we saw triumphantly tropical in the cold
rainy summer of St. Barnabas Road in Cambridge,
how do they do it, the Smiths' doorway and the yard
next door purple with them, visions of Persephone
and ancient excess, the wild half-unconscious
half-drunken willful excesses of Greeks!

And then I remembered the name, clematis, and couldn't
remember if I'm supposed to say cle-may-tis or cle-mah-
tis, like the man in the song about tomatoes
(you say, I say, let's call), anyhow, that flower,

and then I couldn't understand why I was worrying
about the names of flowers or the names of anything
or music or even the flower itself, Greeks and all
their purple antics, their raving gates and trances,
wild throats receiving and decanting seeds from
all the worlds above they meant by "Gods,"

and why should I be thinking about the gods or even winter
when there are men and women who have no homes
with or without flowers on the wall, men and women
who have no history except what happened to them
last night, in the street, when another man
or another woman, said, nameless, or did, motiveless,
this thing, what thing, gave, or took, or struck,
or in the common way of bleary midnight New Year's misery
touched, just touched, and these, without a chair
or a floor to put it on, without a wall,

children only of the wind, who live in the weather
in the unromantic hate-winds of their appetite,
who suffer their own resentment more than their hunger,
whose pain is permanent, hence forgettable, always alone
but never lonely because every human being is their enemy
and a man fighting for his life has no time to be lonely,

and they fight, for their lives, in silence and squalor,
their stupefied eyes almost merry with glowering envy,
and I sit here baffled by the name of purple flowers,
remembering all the girls in my life as they step
naked-footed lewdly up the chill sedate corridors
of the marble museum of my heart, I worship their nakedness
while some man lies in the snow on Sixth Avenue with no shoes,

so dark the flower, shaped like a trumpet, darker
as I peek inside, or walk up down that curving bell
into the sound of what manner of sky they keep there,
who?, in the homeland of that flower whatever its name,
we do what we can and lie down in the dark, and what we cover
ourselves with against the wind is nobody's business,
so dark the flower, so dark the heavy traffic of names.

from *O.blēk*

JANE KENYON

Let Evening Come

◇   ◇   ◇

Let the light of late afternoon
shine through chinks in the barn, moving
up the bales as the sun moves down.

Let the cricket take up chafing
as a woman takes up her needles
and her yarn. Let evening come.

Let dew collect on the hoe abandoned
in long grass. Let the stars appear
and the moon disclose her silver horn.

Let the fox go back to its sandy den.
Let the wind die down. Let the shed
go black inside. Let evening come.

To the bottle in the ditch, to the scoop
in the oats, to air in the lung
let evening come.

Let it come as it will, and don't
be afraid. God does not leave us
comfortless, so let evening come.

from *Harvard Magazine*

KARL KIRCHWEY

The Diva's First Song (White's Hotel, London)

◇ ◇ ◇

The windows have their watered silk
Hangings: my voice hardly comes back

To me at all. The carpet's maze
Of brilliant tufted wool allows

My feet to linger when a note
Wanders chromatic or is covered;

And with the fine tip of a sable
Brush, these walls have been veined like marble

(Though they are wood) or dressed in plumes
And eyes like peacock feathers, flames

Of varnish like an instrument,
Braided like hair, parted like raiment,

Given every texture but the knot
Of what they are: and this is art.

Each morning the maid knocks and fills
Three small and different-colored vials

By the gold taps with lotions for me.
By dusk I've had my bath; they're empty.

I rest and watch the comforter's
Embroidered surf of fruit and pairs

Of birds swarm underneath the lead
Glass clinging in its faceted

Bunches that stains the bedboard wall
With a soft rainbow aureole.

As I once saw on Murano,
After the wobble and the glow,

A rondure and a clarity
Grow from the breath of men, so I

Practice the drop and gust of line
Until at last it is made clean

Of me. As in glass facing glass,
My image almost disappears.

from *Partisan Review*

Marriage Song

◊ ◊ ◊

with commentary

We begin with the osprey who cries, "Clang, clang!"
Which is the sound of the door of marriage slamming.
Our metaphor sits on a nest, surrounded
By blooming succulents; ospreys, like swans, mate once.
For form's sake they appear in public together;
Because she and her spouse play separate roles
They will forgo connubial bliss if necessary
To save their feathered souls.

Complementary image: young, pale, scared,
Has menstruated once, sequestered in a cave,
Miss Chou Dynasty, under lock and key
Thus to preserve her sacred chastity,
Knows that some day her Prince will come.
But this occurs between stanzas two and three.
Thus far she is only a dream in his questing eye.
He doesn't come, he just breathes heavily.

The principal commentaries differ here:
Mao-hang believes the lady tossed from side to side
In bed with long long thoughts of separation.
A respected version claims that the aging bride
Dutifully tried to recruit the limberest dames

For her still-randy spouse, states earnestly
That she worried about the good ones getting away
—or so the followers of Confucius say.

But what, Students, was the intention of the Poem
Before the moral scholiasts worked it over?
The text obscure: was it maid or matron here?
Did not our Princess roll from side to side
Alone with long long thoughts of her absent lover,
Reluctant, yes, to pick out next year's successor
Yet feeling perhaps it was better to marry *and* burn
Than to stay yearning in that cave forever.

Now cry desire, shake silver tambourines
To cue the strings of gypsy violins
As the Fisher-Prince mates with his fluttering Bride.
O her chaste joy! She will hold him in her bosom
(suckle her spouse in dream), then toss and turn . . .
The girls glide out of reach like water-lilies
Slipping along the current of the stream.
Though Pound and Waley speak of zither and gong
In truth our modest heroine bursts into song:

"Alone, I become virginal again.
I know the cave, I learn the cave within.
And you, my Lord, are somewhere out of reach.
I hear your breathy sigh: the aging man
Tuning his lute in our remotest room.
Beside myself at last, I think and think
Of ospreys on their island, dark of wing,
Snow-breasted, and transfixed in abstract love."

from *Antæus*

123

KENNETH KOCH

A Time Zone

◇ ◇ ◇

On y loue des chambres en latin Cubicula locanda.
Je m'en souviens j'y ai passé trois jours et autant à Gouda
Apollinaire, "Zone"

A light from the ceiling is swinging outside on Forty-second
Street traffic is zinging
Collaborating on The Construction of Boston is interesting
To construct the city of Boston Tingueley is putting up a big
wall
Of gray sandstone bricks he is dressed in a French ball
Gown he puts the wall up during the performance
His costume is due to art and not to mental disturbance
Now the wall ten feet high is starting to tremble
People seated in the first rows run back for shelter
However the bricks stand firm Niki de St. Phalle dressed as
Napoleon
Shoots at a Venus full of paint with a miniature (but real)
cannon
Rauschenberg's rain machine's stuck it gives too much
moisture
People look very happy to have gotten out of the theater
People ask that it be put on again but it can't be done
Tingueley with his hand bleeding says Boston can be
constructed only once
And that is the end of that
Next day the Maidman Theatre stage is flat
I like the random absurdity of this performance

124

Done only once with nineteen-sixty-two-and-art romance
I meet Niki four years earlier in France in the spring
Five years before that I am with Janice and Katherine
In Greece two thousand years ago everything came crashing
We stand and try to imagine it from what is still standing
Years before this in Paris it's the boulevard Montparnasse
Larry Rivers is here he is living with a family that includes a
    dwarf
We are talking I have a "Fulbright" with us is Nell Blaine
I am pulled in one direction by Sweden in another one by
    Spain
The idea of staying in Europe jolts me gives a convincing
    jerk
It's New York though where most of my friends are and the
    "new work"
Today with Frank O'Hara a lunch connection
The Museum of Modern Art is showing its Arp collection
Frank comes out of the doorway in his necktie and his coat
It is a day on which it would be good to vote
Autumn a crisp Republicanism is in the air tie and coat
Soon to be trounced by the Democrats personified as a slung-
    over-the-shoulder coat
Fascism in the form of a bank
Gives way to a shining restaurant that opens its doors with a
    clank
However before being taken into this odoriferous coffer
A little hard-as-a-hat poem to the day we offer
"Sky/woof woof!/harp"
This is repeated ten times
Each word is one line so the whole poem is thirty lines
It's a poem composed in a moment
On the sidewalk about fifteen blocks from the Alice in
    Wonderland Monument
Sky woof woof! harp is published in Semicolon
Later than this in this John Myers publication
O'Hara meanwhile is bending above his shirt
His mind being and putting mine on being on International
    Alert

There's no self-praise in his gossip
Which in fact isn't gossip but like an artistic air-trip
To all the greatest monuments of America and Europe
Relayed in a mild excited wide open-eyed smiling
    conversational style
Larry he says and Larry again after a while
He is crazy about Larry these two have a relationship
That is breaking the world's record for loquaciousness
I first meet Larry on Third Avenue
The El goes past and it throws into my apartment rust dust
    soot and what-have-you
Larry has a way of putting himself all out in front of himself
And stumbling through it and looking good while seemingly
    making fun of himself
This is my friend Larry Rivers says Jane Freilicher
She lives upstairs Larry is a sometime visitor
He is dedicated at this moment entirely to drawing
Abstract split-splot and flops and spots he finds a blur and
    boring
Give me a glass of pencil that hath been
Steeped a long time in Delacroix and Ingres nor does he
    neglect Rubens
He is drawing up a storm in his studio working hard
A little bit earlier he and Jane and others are bouleversés by
    Bonnard
Bonnard show at the Modern Museum
I meet these people too late to go and see them
I am of New York not a native
I'm from Cincinnati which is to this place's nominative like a
    remote dative
In 1948 from college I come here and finally settle
The city is hot and bright and noisy like a giant boiling kettle
My first connection to it aside from touristy is sexual
A girl met here or there at first nothing serious or contextual
That is earlier now I'm here to live on street subway and bus
I find people exciting unrecognizable and of unknown-to-me
    social class
Finally they start to come into focus

For a while it's like being at a play I may have the wrong
    tickets
On West Tenth Street now I am firmly settled in New York
I am a poet je suis poète but I'm not doing very much work
I'm in love with a beautiful girl named Robin
Her father has a hand-weaving factory he gives me a job
    winding bobbins
It is a one-floor loft in the garment district on Thirty-first
    Street
Pat Hoey visits someone next door on snow-white feet
Pat and I like to go to the ballet at the City Center
I get "Balanchined" as in a wine-press all Jacques d'Amboise
    has to do is enter
My poetry is somewhat stuck
It's taking me a little while to be able to write in New York
My painter friends help and what I am reading in the library
It is not the contemporary antics this happens later of John
    Ashbery
This shy and skinny poet comes down to visit me from
    "school"
When he and Jane Freilicher meet it's as if they'd both been
    thrown into a swimming pool
Afloat with ironies jokes sensitivities perceptions and sweet
    swift sophistications
Like the orchids of Xochimilco a tourist attraction for the
    nations
Jane is filled with excitement and one hundred percent ironic
This conversation is joy is speed is infinite gin and tonic
It is modernism in the lyrical laconic
Our relationship's platonic
With what intelligence linked to what beauty linked to what
    grassy gusty lurch across the canvas
Jane and her paintings I realize once again happiness
Huh? is possibly going to be available after long absence
Here today in a gray raincoat she appears
The style is laughter the subject may be a cause for tears
Larry has some of the qualities of a stand-up comic
He says of John Myers John Myers he always calls him that

John Myers never John John Myers says he isn't fat
Well he doesn't have a fat EAR but look at his stomach
And oft at a party back his head he throws
And plays the piano singing a song he made up "My Nose"
His nose bothers and is thus conquered by Larry Rivers
He's doing a Bonnardesque painting it's so good it gives me
    "recognition" shivers
It's a room filled with women with somewhat beautiful
    fishlike graces
Mostly orangey-yellow they have sexy and sleepy looks on their
    faces the thick
Oil paint makes it look as if you'd stick
To it if you got next to it it also looks very spacious
Now Larry is sitting and smiling he is copying an Ingres
His hand is shaky his lines are as straight as coat hangers
Why don't you I say rather dumbly put something witty in
    your work
No Kenneth I can't he says prancing around like a funny Turk
Charcoal in one hand and making a little gesture with the
    other
One Sunday I go with him to the Bronx to visit his sister and
    his mother
Here I am with Larry's sister and his mother
Sitting in the kitchen above us is a motto
Joannie is blonde her brunette friend is warm and flushed as
    a risotto
I rather fancy her and Larry's mother fancies it stupid
To have invited this girl at the same time as me so interrupting
    the arrow of Cupid
Posing for Rivers his mother-in-law Berdie before a screen
Posing for her son-in-law this woman full and generous as the
    double issue of a magazine
The French *Vogue* for example or the *Ladies Home Journal*
Frank thinks her marvelous he finds the sublime in her di-
    urnal
Larry is making a leafy tree out of metal
Here is his Jewish version of Courbet's painting of a funeral
Jane loves Matisse and is a fan of Baudelaire

In these paintings she is working on a secret of yellow blue and
    pink air
She and Larry make a big painting together
Larry with an unmeditated slash Jane with the perpetuity of
    a feather
That in a breeze is trying to pull itself together
I'm looking at the finished product it's rather
    de Kooningesque
Being de-Kooning-like some way is practically of being a New
    York painter the test
Here today though is not a de Kooning but one of Jane's it's
    luscious big and feminine
I am inspired by these painters
They make me want to paint myself on an amateur basis
Without losing my poetic status
Jane is demonstrating to me the pleasures of using charcoal
I am copying a Delacroix of a black woman called I think The
    Slave Girl
Erasing makes a lovely mess
It looks like depth and looks like distance
Ink at the opposite end of materials is deliberate and daring
No chance to erase it and oil pastels like wildflowers in a
    clearing
My Aesthetic I only paint for a few years is rather elementary
Get something that looks good looks real looks surprising
    looks from this century
I am sitting at a little table downstairs in the Third Avenue
    apartment
I like buying slabs of masonite and all kinds of equipment
At the Metropolitan on a big wall is a great big Rubens
Of a king and some nobles on horses bigger than cabins
I am walking through the European Collection
With Larry and Jane they're giving it a professional inspection
On drawing paper I'm doing some Seurat-like dotting
I like this even love it but I know it's going to come to nothing
It is invigorating to stand in this studio
John Ashbery comes to visit he is listening to Bob and Ray on
    our radio

It is a small old-fashioned console attacked by salt water
John finds them wheezingly amusing all over the house
      sounds his raucous laughter
He and I "go back" to Harvard College
Now he is sitting at his typewriter in Greenwich Village
He's just finished a poem and he's happy as after a good repast
He is certain this feeling won't last
John is predictably and pleasantly gloom-filled
I've just driven to New York from some place north of
      Bloomfield
I'm an hour and a half late
This enables John to finish his poem as I with mixed feelings
      find out
"The Picture of Little J. A. in a Prospect of Flowers"
He made good use of this couple of wasted hours
Dick gives Genevieve a swift punch in the pajamas
It's a vault over W. C. Williams and a bypass of Dylan Thomas
He is still sitting at his little portable
Being because of my poem-causing lateness exceptionally
      cordial
We are both fans of the old Mystery Plays
We also find each other mysterious in certain ways
This mystery becomes greater as more time passes
Then finally the mystery itself passes
We're at Harvard together
We walk along talking about poetry in the autumn weather
He is not writing much this year but he likes to collaborate
So do I we do a set of sestinas at a speedy rate
Six sestinas each about an animal with one concluding one
      called The Bestiary
There is also a three-page poem in which all lines rhyme with
      the title The Cassowary
Next we do a poetic compendium called The New York Times
September Eighth Nineteen Fifty-One both with and without
      rhymes
Our poems are like tracks setting out
We have little idea where we're going or what it's about

I enjoy these compositional duets
Accompanied by drinking coffee and joking on Charles and
Perry streets
We tell each other names of writers in great secret
Secret but absolutely no one else cares so why keep it
We're writing a deliberately bad work called the
Reconstruction of Colonial Williamsburg
In a feeble attempt to win a contest the style is the Kenyon-
Review absurd
Larry and Jane propose to me renting a house in Easthampton
We go sizzling out of the city with the rapidity of a flu
symptom
No this is actually a year later my memory missed it
I now go to California to be a "teaching assistant"
This year goes by I meet the girl who is later my wife Janice
I love to kiss her and to talk to her very often it's talking about
my friends
I also talk a lot about "Europe" and France
She's a little deflating and tells me that to be a great poet
I have to do something she tells me but I forget exactly what
I think have for all my poems some sort of system
I am shaken but still feel secure in my avant-garde wisdom
East Hampton glaringest of Hamptons Hampton of sea shine
of de Kooning and of leaves
Frank's visiting we're composing a poem he tugs at his sleeves
It is a Nina we are composing it is a Nina Sestina
For Nina Castelli's birthday her adorable sixteenth one
This year this month this week in fact Frank writes "Hatred"
A stunning tour-de-poem on an unending roll of paper
It makes going on forever seem attractive
Writing in the manner of O'Hara means being extremely
active
Twenty people are over then thirty now about forty
Zip Frank sits down in the midst and types out a poem it
doesn't even seem arty
I try it out with little success
It's one of those things the originator can do best

"Hatred" is full of a thundering array of vocables
From it straight through to the Odes Frank's talent is
    implacable
Now here he is holding out to me a package
Of Picayunes he taps one on his kneebone-covering khakis
Finally we have a poem for Castelli's daughter
Moonlight dissolve next day we're visiting Anne and Fairfield
    Porter
Fairfield is in his studio a mighty man
Posing like fluttering then settling sea birds around him Jerry
    Katie Elizabeth and Anne
He has opinions that do not waver
On his canvases he creates a bright and wholesome fever
Flowers like little pockets of yellow and pink pigment
Are aspiring up to a tree or a wall or a house like a sunlight
    shipment
At a John Cage concert there is hardly a sound
It's the paradise of music lost and music found
I find it pure and great as if a great big flash of light were
    going off underground
Satie and Webern are hitting me in the head and so finally
    with The Cantos is Ezra Pound
Frank and I are writing very long poems
Long is really the operative word for these poems
His is called Second Avenue mine When the Sun Tries to Go
    On
I don't know where I got the title
I'm working on it every afternoon the words seem to me
    arriving like stampeding cattle
It's not at all clear but for the first time in my life the words
    seem completely accurate
If I write for three hours I allow myself a cigarette
I'm smoking it's a little too much I'm not sure I can get
    through it alone
Frank and I read each other segments of these long works daily
    on the phone
Janice finds it funny now that I've dropped this bunch of pages

That I can't get them back in the right order well I do but it's
    by stages
It is April I have a job at the Hunter College Library
I come down to the Cedar on a bus hoping to see O'Hara and
    Ashbery
Astonishingly on the bus I don't know why it's the only
    occasion
I write a poem Where Am I Kenneth? It's on some torn-out
    notebook pages
The Cedar and the Five Spot each is a usable place
A celebrated comment Interviewer What do you think of
    space? De Kooning Fuck space!
In any case Frank is there he says he likes Where Am I
    Kenneth?
I carry this news home pleasantly and the poem it mentions
    her to Janice
John's poem Europe is full of avant-garde ardor
I am thinking it's making an order out of a great disorder
I wonder at what stage in life does this get harder
The Cedar Bar one hardly thinks of it is what may be called
    a scene
However one closed to the public since no one goes there to
    be seen
It is a meeting place for the briefest romances
And here is Norman Bluhm at the bar saying Who cares about
    those nances?
And here he is shoving and here is de Kooning and there is a
    beer
Being flung at someone Arnold Weinstein or me through the
    smoke-talky atmosphere
Of this corner booth
Voici Guston and Mitchell and Smith and here on top of
    everything is Ruth
Kligman being bedazzling without stop
She writes a poem with the line At the bar you've got to be
    on top
Meanwhile tonight Boris Pasternak

Is awarded the Nobel Prize and is forced to give it back
Frank O'Hara is angry there seems both a flash and a blur in
    his eyes
Kenneth we've got to do something about Pasternak and the
    Noble Prize
What? well we ought to let him know
That we support him Off flies a cable into the perpetual snow
Dear Boris Pasternak We completely support you and we also
    love your early work
Signed puzzlingly for him in the morning's glare if he ever
    receives it Frank O'Hara and Kenneth Koch
Staging George Washington Crossing the Delaware
Alex Katz comes up looking like a pear
He has some white plywood boards with him he says where
Shall I put this stuff and a big bare
Wall is the side of their emplacement No chair
For Alex painting and cutting And now they're there
The seven soldiers one cherry tree one Delaware crossing boat
Hey hey Ken cries Alex I've done it
I've made you a set for George Washington Crossing the
    Delaware
The British and American armies face each other on wooden
    feet
I write this play in our apartment on Commerce Street
I am working in the early afternoon and stay up late
Dawn is peeling oranges on top of the skyscrapers
On the stage a wall goes up and then it's taken down
And under the Mirabeau Bridge flows the Seine
Today Larry and Frank are putting together "Stones"
It's a series of lithographs
Larry puts down blotches violently they look like the grapes
    of wrath
Frank is smoking and looking his best ideas come in transit
He stares gathers his brows puffs looks up he has it
I walk the nine blocks to the studio he says Come in
New York today is white dirty and loud like a snow-clogged
    engine

Huge men in undershirts scream at each other in trucks near
    Second Avenue and Tenth Street
De Kooning's landscapy woman is full of double-exposure
    perfections
Bob Goodnough is making some small flat red corrections
Jane is concentrating she's frowning she has a look of happy
    distress
She's painting her own portrait in a long-sleeved dark pink
    dress
I'm excited I'm writing at my typewriter it doesn't make too
    much sense

from *The Paris Review*

JOHN KOETHE

Morning in America

◇   ◇   ◇

It gradually became a different country
After the reversal, dominated by a distant,
Universal voice whose favorite word was *never*,
Changing its air of quiet progress into one of
Rapidly collapsing possibilities, and making me,
Even here at home, a stranger. I felt its tones
Engaging me without expression, leaving me alone
And waiting in the vacuum of its public half-life,
Quietly confessing my emotions, taking in its cold
Midwinter atmosphere of violence and muted rage. I
Wanted to appropriate that anger, to convey it, not
In a declamatory mode, but in some vague and private
Language holding out, against the clear, inexorable
Disintegration of a nation, the claims of a renewed
Internal life, in these bleak months of the new year.
That was my way of ruling out everything discordant,
Everything dead, cruel or soulless—by assiduously
Imagining the pages of some legendary volume marked
Forever, but without ever getting any closer. As I
Got older it began to seem more and more hopeless,
More and more detached—until it only spoke to me
Impersonally, like someone gradually retreating,
Not so much from his life as from its settings,
From the country he inhabits; as the darkness
Deepens in the weeks after the solstice.

from *American Poetry Review*

Work Song

◇   ◇   ◇

My name is Henri. Listen. It's morning.
I pull my head from my scissors, I pull
the light bulb from my mouth—Boss comes at me
while I'm still blinking.
Pastes the pink slip on my collarbone.
It's O.K., I say, I was a lazy worker, and I stole.
I wipe my feet on his skullcap on the way out.

I am Henri, mouth full of soda crackers.
I live in Toulouse, which is a piece of cardboard.
Summers the mayor paints it blue, we fish in it.
Winters we skate on it. Children are always
drowning or falling through cracks. Parents are distraught
but get over it. It's easy to replace a child.
Like my parents' child, Henri.

I stuff my hands in my shoes
and crawl through the snow on all fours.
Animals fear me. I smell so good.
I have two sets of footprints, I confuse the police.
When I reach the highway I unzip my head.

I am a zipper. A paper cut.
I fed myself so many times
through the shredder I am confetti,
I am a ticker-tape parade, I am an astronaut
waving from my convertible at Henri.

Henri from Toulouse, is that you?
Why the unhappy face? I should shoot you
for spoiling my parade. Come on, man,
glue yourself together! You want so much to die
that you don't want to die.

My name is Henri. I am Toulouse. I am scraps
of bleached parchment, I am the standing militia,
I am a quill, the Red Cross, I am the feather
in my cap, the Hebrew Testament, I am the World Court.
An electric fan blows
beneath my black robe. I am dignity itself.

I am an ice machine.
I am an alp.
I stuff myself in the refrigerator
wrapped in newsprint. With salt in my heart
I stay good for days.

from *The New Yorker*

LAURENCE LIEBERMAN

Dark Songs:
Slave House and Synagogue

◇ ◇ ◇

(St. Eustacious, Summer 1989)

1.

A few museum florid paintings by unknown
colorists, but mostly sketches
    in private family albums tell the story—
we children more inclined to trust
    tales we heard of slave days on Granddad's knee
at bedtime than the remote sagas
    we find in our school books today . . . A shipment
of new slaves came, all at once,
    several boatfuls clumped in a caravan:

    serfs in one lead vessel, an echelon or two
above their comrades in chains
    in rear ships, parallel teams of rowers
puffing at the oars to speed
    those sail-masted, multi-sail-driven craft.
The privileged half-freed advance
    troop, whether promoted by bribes, loyalties,
friendship, sexual favors,
    family rank honored across generations,

or sheer beauty and power of person—those few,
alone, were earmarked for serf
    status: no, not branded or pegged like livestock,
but targeted for low rank jobs.
    Perhaps no more than four hundred per installment
(from Ghana, Rhodesia), leg-cuffed,
    they were herded like steer—while that vanguard
of cooks, domestics, saddle-
    horsers, disembarking first, arranged floor mats

    to sleep the maximum number per human stall
in the deep low-ceilinged bins
    of the two-story slave quarters. Chefs, tailors,
laundresses, who slept in makeshift
    huts or tents in the rear yard, had, at least,
some leg room, *private bodyturn space.*
    In the slavehouse itself, all girls and ladies
were ensconced upstairs, while men
    and boys were marooned to the ground floor.

2.

    When both levels
        grow full to capacity, most slaves
    are sandwiched in boxy
        tight jamups—vertical by day,
    horizontal
    by night: except for sharp jabs in belly, neck, eyes
        or tenderest parts (breasts, genitals),
    you often don't know your neighbor's knees, elbows,
    bony appurtenances
        (keen-edged, wiry, if underfed on sea
        voyage, as like as not)
    from your holy own;

but your howls
and smart pains—excruciating, most,
of whip's lash—define you,
no confusing your boneaches
muscle spasms,
nausea, or skin rash rawness with your floormate's
scorched hide: when skin and bone's
so mashed, mine into the other's, I into Thou,
agonies keep self
intact; tiniest remove between Spirit
entity and entity saves.
Who we be survives. . . .

Some weak slaves,
afflicted with permanent squared
shoulder, humped back,
limbs flattened and malformed,
were disabled
by the crunch of bodies; no few lads suffocated
between more muscular hall mates,
none to blame. At intervals, when slavehouse
quotas ran amok,
open market ships, from South America
and other more distant ports,
arrived: bids for slaves

at townsquare
auction commenced by first light; each
half dozen, or thereabouts,
placed on front doorstoop auction
block, in cluster;
some bidders coerced by shrewd auctioneer to purchase
a mixed gaggle of males, females,
young and old, as one indivisible unit—to speed up
haggling over prices,
finicky tooth checks, sight and hearing tests
as if man needed model-perfect
molars, 20/20 sight,

                just to chop
            and husk cane all day in the fields;
        or lass glamour-shaped hips
            and breasts just to scoop proper
        bounteous handfuls
        of cotton. Each flock might boast a matchless beauty,
            or prize strongarm—most slaves sold
        for export to distant shores, Statia being chief
        transshipment center
            for humans, and nonhuman goods, alike,
            throughout the Antilles chain
    of isles. . . . Before selloffs

            in human meat
            markets, a normal day in the yards
        finds cooks, like modern
            caterers, stacking huge supplies
        of fast-food grub,
        laundresses hauling wagons and carts with mountains
            of soiled sackcloth pullovers, baggy
        shapeless blouse and shorts, all alike in style,
        dull yellowish gray,
            loose crosshatched weave of material;
            a few sizes are to be stretched
    to cover widest spectrum

            of body shapes,
            women and men in identical garb,
        little telling them apart. . . .
            I peer into the two-story-deep
        structure, thin bricks
        marvelously even-mortared, still intact today
            but for the very few crumbled
        or missing slim yellow units; those narrow
        interior hallways
            resemble storage bins or blank vats
            in grain elevators, hardly
    fit stable for livestock,

much less brain-
   bearing-mammal biped repository;
so few narrow windows, shrunk
      to prevent runaways, perhaps,
are raised too high
to collect inflow of trade winds, no East-West match up
      for air streams or ripples of cross-
ventilation: if the inmates weren't asphyxiated
by closest body
      cramping, that crush of backs and hips,
      they might choke on stale fetors,
so noxious was the stench. . . .

3.

Josser Daniel, my tutor, points across the road,
shoreside, directly opposite
Ye Olde Slave House: yet another shipman's stock
quarters fallen into disuse,
   idle for one hundred years or more, boarded-up.
This was "de Guvment Guardhouse
   and Constabulary joined" (court, too, I suppose,
all functions of arrest, trial
      & jail terms centralized for speedy work shifts) . . .

When British Rear Admiral Rodney laid siege
to Statia, he plundered the gold-
   and-silver vaults. Statia, dubbed *Golden Rock*,
had been the wealth jugular—
   sea trade megalopolis of the whole Eastern
Caribbean—for decades.
   Like today's duty-free Colonies, espoused
for their money laundering
   schemes via offshore banks, Statia was haven

for tax evaders at home, drawn to price steals
on ritziest goods the Continent
    shipped abroad, at bargain basement markoffs.
Quick as Rodney shut down the Port
    with his naval blockade, he set about to fleece
all wealthy merchants—then tried
    to win sympathizers among the local poorfolks.
But a few outspoken mavericks
    painted him History's worst *blackguard, pirate*

barbarian, quoting wild biblical parallels
in both Old and New Testaments
    (so oral historians tell), packed to deliver
the most stinging word portraits
    of his "atrocities" you can imagine, the sole
weapon any might wield against him.
    Sir Rod held all the guns. But ah, what threats
they mustered! The few unnamed—
    though prestigious—writers in their midst

    would spread poison about him to a World Press
(such Global media exchange as
    was viable 200 years back): they'd brand him
close kin to Attila the Hun!
    Since his most acid and eloquent accuser
was a prominent Jew, Rod staged
    a surprise police raid on a Friday night
Shabbas Service—in full swing
    in the Upper Town Oranjusted synagogue.

    Ha! Sham holy service, a covert political
town meeting, in disguise, Jews
    plotting sabotage against occupation forces,
so Rodney would bluster and plead
    in his own defense, years later in High Court,
when he answered to charges sworn

upon him into the docket by Queen's Councilor:
ACTS OF MASS ANTI-SEMITISM
AND RELIGIOUS CALUMNY disgracing the Crown.

4.

   Rodney's armed guards,
 undetected, surround the old Synagogue
   where all but a smidgin of some three-hundred-odd
     adult Statian Jews
   are congregated, arrest them en masse
(not a soul among them can slip
     through Rodney's net), and swiftly transport the lot
   to this Guardhouse, three ships at the ready, armed to gunnels'
galley teeth, all sails furled to deport them—
   the whole Congregation:
     chainlocked indoors, thrashing and howling, for fear
   they be pilloried, throttled, lynched, or rent
         by firing squads

   at daybreak. . . . Before dawn,
 they're whisked to the pier, ropetied in threes
   or foursomes, mouths gagged, heads bag-covered
     to cloak their faces
   from stray passersby (though all citizens
are warned by Curfew Broadsides
     to stay indoors or risk police detainment,
   not to say sniper fire); those who resist, the hysterics,
flinging themselves sideways or backwards on the wharf,
   are dragged aboard
     by their heels, heads clumping like loose potatoes
   in the sacks; those upright, the stoics,
       are stampeded

   from dock to shipdeck—
 the whole forced exodus carried off, lickety
   split, in ten minutes flat. . . . Thus, the near bulk

of Island Jewry,
    third and fourth generation Dutch families
who hail back to the civic
        roots of Colonial days, are Shanghaied, lugged
    to twelve-miles-distant St. Kitts, abandoned on woodsy
shoreline: huge death bounties sworn on their heads,
        if their postered mugs
            be spotted in Statia . . . Sir Rodney's return home,
        months hence, greeted by scathing headlines
                in London Press:

    ATTACKS ON DUTCH JEWS
    DEPLORED BY HOLLAND, Admiral Rodney's conduct
        in Statia viewed as "heinous, verging on Holy War,
            and UN-BE-COM-ING
        to any agent of Her Majesty the Queen
on the High Seas," these charges
            upon Rodney's honor carrying far more sting
        than vandalism, pillaging, or no-holds-barred piracy
(the latter, just the spoils of war by a turn
        of the tongue); no record's
            extant that Rodney had slain even one Jew—
        but his impulse to wipe the whole Isle's
                Jew-smudged slate

        clean, at a single stroke,
    smacks of the Third Reich's mass roundups. Secret
        abduction of Jews in trucks, railway boxcars, army
            transports to the camps;
        their sly, devious ruses to keep pervasive
body-snatching under wraps
            for those many months. . . . Why, despite Rod's
        early departure, did so few Jewish deportees ever return
to Statia? Perhaps the small nation's strand
        bore his taint in offshore
            mists, a noxious fume of ill spirit hung
        suspended in the ghostly sea air . . .
                Today, I explore

the awesome blank ruins
of Synagogue where the worshipers were entrapped,
a grand void since their going, perhaps never once
immersed in formal prayer
after that day; these walls may never again
have been graced with Cantor's
voice waves, or pupil's mime-whispered breath
chants of Old Testament prayer, some murmured orthodoxy
of those displaced Jerusalemites smitten
from this sad haven
ever afterwards . . . And do I hear, again, the song
of dovening, Cantor's sweet lullaby
of trilled scripture,

the youngest children, ·
students of Hebrew reading from the back
of the holy book toward the front, their fingers
groping as they trace
those richly rounded letters of Hebrew script
alphabets from right to left
while they repeat, soundlessly, with their lips
the Cantor's operatic blessings . . . *Driven, blindfolded
and gagged, bag-shroud-faceless from homeland,
a family of spirits,
dug up by their roots, torn from the soil & hurled
across the sea, from one tiny Carib
outpost to the next.*

from *Pequod*

At The Classics Teacher's

◇ ◇ ◇

You gave us phlox, blue-rose, burst on the marble
table in the backyard, the word in bloom like the sound
fire makes when it leaps—*phlox*—into being.

Our friend has gone to sleep, blue-white, this evening
on the black grass. Beside him, a pine-green spotlight falls
where, torchlight, the kerosene shines. There are no clouds.

Cloud-gray phlox in front of us, though. Not everything's lost,
not everything's shaken. Your clean, safe-surrounded house
has a back door into its garden. Your pinks have blue-gray

leaves. Your broken porch has a strong false floor. There's a place
to hide just behind the trellis covered in larkspur. Across
two rivers and fifty miles, our tiny great city is crowned

in acres of gray-pink light. It smokes, it could be on fire,
with all its division and anger. Night is making it loud
even now, but we don't hear it. In the garden tonight we're turned

to another city—cities: How the ex-queen Hecuba cried *oimoi* over
captured daughters and two dead sons. How Troy was flicked from its
pyre of ashes and became Rome. How S. Weil proved that hounding

force, like hounding charity, turns its object to stone. Our friend
turns over and wakes up, mentions the stars. He laughs aloud: "Found
it." He's forgotten, he says, the whole sky except for the Bear,

the Dipper, after all this time. "Look." We look, we gaze, we stare
at the ones we see and the ones we cannot see. You laugh, and send
us looking for Cassiopeia on her visible chair. We allow

as she might be somewhere. Those poor sailors, believers, swimming
cousins, their stars arranged into patterns they could understand—
how they longed, like fossils in water, to stay in mind,

their impression buried in mud of a certain kind.
We debate their conjugations, their words like men and women,
yoked to sense. How is it that the word "to bear," as in pounds

of burden, in the present (*fero*) was not at all like the word
"to bear" in the past (*tuli*), the "perfect"? We do not know,
but we can guess. And how are the slaves who bear our peace?

If we do not know, we do not know. We can guess, at the very least.
You were positing how to move a kind of knowledge into the world,
how Virgil, off on his farm in wartime, reported the sounds

of bees, soil, reaping. You stepped indoors for something: "Wait
right here." Our friend (you should know) said some words about
you. Then you came out with water, ice, sugar, lemons.

Catullus and his supper guests who had to bring their own provisions
didn't drink like this. All nose and mouth, we inhaled, we drank
what only in your buried garden tastes whole and round.

from *The New Yorker*

J. D. McCLATCHY

An Essay on Friendship

◇ ◇ ◇

Friendship is love without wings.
French proverb

I.

Cloud swells. Ocean chop. Exhaustion's
Black-and-white. The drone at last picked up
By floodlights a mile above Le Bourget.

Bravado touches down. And surging past
Police toward their hero's spitfire engine,
His cockpit now become the moment's mirror,

The crowd from inside dissolves to flashbulbs.
Goggles, then gloves, impatiently pulled off,
He climbs down out of his boy's-own myth.

His sudden shyness protests the plane deserves
The credit. But his eyes are searching for a reason.
Then, to anyone who'd listen: "She's not here?

But . . . but I flew the Atlantic because of her."
At which broadcast remark, she walks across
Her dressing room to turn the radio off.

Remember how it always begins? The film,
That is. *The Rules of the Game*, Renoir's tragi-
Comedy of manners even then

Outdated, one suspects, that night before
The world woke up at war and all-for-love
Heroes posed a sudden risk, no longer

A curiosity like the silly marquis's
Mechanical toys, time's fools, his stuffed
Warbler or the wind-up blackamoor.

Besides, she prefers Octave who shared those years,
From twelve until last week, before and after
The men who let her make the mistakes she would

The morning after endlessly analyze—
This puzzle of a heart in flight from limits—
With her pudgy, devoted, witty, earthbound friend.

II.

—A friend who, after all, was her director,
Who'd written her lines and figured out the angles,
Soulful *auteur* and comic relief in one,

His roles confused as he stepped center stage
(Albeit costumed as a performing bear)
From behind the camera—or rather, out

Of character. Renoir later told her
The question "how to belong, how to meet"
Was the film's only moral preoccupation,

A problem the hero, the Jew, and the woman share
With the rest of us whose impulsive sympathies
For the admirable success or lovable failure

Keep from realizing the one terrible thing
Is that everyone has his own good reasons.
The husband wants the logic of the harem—

I.e., no one is thrown out, no one hurt—
His electric organ with its gaudy trim and come-on,
Stenciled nudes. His wife, who's had too much

To drink, stumbles into the château's library
And searches for a lover on the shelf just out
Of reach, the one she learned by heart at school.

The lover, meanwhile (our aviator in tails)
Because love is the rule that breaks the rules,
Dutifully submits to the enchantment of type.

If each person has just one story to tell,
The self a Scheherazade postponing The End,
It's the friend alone who, night after night, listens,

His back to the camera, his expression now quizzical,
Now encouraging even though, because he has
A story himself, he's heard it all before.

III.

Is there such a thing as unrequited
Friendship? I doubt it. Even what's about
The house, as ordinary, as humble as habit—

The mutt, the TV, the rusted window tray
Of African violets in their tinfoil ruffs—
Returns our affection with a loyalty

Two parts pluck and the third a bright instinct
To please. (Our habits too are friends, of course.
The sloppy and aggressive ones as well

Seem pleas for attention from puberty's
Imaginary comrade or the Job's comforters
Of middle age.) Office mates or children

Don't form bonds but are merely busy together,
And acquaintances—that pen pal from Porlock is one—
Slip between the hours. But those we eagerly

Pursue bedevil the clock's idle hands,
And years later, by then the best of friends,
You'll settle into a sort of comfy marriage,

The two of you familiar as an old pair of socks,
Each darning the other with faint praise.
More easily mapped than kept to, friendships

Can stray, and who has not taken a wrong turn?
(Nor later put that misstep to good use.)
Ex-friends, dead friends, friends never made but missed,

How they resemble those shrouded chandeliers
Still hanging, embarrassed, noble, in the old palace
Now a state-run district conference center.

One peevish delegate is sitting there
Tapping his earphones because he's picking up
Static that sounds almost like trembling crystal.

IV.

Most friendships in New York are telephonic,
The actual meetings—the brunch or gallery hop
Or, best, a double-feature of French classics—

Less important than the daily schmooze.
Flopped on the sofa in my drip-dry kimono,
I kick off the morning's dance of hours with you,

Natalie, doyenne of the daily calls,
Master-mistress of crisis and charm.
Contentedly we chew the cud of yesterday's

Running feud with what part of the self
Had been mistaken—yes?—for someone else.
And grunt. Or laugh. Or leave to stir the stew.

Then talk behind the world's back—how, say,
Those friends of friends simply Will Not Do,
While gingerly stepping back (as we never would

With lover or stranger) from any disappointment
In each other. Grooming like baboons? Perhaps.
Or taking on a ballast of gossip to steady

Nerves already bobbing in the wake of that grand
Liner, the SS *Domesticity*,
With its ghost crew and endless fire drills.

But isn't the point to get a few things
Clear at last, some uncommon sense to rely
Upon in all this slow-motion vertigo

That lumbers from dream to real-life drama?
You alone, dear heart, remember what it's like
To be me; remember too the dollop of truth,

Cheating on that regime of artificially
Sweetened, salt-free fictions the dangerous
Years concoct for nostalgia's floating island.

V.

Different friends sound different registers.
The morning impromptu, when replayed this afternoon
For you, Jimmy, will have been transcribed

For downtown argot, oltrano, and Irish harp,
And the novelist in you draw out as anecdote
What news from nowhere had earlier surfaced as whim.

On your end of the line (I picture a fire laid
And high-tech teapot under a gingham cozy),
Patience humors my warmed-over grievance or gush.

Each adds the lover's past to his own, experience
Greedily annexed, heartland by buffer state,
While the friend lends his field glasses to survey

The plundered gains and spot the weak defenses.
Though it believes all things, it's not love
That bears and hopes and endures, but the comrade-in-arms.

How often you've found me abandoned on your doormat,
Pleading to be taken in and plied
With seltzer and Chinese take-out, while you bandaged

My psyche's melodramatically slashed wrists
(In any case two superficial wounds),
The razor's edge of romance having fallen

Onto the bathroom tiles next to a lurid
Pool of self-regard. "*Basta!* Love
Would bake its bread of you, then butter it.

The braver remedy for sorrow is to stand up
Under fire, or lie low on a therapist's couch,
Whistling an old barcarole into the dark.

Get a grip. Buckle on your parachute.
Now, out the door with you, and just remember:
A friend in need is fortune's darling indeed."

VI.

Subtle Plato, patron saint of friendship,
Scolded those nurslings of the myrtle-bed
Whose tender souls, first seized by love's madness,

Then stirred to rapturous frenzies, overnight
Turn sour, their eyes narrowed with suspicions,
Sleepless, feverishly refusing company.

The soul, in constant motion because immortal,
Again and again is "deeply moved" and flies
To a new favorite, patrolling the upper air

To settle briefly on this or that heart-
Stopping beauty, or flutters vainly around
The flame of its own image, light of its life.

Better the friend to whom we're drawn by choice
And not instinct or the glass threads of passion.
Better the friend with whom we fall in step

Behind our proper god, or sit beside
At the riverbend, idly running a finger
Along his forearm when the conversation turns

To whether everything craves its opposite,
As cold its warmth and bitter its honeydrop,
Or whether like desires like—agreed?—

Its object akin to the good, recognizing
In another what is necessary for the self,
As one may be a friend without knowing how

To define friendship, which itself so often slips
Through our hands because . . . but he's asleep
On your shoulder by now and probably dreaming

Of a face he'd glimpsed on the street yesterday,
The stranger he has no idea will grow irreplaceable
And with whom he hasn't yet exchanged a word.

VII.

Late one night, alone in bed, the book
Having slipped from my hands while I stared at the phrase
The lover's plaintive "Can't we just be friends?"

I must have dreamt you'd come back, and sat down
Beside my pillow. (I could also see myself
Asleep but in a different room by now—

A motel room to judge by the landscape I'd become,
Framed on the cinder-block wall behind.)
To start over, you were saying, requires too much,

And friendship in the aftermath is a dull
Affair, a rendezvous with second guesses,
Dining out on memories you can't send back

Because they've spoiled. And from where I sat,
Slumped like a cloud over the moon's tabletop,
Its wrinkled linen trailing across a lake,

I was worried. Another storm was brewing.
I ran a willowy hand over the lake to calm
The moonlight—or your feelings. Then woke

On the bed's empty side, the sheets as cool
As silence to my touch. The speechlessness
Of sex, or the fumble afterwards for something

To say about love, amount to the same. Words
Are what friends, not lovers, have between them,
Old saws and eloquent squawkings. We deceive

Our lovers by falling for someone we cannot love,
Then murmur sweet nothings we do not mean,
Half-fearing they'll turn out true. But to go back—

Come dawn, exhausted by the quiet dark,
I longed for the paper boy's shuffle on the stair,
The traffic report, the voices out there, out there.

VIII.

Friends are fables of our loneliness.
If love would live for hope, friendship thrives
On memory, the friends we "make" made up

Of old desires for surprise without danger,
For support without a parent's smarting ruler,
For a brother's sweaty hand and a trail of crumbs.

Disguised in a borrowed cloak and hood, Christine
Has escaped with Octave the muddle of romance.
It is midnight. They are in the greenhouse, alone

But spied upon by jealousies that mistake
Anxiety for love, the crime that requires
An accomplice. Then, for no reason, *they* mistake

Themselves, and suddenly confess—the twin
Armed guards, Wish and Censor, having fallen
Asleep—to a buried passion for each other.

The friendship shudders. In the end, as if he's pushed
Christine toward a propeller blade for the pleasure
Of saving her, he sends the proper hero

In his place to meet her. His head still in the clouds,
The aviator races to his death, shot down
Like a pheasant the beaters had scared up for the hunt.

Christine, when she discovers the body, faints.
Her husband, the mooncalf cuckold, so that the game
Might continue, acts the gentleman, and thereby

Turns out the truest friend. He understands,
Is shaken but shrugs, and gracefully explains
"There's been the most deplorable accident . . ."

One guest begins to snigger in disbelief.
The old general defends his host: "The man has class.
A rare thing, that. His kind are dying out."

IX.

And when at last the lights come up, the echo
Of small arms fire on the soundtrack next door
Ricochets into our multiplex cubicle.

Retreating up the empty aisle—the toss
Is heads for home, tails for ethnic out—
We settle on the corner sushi bar,

Scene of so many other films rehashed,
Scores retouched, minor roles recast,
Original endings restored, or better, rewritten,

So the stars up there will know what the two of us,
Seated in the dark, have come to learn
After all these years. How many is it now?

Twenty? Two hundred? Was it in high school or college
We met? The Film Society's aficionados-
Only, one-time, late-night *Rules of the Game,*

Wasn't it? By now even the classics
(Try that tuna epaulet) show their age,
Their breakneck rhythms gone off, their plots creaky.

But reflections our own first feathery daydreams
Cast on them still shimmer, and who looks back,
Airily, is a younger self, heedless

Of the cost to come, of love's fatal laws
Whose permanent suffering his joy postpones.
He's a friend too. But not so close as you.

He hasn't the taste for flaws that you and I
Share, and wants to believe in vice and genius,
The sort of steam that vanishes now above one

Last cup of tea—though I could sit here forever
Passing the life and times back and forth
Across the table with you, my ideal friend.

from *Poetry*

Smash and Scatteration

◇   ◇   ◇

I

About a year and a half ago my then girlfriend
Linda's parents came home from an Eric Burdon
concert and found Q.T., their twelve-week-old

black Labrador retriever, dead on the floor
of their den, his muzzle lodged—locked—
inside a box of Screaming Yellow Zonkers.

The TV was on, since Q.T. liked to hear
human voices when Linda's parents went out
without him for more than a couple of minutes.

A young Chinese man in a gleaming white shirt
was standing in front of a tank. Linda tells me
her mother was struck by the fact that Q.T.'s

hungry asphyxiation had probably caused him
to suffer, and that when the camera panned back
there were fourteen or fifteen more tanks.

II

Last month my aunt committed suicide by jumping
from her eighty-second-story bedroom window.
Her third husband had recently died, and she

had been suffering from Alzheimer's disease
and cervical cancer. She apparently smashed through
the triple-ply glass with a miniature dumbbell,

put down the dumbbell and thought about things
for a while, then stepped out the hole.
Buffeted furiously by the Venturi Effect,

she bounced down the side of her building,
the Hancock, for almost ten seconds. When
she finally hit the sidewalk on Delaware

her gray head snapped off and caromed back
up in the air. According to three gore-be-
spattered eyewitnesses, the sidespin imparted

III

to her head by the impact made it kick
back up toward the Hancock in a kind of
American twist. Chris Burden fired a pistol

at a 747. While I was licking her
clitoris and watching her face, Linda seized
her own nipples. I told her my aunt had not

left a note. In shorts and no shirt, Picasso
drew nudes with a light pen. Mick Jagger
slicked back his hair and taunted some corporate

nancies. Chris Burden had himself stuffed
into a duffle bag and dropped in the middle
of the Santa Monica Freeway. Three men burst

into a gallery brandishing automatic weapons
and kidnapped a frail-looking elderly gentleman
by placing a muzzle to his gums and walking him

IV

out the door backward. On that evening's news,
between Gorbymania stories, the elderly gentleman
turned out to have been a confederate, the weapons

authentic. A skinny little guy with black hair
stood his ground as fifteen tanks tried to advance.
In shorts and no shirt, Picasso drew nudes

with a cigarette. During the concert he gave while
Q.T. was gorging himself, Eric Burdon exhibited
his denim-clad crotch in a provocative manner.

Two nights ago on the David Letterman Show
Kevin Costner, the father of four, exhibited
his denim-clad crotch in a provocative manner.

A handsome black model arrested for gang rape
and murder (scar-faced white trash were the culprits)
kissed Madonna. Blood oozed from wooden facsimiles

V

of his model brown eyes. Sporting stigmata
and backlit by twelve burning crosses, Madonna
shimmied lasciviously. Dred Scott Tyler

placed the American flag on the floor
of a gallery. On the wall perpendicular
to the flag were a notebook and pen

along with black-and-white photographs
implying virulent third-world abhorrence
of imperialist behavior perpetrated under

or in the name of the flag. It was convenient
but not necessary to stand on the flag
while writing comments in the book. Other than

written responses were implicitly, some averred
illicitly, invited by Tyler's provocative title:
"What Is the Proper Way to Display the U.S. Flag?"

VI

In *Dick Instruction* two loinclothed men banged a drum
and shot at each other with twenty-gauge shotguns.
Laurie Anderson had an affair with Thomas Pynchon

and collaborated with William S. Burroughs.
Joy Poe was raped by Pete Panek. The reactions
of the audience were videotaped. In *The Long*

Good Friday the bird what gobbed on Eric
slapped 'Arold (Bob Hoskins) across the face.
Hoskins retaliated by shredding Eric's froat

with the jagged shards of a scotch bottle.
Eric's jugular was severed and his blood spurted
onto Hoskins' silk shirt. Hoskins went home

and lathered his muscular chest in the shower
while his moll burned the shirt. David Nelson
painted an average portrait of Harold Washington

VII

wearing women's lingerie and hung it inside
The School of the Art Institute of Chicago.
Tony Jones, the School's new President, summoned

Nelson, a graduating senior, to his windowless
office. He requested that Nelson consider
voluntarily removing the painting in order

to avert a potentially violent confrontation
with members of Chicago's black community
whose rage had been galvanized by half

a dozen aldermen. The interview lasted a couple
of hours. In the end Nelson turned down Jones's
request. The painting was confiscated by Chicago

police officers. It turned out later that evening
that the young man Jones had been interviewing
was Timothy Mostert, David Nelson's roommate.

VIII

James Fox is beaten and stripped and then
beaten again by belt-wielding cockney mafiosi.
A 747 taxies to the end of a runway, preparing

for takeoff. An attractive blond flight attendant
pretends to hassle a handsome serviceman for not
having fastened his seatbelt. Four feet below her,

in the cargo bay inside a tan leather suitcase,
is a boombox laden with Semtex. Randy Newman's
best song continues to be "Gone Dead Train."

Adrian Piper walks through London with WET PAINT
printed on her blouse. Linda Krajacik opens her legs
and lathers her crotch front and rear, singing

to herself about nothing in melodic perfecto contralto.
She scrubs her flushed face with a washcloth, then lufas
her abdomen, breasts, thighs, and sternum. She scrubs

IX

and shaves and daydreams and sings. Then she shampoos
her hair, rinses it, turns off the water. Okay.
She pulls back a translucent curtain. Two scraggly guys

in bandannas are waiting for her in the bathroom.
One guy hands her a towel. The second guy presses
the muzzle of an Ingram MAC-10 against her pink

gums and tells her to put up her hands. "You are
under arrest!" he shouts in immaculate English.
"For what?" demands Linda, raising one hand.

"For the murder of Jose Guillermo Garcia, Celia
de la Serna, Lorenzo Somoza, Manuel Noriega, Joaquin
'Stick' Villalobos, David Hidalgo, Jose Antonio

Morales Carbonel, Pilar Ternera, Roque Dalton Garcia,
Vasco 'Duende' Goncalves, Carmine Sandino, Santino
Corleone, Alvaro Magana, and Jose Rodolfo Viera,"

X

says the guy with the gun. "And so put down that
towel already, you feelthy little *desaparecida*."
"But Dalton Garcia is already dead," counters Linda.

"I'm clean." The guy with the gun says, "We know
        that."
Linda is dripping, gooseflesh has risen, she shivers.
Both hands are raised, the white towel lies on the floor.

The guy who originally gave her the towel now slaps her
across the face, twice, first with the back of his hand,
then with the front, very hard. "We already know that!"

he says. Blackout. Two nights later, at Randolph Street
Gallery, Linda stands on a table in green suede high
heels about two feet apart and pees into a teacup.

A few drops at first, then a clear steady stream
that lasts twelve, fifteen seconds. Not a drop hits
the table. Applause. Wearing a Fearnley tartan kilt,

XI

a Harris tweed jacket and kneesocks, I pretend to
interrogate her after she pees. "Quite bloody finished?"
I say. "I'm pregnant, I think," Linda says. "Not by you."

I say, "But that sounds but medium true."
"Shakespeare?" she says. I shake my head no,
then say, "But speaking of the Bard of Avon,

what's the dirtiest line, by far, ever spoken
on a prime-time network situation comedy?"
She pauses, pretending to think. "Ward,"

says finally, "weren't you a little hard on
the Beaver last night?" There is laughter.
"That's correct," I say, acting astonished.

"Okay, cheesewizz," she says, "what do you call
a Polack in a hundred-dollar hat?" I pretend
not to know. "Pope," she announces. Denim-clad

XII

Catholics prick up their ears. Thumbs-forward hands
on her hips, Linda stands on the table, clad in saucy
green smock and high heels, having already peed

in a chalice-like teacup, downloading blasphemous
info through pink bee-stung lips, unmarried and seven
weeks pregnant. "How are women like dogshit?!"

she snarls a la Vlad the Impaler. "The older they get
the easier they are to pick up!" I am stunned.
"But isn't that precisely the sort of unfunny

'bad joke' that could set feminism back a couple
three weeks?" I inquire. "Yo, tell me about it, Mr.
Premature Ejaculation," she says, whapping her palm

with her fist. "What do fifteen battered husbands
have in common?" I cower and shrug. I don't know.
"They just wouldn't fucking listen!" she sneers.

XIII

They just wouldn't fucking listen is right.
When our son was born seven months later,
we named him John Molloy after Linda's great

grandfather, who was also an artist of sorts, but
lately we've ended up calling him Air Jake or
Buzz or just John. He seems to be getting used

to having such a famous artist for a mother and all
since he spits up and cries less and less when she
uses him in her performances or we take him to see

other people's. Not that we'd leave him at home by
himself after what happened that time to Q.T. I
mean, are you kidding? We even have written a "love

of the game" clause into his contract, which
he's the only guy in the family to have such
a clause so far as I know, at least so far.

from *New American Writing*

The "Ring" Cycle

◇ ◇ ◇

1

They're doing a "Ring" cycle at the Met,
Four operas in one week, for the first time
Since 1939. I went to that one.
Then war broke out, Flagstad flew home, tastes veered
To tuneful deaths and dudgeons. Next to Verdi,
Whose riddles I could whistle but not solve,
Wagner had been significance itself,
Great golden lengths of it, stitched with motifs,
A music in whose folds the mind, at twelve,
Came to its senses: Twin, Sword, Forest Bird,
Envy, Redemption Through Love . . . But left unheard
These fifty years? A fire of answered prayers
Burned round that little pitcher with big ears
Who now wakes. Night. E-flat denotes the Rhine,
Where everything began. The world's life. Mine.

2

Young love, moon-flooded hut, and the act ends.
Houselights. The matron on my left exclaims.
We gasp and kiss. Our mothers were best friends.
Now, old as mothers, here we sit. Too weird.
That man across the aisle, with lamb's-wool beard,
Was once my classmate, or a year behind me.

Alone, in black, in front of him, Maxine. . . .
It's like the "Our Town" cemetery scene!
We have long evenings to absorb together
Before the world ends: once familiar faces
Transfigured by hi-tech rainbow and mist,
Fireball and thunderhead. Make-believe weather
Calling no less for prudence. At our stage,
When recognition strikes, who can afford
The strain it places on the old switchboard?

3

Fricka looks pleased with her new hairdresser.
Brünnhilde (Behrens) has abandoned hers.
Russet-maned, eager for battle, she butts her father
Like a playful pony. They've all grown, these powers,
So young, so human. So exploitable.
The very industries whose "major funding"
Underwrote the production continue to plunder
The planet's wealth. Erda, her cobwebs beaded
With years of seeping waste, subsides unheeded
—Right, Mr. President? Right, Texaco?—
Into a gas-blue cleft. Singers retire,
Yes, but take pupils. Not these powers, no, no.
What corporation Wotan, trained by them,
Returns gold to the disaffected river,
Or preatomic sanctity to fire?

4

Brünnhilde confronts Siegfried. That is to say,
Two singers have been patiently rehearsed
So that their tones and attitudes convey
Outrage and injured innocence. But first
Two youngsters became singers, strove to master
Every nuance of innocence and outrage

Even in the bosom of their stolid
Middle-class families who made it possible
To study voice, and languages, take lessons
In how the woman loves, the hero dies. . . .
Tonight again, each note a blade reforged,
The dire oath ready in their blood is sworn.
Two world-class egos, painted, overweight,
Who'll joke at supper side by side, now hate
So plausibly that one old stagehand cries.

5

I've worn my rings—all three of them
At once for the first time—to the "Ring."

Like pearls in seawater they gleam,
A facet sparkles through waves of sound.

Of their three givers one is underground,
One far off, one here listening.

One ring is gold; one silver, set
With two small diamonds; the third, bone
—Conch shell, rather. Ocean cradled it

As Earth did the gems and metals. All unknown,
Then, were the sweatshops of Nibelheim

That worry Nature into jewelry,
Orbits of power, Love's over me,

Or music's, as his own chromatic scales
Beset the dragon, over Time.

6

Back when the old house was being leveled
And this one built, I made a contribution.
Accordingly, a seat that bears my name
Year after year between its thin, squared shoulders
(Where Hagen is about to aim his spear)
Bides its time in instrumental gloom.
These evenings we're safe. Our seats belong
To Walter J. and Ortrud Fogelsong
—Whoever they are, or were. But late one night
(How is it possible? I'm sound asleep!)
I stumble on "my" darkened place. The plaque
Gives off that phosphorescent sheen of Earth's
Address book. Stranger yet, as I sink back,
The youth behind me, daybreak in his eyes—
A son till now undreamed of—makes to rise.

from *The New Yorker*

Sky of Clouds

◇   ◇   ◇

In that town in October
there was a ritual dressing up, a dance of sorts
that ended in a ballroom where a man laced
into a tight-fitting skirt and low-cut clingy blouse
asked me to dance. I am a woman talking
to you who exist like tinsel, a flash
and flicker at the periphery of my hearing.
On that floor were others
like me and others like him. He had managed
to extrude breasts that felt like
my mother's or my own, and we laughed about
that and the shade of his lipstick
was so close to mine, if we had kissed,
but someone cut in and stole him
from me. If this is shocking, let's say
I wanted to get your attention fast
like a neon sign or the lush trees
where I live. In spring they hang out
their ovaries in red and yellow
clusters, and they don't let you
get away any more than the women who walk
along the highway with only their poverty
and their dark hair let you
miss what they want from you. But
my subject is not what it seems. I want
to explain how it is for me
all the time now whether I'm dancing

or propped on pillows watching
the scarlet streaks of heaven, the orange
fronds of the weather. The birds
kill me with their singing, the saddest songs
are sung at sunset, and I stir the ice
in my drink and let it go, remember
and let it go, which is what the wind
does with everything I love. Sometimes,
I can't help it, I have to
get in the car and play toccatas and fugues.
I have to look at the clouds,
fat ladies on their couches, the green
and gold tassels of a sumptuous life
that keeps changing its liqueurs and girdles,
the slow slide of its trombones. Over the ocean
pelicans plummet, so heavy
with desire, it sinks them deep
as rivets, as pile drivers into
whatever catches their eye for the moment.
And after heavy rains, when the egrets
settle on the gardens, cramming
their beaks with the shrill
cries of the frogs, I think
I could do that too, I could be gorgeous and cruel.
But it's more magnanimous than that.
Right now clouds are what is going on, and after
the clouds come violet and blue. The deep
purples, the lavish tangerines
so extreme, you suspect this isn't happening,
this has been touched up. Flaming
effluvium, wells in the music
where sound bubbles, and you slide down
or through, brown rings within lime
rings, ferriferous bracelets.
Toward this hour a dark gray wading
bird comes to drink the water in the swimming pool,
a saliva color restores to the mouth. *Hello,
strange bird, with a taste for chlorine.*

Very slowly, as if arthritic, it dips
deep into its own transparency. I think
it drinks. I think it is not a mechanical
prank someone has left there. Its
throat muscles are moving.

from *Provincetown Arts*

Benedick's Complaints

◊ ◊ ◊

MUCH ADO ABOUT NOTHING

Burn my study for it holds no friends.
Who says one fathers the self for others?
Remember, Lady Disdain cannot die for you.
Courteous turncoats love women's happiness.
After sober custom who scratches the tongue?
Sighing away Sundays, put on a suspicious cap.
Savage bulls too often fall from faith.
Heavenly tuition's paid for hard lessons.
Twisting fine stories, the present practice.
Hearing of reason we use discontent as a muzzle.
Apes in hell likewise betrothed to unquiet.
The cook's mind filled with earth like supper.
Valiant dust no longer dances out answers.
Impossible slanderers eat the fool's partridge.
Hearts with tongues can always sell bullocks.
Silent heralds steal mirth and matter from all.
Dancing stars come on time's last crutches.
Argument and scorn soil this fantastic banquet.
Sheep from men's bodies counterfeit passion.
The hit fox devours tender blood like oysters.
There's fear and trembling in Messina.
Trust expectations, sport of the sadly born.
Mend distractions with paper brains, paper bullets.
Pain's message runs like fish after bait.
Consuming wrong becomes Cupid's trap.

The taming hand starts fire in the ear.
Sad money like a sighing ache is fancy's disguise.
Deaf hobbyhorses at cold midnight face upward.
Hanging dogs bark out man's shame and reproach.
Behind the horse one cannot find wantonness.
Every luxurious bed holds unknown loins.
Gone though here, Count Conflict condemns.
Recorded as an ass, he received no burial.
Caring cats, we refuse to see the doctor ape.
Hard words will not grow into a rhyming plant.
Sir God, please stop dealing in bruised hope.

from *Western Humanities Review*

Protracted Episode

◊   ◊   ◊

Then I saw one who, biting at himself,
dodged at us through the traffic. His plastic neck
stretched so his jaws could reach his shining buttocks:
cunningly made. And as he chewed he said,

"It's no unworthy task to create a speech
that ignores everything this time thinks true:
helpless patterns and correspondences,
the machine of age and endlessness of death.

This speech would be the song of an old man
praising his own eroded voice as though
it were the glory of mountains and the withered
centuries, his bleached bones were their bright snow.

But to project this man, his voice, his song,
is to confess the other speech. He is only will
yearning both to forget what should not be
and cut a swath through it with his sharp brow.

He is a voice that wonders while the flies
circle the bearded grass-tips and the stars
burst on the mountains—wonders all the time,
chanting perplexity and willing praise."

So many tears then filled me as we stood
in a bank's shadow, and so much desire
to guard these words, I quit my guide and journey,
came back, and tried to remember all my days.

from *Southwest Review*

Lunchcounter Freedom

◇ ◇ ◇

I once wanted a white man's eyes upon
me, my beauty riveting him to my slum
color. Forgetting his hands are made for my
curves, he would raise them to shield his eyes
and they would fly to my breasts with gentleness
stolen from doves.

I've made up my mind not to order a sandwich on
light bread if the waitress approaches me
with a pencil. My hat is the one I wear
the Sundays my choir doesn't sing. A dark
bird on it darkly sways to the gospel music,
trying to pull nectar from a cloth flower.
Psalms are mice in my mind, nibbling,
gnawing, tearing up my thoughts.
White men are the walls. I can't tell anyone
how badly I want water. In the mirage that
follows, the doves unfold into hammers.
They still fly to my breasts.

Because I'm nonviolent I don't act or
react. When knocked from the stool
my body takes its shape from what
it falls into. The white man cradles
his tar baby. Each magus in turn.
He fathered it, it looks just like him,
the spitting image. He can't let go of

his future. The menu offers tuna fish,
grits, beef in a sauce like desire.
He is free to choose from available
choices. The asterisk marks the special.

from *Gargoyle*

Edward Hopper's Nighthawks, *1942*

◇ ◇ ◇

The three men are fully clothed, long sleeves,
even hats, though it's indoors, and brightly lit,
and there's a woman. The woman is wearing
a short-sleeved red dress cut to expose her arms,
a curve of her creamy chest; she's contemplating
a cigarette in her right hand, thinking that
her companion has finally left his wife but
can she trust him? Her heavy-lidded eyes,
pouty lipsticked mouth, she has the redhead's
true pallor like skim milk, damned good-looking
and she guesses she knows it but what exactly
has it gotten her so far, and where?—he'll start
to feel guilty in a few days, she knows
the signs, an actual smell, sweaty, rancid, like
dirty socks; he'll slip away to make telephone calls
and she swears she isn't going to go through that
again, isn't going to break down crying or begging
nor is she going to scream at him, she's finished
with all that. And he's silent beside her,
not the kind to talk much but he's thinking
thank God he made the right move at last,
he's a little dazed like a man in a dream—
is this a dream?—so much that's wide, still,
mute, horizontal, and the counterman in white,
stooped as he is and unmoving, and the man

on the other stool unmoving except to sip
his coffee; but he's feeling pretty good,
it's primarily relief, this time he's sure
as hell going to make it work, he owes it to her
and to himself, Christ's sake. And she's thinking
the light in this place is too bright, probably
not very flattering, she hates it when her lipstick
wears off and her makeup gets caked, she'd like
to use a ladies' room but there isn't one here
and Jesus how long before a gas station opens?—
it's the middle of the night and she has a feeling
time is never going to budge. This time
though she isn't going to demean herself—
he starts in about his wife, his kids, how
he let them down, they trusted him and he let
them down, she'll slam out of the goddamned room
and if he calls her *Sugar* or *Baby* in that voice,
running his hands over her like he has the right,
she'll slap his face hard, *You know I hate that: Stop!*
And he'll stop. He'd better. The angrier
she gets the stiller she is, hasn't said a word
for the past ten minutes, not a strand
of her hair stirs, and it smells a little like ashes
or like the henna she uses to brighten it, but
the smell is faint or anyway, crazy for her
like he is, he doesn't notice, or mind—
burying his hot face in her neck, between her cool
breasts, or her legs—wherever she'll have him,
and whenever. She's still contemplating
the cigarette burning in her hand,
the counterman is still stooped gaping
at her, and he doesn't mind that, why not,
as long as she doesn't look back, in fact
he's thinking he's the luckiest man in the world
so why isn't he happier?

from *The Yale Review*

Chronic Meanings

◊   ◊   ◊

The single fact is matter.
Five words can say only.
Black sky at night, reasonably.
I am, the irrational residue.

Blown up chain link fence.
Next morning stronger than ever.
Midnight the pain is almost.
The train seems practically expressive.

A story familiar as a.
Society has broken into bands.
The nineteenth century was sure.
Characters in the withering capital.

The heroic figure straddled the.
The clouds enveloped the tallest.
Tens of thousands of drops.
The monster struggled with Milton.

On our wedding night I.
The sorrow burned deeper than.
Grimly I pursued what violence.
A trap, a catch, a.

Fans stand up, yelling their.
Lights go off in houses.
A fictional look, not quite.
To be able to talk.

The coffee sounds intriguing but.
She put her cards on.
What had been comfortable subjectivity.
The lesson we can each.

Not enough time to thoroughly.
Structure announces structure and takes.
He caught his breath in.
The vista disclosed no immediate.

Alone with a pun in.
The clock face and the.
Rock of ages, a modern.
I think I had better.

Now this particular mall seemed.
The bag of groceries had.
Whether a biographical junkheap or.
In no sense do I.

These fields make me feel.
Mount Rushmore in a sonnet.
Some in the party tried.
So it's not as if.

That always happened until one.
She spread her arms and.
The sky if anything grew.
Which left a lot of.

No one could help it.
I ran farther than I.
That wasn't a good one.
Now put down your pencils.

They won't pull that over.
Standing up to the Empire.
Stop it, screaming in a.
The smell of pine needles.

Economics is not my strong.
Until one of us reads.
I took a breath, then.
The singular heroic vision, unilaterally.

Voices imitate the very words.
Bed was one place where.
A personal life, a toaster.
Memorized experience can't be completely.

The impossibility of the simplest.
So shut the fucking thing.
Now I've gone and put.
But that makes the world.

The point I am trying.
Like a cartoon worm on.
A physical mouth without speech.
If taken to an extreme.

The phone is for someone.
The next second it seemed.
But did that really mean.
Yet Los Angeles is full.

Naturally enough I turn to.
Some things are reversible, some.
You don't have that choice.
I'm going to Jo's for.

Now I've heard everything, he.
One time when I used.
The amount of dissatisfaction involved.
The weather isn't all it's.

You'd think people would have.
Or that they would invent.
At least if the emotional.
The presence of an illusion.

Symbiosis of home and prison.
Then, having become superfluous, time.
One has to give to.
Taste: the first and last.

I remember the look in.
It was the first time.
Some gorgeous swelling feeling that.
Success which owes its fortune.

Come what may it can't.
There are a number of.
But there is only one.
That's why I want to.

from *Temblor*

ROBERT POLITO

Evidence

◊ ◊ ◊

It was one of those spots you get in. If I said some more
about "personal" I would be making a mystery of it, and that's bad.
                                                    Double Indemnity

1.

The blood-red drapes were there,
but they didn't mean anything.

On our first full night together
—Fought for; ecstatic—

Riding on desire like a drug,
Too frightened, too thrilled, to let go,

Although undone by the night,
Drained, empty, coveting sleep like a drug,

I kept driving on, never to sleep,
So that, sometime in the night, I might watch you sleep—

But I must have dozed off—
Because I came to dreaming

I was in my own bed, alone,
Flames chewing the walls of my room

—Lord Byron, on his "treacle-moon,"
Roused by firelight through the crimson curtain
Of a four-poster, determined:
"I was fairly in hell, with Proserpine lying beside me—"

But hell, here . . . in our hotel, on West 44th Street?
I roll over to wake you; then stop—

Through the greasy, polyester drapes, the color
Of movie-blood,

Bare bulbs in the airshaft glow
Like a plug-in, portable fire from Sears . . .

—Hell, I told myself, is outside;
And starts tomorrow.

On my way to kiss your hand,
You stir, raise up, look past me,

Groan once—
Then drift off again.

2.

"Winter, and I feel the circles of my world
Contract . . . Soon it's boots and leg-warmers—
Do you care if I become taller than you?
I guess horizontal it doesn't matter."

*

"I want to break out of all the rules, not just
The ones everybody does. There's nothing interesting
About infidelity—let's go way beyond that!"

*

"He makes me laugh by telling jokes
Or doing 'funny' things on purpose . . .
I feel I make him laugh mostly not on purpose.
Sometimes it seems confusing—"

*

"What got you interested? It's partly a question of *why me* . . .
Don't worry, though, I'm too curious to skip this one—
Hold on tight it's faster than the speed of light!"

*

"I listen to basketball games on the radio
In the car—you love Frank Sinatra;
It could be amazing . . .
But why am I doing this? I love my husband."

3.

*He was a big blocky man, about my
size, with glasses, and I played him exactly
the way I figured to.*

—July. Noon. Lunch. Sun
Like a slap to the back of the neck.
Heat in visible coils above the street;
Mirage shaded in the fine brown dust
Of an adjacent construction site
A tin umbrella tensely unfold-
Ing over this sidewalk table
Or the beers I've ordered
Won't shield us from,
As the Rival collapses into his seat—
My friend; her husband;
Earnest, affable, if a little
Slow   *no*

191

porcine   vacant   swelling
over mugs & napkins   balloon i'm twitching
to pop   what do i what does she
see

Looking around: Next to us, frowning
Over folders, broadsides, infinite Xeroxes,
Stopping to count each new line on his fingers
A red-eyed poet shakily fills
In the squares of a notebook stamped RECORD;

A young woman in a pink sundress
Raises the *Globe* against the light:
Nominee and also-rans compete
On page one with the Jacksons' "Victory" tour
And RADIOACTIVE MAN LOOSE IN CITY.

Fiercely I keep my Ray-Bans
Plastered to my face;
So that what I don't hear myself saying
Won't burn through—
you think i'm kidding   you think   i'm crazy
i got a bomb strapped to my crotch   hear the
ticking   everybody
here   just bought a one-way ticket   Sirens cut the air—

A water glass pitches over as workers return to their machines.
No other evident signs of alarm.

4.

". . . We've got to be brazen!
That day, way back, when I wore the blue skirt,
I was guessing you'd approve of something 'stylish'—
I wasn't thinking about *legs*."

*

"This might have to stop
If we decide to have a baby—
Or perhaps I'll just take my chances . . .
Thanks for being so lovely this weekend."

*

"You and I need to live in the real world;
I get afraid that you are looking for fantasies,
That the actual stuff won't be enough . . . if I think of this going on
It's got to fit some life of ours, it can't *be* our life."

*

"But I keep getting images of smashing up,
Body to body, explosions in the night, flames engulf
The house . . . I always have a tremor—
Should I try to keep a bit more distance?"

*

"Could you destroy my letters?
I'd feel better and freer about writing—
I don't want you to be hit by a truck
And . . ."

5.

LAST TIMES: NOON

Spring, 1981

Sharp insistent ringing. The alarm? No. Who's
At the door I drift to in a fog,
As my old teacher stumbles in—
Last day of his visit, always the worst.

"I got the papers," he says; plus,
I see, tea, headcheese, some books,
Whatever it took to postpone his hangover
—Watery eyes, sea-blue and uncertain; rolling
Walk like a sailor's (up all night,
I slept in when he went prowling at dawn);
Voice hoarse, and too intent on being understood:

"I've only had a few shandies, for Christ sake.
Don't think I do this all the time at home."

I fill a kettle, take down plates;
As he recites or invents items in the news:

—*Telepathic Twins Separated At Birth*; embarrassing celebrity
Deaths; highjinks of animal mimicry;
*JFK Alive In Geneva Hospital; Aphasic Murders Mother
With One Hand As The Other Struggles To Stop Him*—

Then more drinks; telephone calls;
More Ramones, Beach Boys, show tunes;
A nap before his long drive home . . .

Day lost in a daze like so many of our days.
Until the next time;

—Until, weeks later, just home from work,
The phone ringing as I enter the apartment:
"I have very bad news—Mark was killed last night."

Mark *killed*, I find myself thinking—

In a bar . . . ? Mugged . . . ? A knife? Gunplay?

Mark? Come on—
This is too *West Side Story*.
Has to be one of his jokes.
"Who are you?
Who put you up to this?"

As   *broken steering column   too much wine   stone wall*

Careen past before
Crashing to a stop.

6.

"EVIDENCE"

> *Believe me it's an awful thing to kibitz on a man*
> *and his wife, and hear what they really talk about.*

—August. Cape Cod. Bluffs. Vines,
Grass, a few stunted birches where what's left
Of a cliff rises to divide the ocean
From the parking lot of the Atlantic
Bar & Grille. On the corner of two dead-
End streets an exposed "chalet." She watches him
Write a letter: greetings, bus schedule,
Directions. Out of a morning's
Fog their houseguest looms—he and she and he
Share a cottage for a week.

. . . A rattle of leaves overhead.
Three trees hooked by the wind beget an inclining L
For a pair of hammocks—
Jane, restless, chats and swings
As the spare Tarzan stalks a book inside;
Shape we live in,
Shaping the way we live.

Sunset strolls to the adjacent watering hole . . .
LIVE BANDS! Drunk, dead-eyed locals.
Jokey dancing, leading, unsteady talk—
Remarkable, unremarked disappearances.
. . . We sober up in the dark
With loud, reckless swims—on a dare
Who will hazard the most?
One night straining to the warning buoys
That loop the bay in a clanging, iridescent necklace.

she's stronger than she looks   pulling him
out of the backseat while I guide her with a pocket flash
blind triple-turns   no sign   his lights out on vodka
doctored with tuinals   tomorrow's hit and run
G-L-R   G-L-R-R-K   already drowning in vomit

Florid and shaky over breakfast . . .
Sleepy jabberings, half-sentences droned
As through a stroke . . . His fingers probe
A rat's nest of uncurling hair,
Yanking, pressing, twisting,
Before exploding in a squall
Of splashy pamphlets and a project—
"Any takers for diving lessons at that marina we passed?"
. . . Her thesis; my . . . hangover;
Waving our hands, shaking our heads,
We sink into the "extra" room,
Scavenge for pleasure . . .
Hooks that tear through flesh
Even as they bind it.

Later, out for a walk with her Nikon,
We stumble on our own project: "Evidence—
The Oblique Account of an Illicit Affair,"
Each photograph like a Dutch Interior
With its own tacit narrative:
My hand gripping her thigh, moving with
The muscle as she stretches for the clutch . . .

An empty, ruined bed,
Three departing shadows . . . And then stumble off again, grinning—
"But who would shoot the pictures?"

helter skelter dead in the middle of relating
a joke about who killed david kennedy i leap
heels over head into the front seat cracking
the steering column and launching the datsun
hell and high water into the grill of an unsuspecting jeep
'JAWS OF LIFE' CAN'T SAVE 3 TANGLED IN FREAK CAPE CRASH

Another night . . . Exhaling concentration,
With both hands she stirs the pot to a boil . . .
Through the water she studies my face,
Then his, as she poles, blending
The contents of a small sack I filled in Chinatown
With the full basket he hauled dripping from the docks;
Black mushrooms, pared pork, water chestnuts stroke
Past baby shrimp and scallops—
Blowing once, twice, to cool
What she's of two minds to swallow
. . . Hot and sour bouillabaise?
"My wife," he says, rubbing his abdomen.

I linger after they go to bed.
Killing Heinekens; spinning records—
Mixing standards from their traveling collection
With my own deadpan presents: "I Stand Accused,"
"Dark End of the Street," "Getting Mighty Crowded,"
"He'll Have to Go."

It was late, now, and the rain
made the night darker . . . tipsy, i kept tripping
and sliding . . . I didn't know he was there
until he spoke—until a match flared and raised up
to a face beneath a slouch-brimmed hat . . .
that, i said, is a good way of getting killed—
cut the tough guy stuff, he spat back . . . listen,

i've known about you two for a long time . . . don't explain—
things happen that way . . . hey—we fall
into our lives . . . but don't you want to get off
this merry-go-round? . . . yeah, she knows
i'm talking to you . . . look, here are my keys—
catch—why not . . . take a spin someplace. . . .

On my way to the bathroom
I stop outside their bedroom door—

In the living room a guitar feeds back,
The hot distorted notes soar and scud
Before they're ripped back into the rhythm—

On the porch bushes scratch at the screen,
Heaving like the sea after a high wind—

Through the window beams from a wandering car
Climb the wall—

A rattle of leaves overhead—

August. Cape Cod. Bluffs. Vines,
Grass, a few stunted birches where what's left . . .

7.

"BACKWARDS AND FORWARDS"

"Passion, it's so much bigger
Than sex; a certain level of anticipation,
Unexplored limits—

And you don't do that with someone you've known 10 years.

It's the music too—live,
When I catch the jolt through the floor—
And I just don't feel I'm here anymore.

But you don't want to be on edge all the time either . . .

This probably won't get any easier—
Passionate encounters tend to become addictive."

*

"That Sunday I wasn't sure anything would happen . . .

It was like sitting through a thunder and lightning storm—
Except no rain.

I love your accent—but oh my God,
If we keep talking
We might like each other—

And then there wouldn't be loopholes,
Or excuses, or good one-liners . . .

Write me at work—I hate to think this ends
Getting mail from you."

*

"Next week I'm having lunch
With a man I haven't seen in—holy shit, is it 12 years?
I could tell I was making him crazy
Over the phone. We'll see . . .

I never return to the scenes of past crimes.

The idea of a relationship
That's basically a friendship with the odd sexual
Moment thrown in
Is unbelievably appealing to me—

But I've never pulled it off."

*

"Listen. We've got to have a big talk.
I'm hating having to lie all the time—
And I'm starting to make comparisons . . .
It's getting me crazy.

I know that if I told him
He'd make me stop seeing you
—Or go—
And I'm just about certain what I'd do . . .

Listen. I don't like myself this way.
This hurts me too. Listen!"

8.

LAST TIMES: NIGHT

Fall, 1979

Stayed away for days;
unable to imagine,
refusing to think about

how easy it should be
to get up, shower, dress
and bus across town

to watch an old man gaining
years by the hour, shrinking,
bottle dripping

nourishment,
machines feeding poisons into swollen
wasted arms,

twisting and rolling as he repeats
rhythmically, dimly,
"God, oh, God,"

to the dropped ceiling;
stuck on the words
the way a falling climber

bites the rope
rock chewed through miles above;
invoking nothing;

just as on his last night, 3 A.M.,
the phone kept ringing and ringing
—could only be

mother, alone at the hospital,
dialing back
as soon as she hangs up

crazy to hear herself say:
"If you want to see your father
die—this is it—he's stopped talking."

9.

"CLUBLAND"

I hung up . . . That night I did something
I hadn't done in years. I prayed.

A barrel in the kitchen
Waits to receive the bottle I'm drinking;
At the bottom of the barrel
Other bottles—

               The phone I keep picking up,
               Dialing only to hang up—

Rocking chair, glasses, ears, nose, chin,
Double in the double-pane window;
Doubled again by the Guinness—

        A leather bar gone to hell—

Smoke uncoiling in cool ribbons from a semicircle
Of overhead lamps, each white-hot and unblinking; no light-
Show here, only shooting star B.U. girls trailing
Glitter, as they dance,
Flashing studded belts, smiles, and fuck-me shoes
Toward the band that, inches away, twitches and pulses
Over them. Their boyfriends, cast off in groups by the P.A.,
Gape and drink, flexing spandex or fingering
Chords on the necks of their beers . . . All alone in a corner,
Two slumming models in his and her matching
Jackets, haircuts, and eye shadow, tease
A blackened mirror that once unriddled
Ramrods, fist fuckers, and rough trade,
Their fierce codes—keys, insignia, colored
Handkerchiefs—as sly and unequivocal as a Church Father's.

When the first ragged act's history,
The swaggering frontmen, identical twins, wheedle
Drinks from the kids near the stage;
My date, a local music critic, points
At a Siouxsie Sioux lookalike
Parked by the dressing room door—
"One night the guitar player
Got trashed enough to take her home.
When he was through, he disappeared to take a piss,
But sent his brother back;
Then he screwed her too . . .
She still doesn't know this happened!"

Between sets the show goes on—Lao Tse,
Timeless neighborhood fixture, pushing
80 but boyish in his olive toupee
And leather pants, demonstrates Tai Chi
Before a jar of plastic flowers
He's offering to the next group, his favorite;
My date scampers past with Anton
—Unflappable "manager" of Scurvy the Bat,
He'll play rhythm in the Wild Motel Dwarfs Friday and Saturday,
230 lbs. of game good cheer—
"I'm picking up a press kit, sweetie,
I'll be back in a coupla minutes."

Squirming onto a stool by an idle Ms. Pacman,
I almost elude the middle band:
Icy synth-wizards into random pain . . .
Later, I cruise the aisles,
Shadow a pretty skinhead
Combing out her friend's hair—
"Can you believe all the cute guys here?
I keep wanting to go up to them
And scream, I love you, can I have your baby!"

House lights already up, a breakneck Scurvy
Careers into the final encore
As my date returns with a thick envelope and a cassette—
"Come on, let's go back to my place."

From the window of a 7–11 by the cabstand
The Weekly World News *reassures*
THERE IS SEX AFTER DEATH MEDIUMS SAY.

On my lap through the Back Bay—
"Anton called me a gossip . . . Can you believe it?
The people I tell things to don't tell other people!

. . . Oh Robert . . . I'm so bad . . .
I went back to his house for a tape,
Sorta drunk, so I jumped on his bed—
Then I fucked him . . .
Don't look at me that way,
Like you're going to be sick . . ."

On the floor of her apartment she turns
And licks the last dot of white powder off a record jacket—
"God, I never made it with two people
On the same day before. . . .

What are you doing here?

One more beer
And I want to go to sleep . . .

Do you think I should take a Valium?

Please stay . . .

Sorry . . . I'm really wasted."

Rocking chair, glasses, ears, nose, chin,
Double in the double-pane window;
Doubled again by the Guinness—

I watch the Guinness bottle spin in the air,
Arc toward one of my faces;
I watch my features duck and blur
When it bounces back into my chest—

        The phone I keep picking up,
        Dialing only to hang up—

A barrel in the kitchen
Waits to receive the bottle I'm drinking—

10.

LAST TIMES: MORNING

First snow of the year, but late; and
Light, blowing in the empty sunny street . . .

      Unrelenting sun,
Bearing down through a high, round window,
Hacks out and trims a small stage,
Then pierces the bed like a spotlight;
As last night's impatient forces
—Overdressed, underrehearsed actors
With names like "Desire" and "Necessity"—

Play themselves out.

Her new curls, blond streaks
And patches, settling as she talks;

Eyes clouding over;
Then wetly brightening;
As they watch him
Watching her do what she says she has to do;

Her "we thought we could save each other":

Head shaking no;
Her long arm cutting through
His *"but can't we still"*—

Until all clears.

The storm's ending; whatever stirs and gusts
Scatters
Over the same rolling, motionless drifts.

—But with nothing else
To do or say;
No audience but themselves:
Once more, for old time's sake?

"We can't—it would be too sad."

                              "I know.
Every minute I'd be thinking, this is the last time."

11.

   "Dear R—

   I know I should have called but for various reasons I have been
feeling tired & feeling a need to see the center of things.
   I also haven't changed my mind.
   Maybe you're right about some things but now I feel I want
my life to be as smooth & easy as possible.

I want to concentrate on digging deeper alone & not on scattering myself around.

The new career thing seems very important & exciting to me & needs attention.

I am sorry but I just couldn't face having a conversation about it all.

I just didn't want to feel I was letting you down.

I am tired of letting people down.

I'm feeling frayed & must just burrow in someplace safe.

For whatever reasons that's the story."

12.

*What you've just read, if you've read it,
is the statement.*

The story behind the story

In Weegee's photograph
It's all black and white.
—"Weegee the Famous," prowling Manhattan after
Midnight for the *Daily News,* his studio
A restless Black Maria driven by instinct
And a police radio; his high speed
Infrared film—newly developed
For reconnaissance flights—would expose lovers
From the protective gloom of 3D movie houses,
Or on summer nights, shameless, in the sand at Coney Island
—A lone young woman gazes down
From a lifeguard's watchtower, chewing the tips of her fingers . . .

The story behind the story

In "Victory Celebration 1945"
The furtive, unfair flash locks on
A no-longer-young sailor and the dark body of a woman
(Her features swallowed up by his) locking into
A kiss, abrupt and jittery—

Her right hand holding fast to a thick comb,
In his left the still burning end of a war-issue cigarette;

Fingers embroiled in her hair, her other arm is caught
Between them—thrusting him back, or urging
Him in and closer, as his face
Cut by fatigue or dissipation or laughter
Presses her lips, or down into her neck;

Over their shoulders a grinning civilian in a straw hat,
Pleased with the victory, or with himself
Like a deaf-mute in a telephone booth,

As above them a soldier has drifted by—
"At ease," hands firmly in his own
Pockets, legs stiffening
Or about to carry him away—

And turned: Face puffy with desire,
Mouth tight, even; his envy at odds
With the grim sense he's seen them before,
His eyes lock on the celebrating couple—

       At the clear center whose edges fade,
Not me looking down at them;
But back into the flash and shadow of our few minutes
Hand in hand down a crowded avenue, oblivious
Of detection, running—;

Another story   behind the story.

from *Pequod*

Night Subway

◊   ◊   ◊

The nurse coming off her shift at the psychiatric ward
nodding over the *Post*, her surprisingly delicate legs
shining darkly through the white hospital stockings,
and the Puerto Rican teens, nuzzling, excited
after heavy dates in Times Square, the girl with green hair,
the Hasid from the camera store, who mumbles
over his prayerbook the nameless name of God,
sitting separate, careful no woman should touch him,
even her coat, even by accident,
the boy who squirms on his seat to look out the window
where signal lights wink and flash like the eyes of dragons
while his mother smokes, each short, furious drag
meaning *Mens no good they tell you anything—*

How not think of Xerxes, how he reviewed his troops
and wept to think that of all those thousands of men
in their brilliant armor, their spearpoints bright in the sun,
not one would be alive in a hundred years?

O sleepers above us, river
rejoicing in the moon, and the clouds passing over the moon.

from *The New Republic*

209

Into the Open

◇ ◇ ◇

How forlorn and lost
they must have looked, the mahogany deer
carved on the cabinet,
peering forth from the trailing
vines and foliage, antlers
intertwined, their bodies forever
suspended, frozen
as if jacklighted, as if, having come
so far to the edge
of the forest,
they couldn't bear to enter
the room, with its stale air,
the claw-footed sofa. Coaxed
from the wood, whittled,
these fallow deer, clustered
around the keyhole, guardians
of some mortal secret. . . .

It was a woman's hand, I think,
that turned the key
to lock away some token, hidden perhaps
in her underclothes, lying under
her corset, its hooks
and eyes open. I like to believe
it was she, needing
consequence, image, passion,
who placed the china figurines

in the curio cabinet, almost touching,
the shepherdess and the sweep,
vivified, at least for a moment,
by closeness. Once they were slip
in a single bowl, poured
into molds of equal measure,
and set on the topmost
shelf together—she with a rose
pinned to her bosom, a gilded crook
beside her, but no sheep walk
to cross, no flock to tend to,
and he in pitch-black clothes,
holding ladder and broom,
his face glowing,
having swept, as yet, no nooks,
no hearth, no ingles.

Day after day, lifted up, dusted,
placed on the shelf closer
and closer, the shadow of one
sometimes falling across the other,
they felt the shape
that love can take—the form of one
lying darkly upon the other—
and though you might say
they were only dolls, their features
glazed, their bodies rigid,
they, too, are of the earth, and I,
for one, have come to believe
in the primal sadness
of a divided substance. Oh, come

to me now, toting your ladder,
and we'll go, as they once did,
past the opening night
at the dolls' theatre,
past the one-act play of star-crossed lovers,
past the household creatures—

                                    the potpourri jar
                  exuding sweetness, the captured knight
                                 and the ivory castle,
                    the knave of hearts
                             doubling with self-love—
        and I'll take you with me over the doused embers
                                   into the dark heart
                               of the stove,
               where we'll climb together toward the stars
                          bracketed inside the chimney,
                    past firebrick and flue
                             into the stratosphere.

        from *The New Yorker*

JACK ROBERTS

The New Reforms

◊ ◊ ◊

for Robert and Helene Atwan

Those were fluid days. And the wind that met us
As we turned into the street which traced
The line of conquest sang of pleasant rains.

On the steps of the public library,
Vendors talked only of the lost caravan.
Then, we thought of you almost constantly.

If there had been an opening, a rent
In the arras, there was no way of knowing.
That night the martins grew silent in their nests.

In the square the lines began to soften.
And all around us space became something
No longer to be feared. We could see

Everything. That was not the problem.
The difficulty lay in seeing further,
Beyond what we always saw: the showgirls,

The luncheonettes, the tiny pools themselves,
Which had never failed until now to waken
All sorts of feelings. These pass from our minds

As one passes from the lobby unobserved
And having found some quieter spot, looks once
Around, and lights a cigarette. The builders

Grow old and move away, leaving no plans
For those who remain; far too damaged
To repair, these walls admit a stranger light.

Our newest maps reflect the coastal changes.
Beneath the shore estates, the rock shifts
Another inch; a great cornice falls away.

I follow highways north along the sea,
Through mossy headlands verging on the sea.
I am lost and will not know my place again,

Carried along by some other power
Toward regions of ice; behind me only love
Stretched tight as deerskin across continents.

And though I could blame the cartographers,
Was it their fault they had hoped to create
A landscape untouched by the old failures

That touch us even as we fail so that
It all had the sense of a Hollywood
Ending. You know the one I'm thinking of.

It's where the Creature alone as before,
The blonde girl having been taken from him,
Moves off toward the tarpits. He knows even then

He won't be coming back. Slowly submerging,
He takes one last look back—there may be peace—
At the lovely world he is losing.

from *Sites*

DAVID ST. JOHN

Merlin

◇ ◇ ◇

Italo Calvino (1923–1985)

It was like a cave of snow, no . . .
More like that temple of frosted, milk-veined marble
    I came upon one evening in Selinunte,
Athena's white owl flying suddenly out of its open eaves.
    I saw the walls lined with slender black-spined
        Texts, rolled codices, heavy leather-bound volumes
Of the mysteries. Ancient masks of beaten copper and tin,
    All ornamented with rare feathers, scattered jewels.
His table was filled with meditative beakers, bubbling
        Here and there like clocks; the soldierly
Rows of slim vials were labeled in several foreign hands.
    Stacks of parchments, cosmological recipes, nature's
Wild equivalencies. A globe's golden armature of the earth,
        Its movable bones ringing a core of empty
    Space. High above the chair, a hanging Oriental scroll,
Like the origami of a crane unfolded, the Universe inked
        So blue it seemed almost ebony in daylight,
The stars and their courses plotted along its shallow folds
    In a luminous silver paint. On an ivory pole,
        His chameleon robe, draped casually, hieroglyphics
Passing over it as across a movie screen, odd formulas
    Projected endlessly—its elaborate layers of
Embroidery depicting impossible mathematical equations;
    Stitched along the hem, the lyrics
Of every song one hears the nightingale sing, as dusk falls

On summer evenings. All of our stories so much
Of the world they must be spoken by
A voice that rests beyond it . . . his voice, its ideal melody,
Its fragile elegance guiding our paper boats,
Our so slowly burning wings,
Toward any immanent imagination, our horizon's carved sunset,
The last wisdoms of Avalon.

from *Antæus*

SHEROD SANTOS

Two Poems

◊   ◊   ◊

I

Early morning, a woman sits up in bed
With a cup of coffee and an ashtray
In her lap, though she isn't smoking
And the coffee has long since cooled.
For the last two months she and her husband
Have slept in separate rooms, and now,
By habit, it's decided this room is "hers."
Outside, the sky is overcast, as it usually is
In the mornings in the fall, and there's
A stillness on the world, which for once
She doesn't find threatening. Beyond her window
A sparrow is furiously tearing away
At the wildly overgrown lantana bush,
Stabbing at its inky, blue-black berries,
Some of which fall onto the window ledge
Already badly stained. Before entering
Her room—he's dressed for work and probably
In a hurry—her husband pauses and shuffles
His feet as though wiping his shoes on a mat.
At the sound this makes, she looks up at him
Undisturbed, and so manages once more
To turn a loss into the semblance of a loss.

II

Weeks, maybe months, have passed and just
Outside the kitchen door he's standing
On our new redwood deck listening to the owls,
Who call, or answer, or resign themselves
To a mounting dark in the woods behind our house.
The more he listens, the more they call.
Seeing what his life has come to—how else
To say it now?—perhaps it's not too much
To think: Things might get a little better
In time. Time, all the while, sliding
Past like a calm sea beneath those boards. . . .
No, standing there he seems to incline
Toward something that inclines toward him:
The beginning of hope. The beginning of sorrow.
Something hunted deep within the forest
Of his affections. It's an hour he'd like
To preserve somehow, but already the dark
Has begun to lap against the lowest rungs
Of the railing. A small moving. Wind
In the trees. Salt wetness and bright stars.

from *The New Yorker*

LLOYD SCHWARTZ

Leaves

◇ ◇ ◇

1.

Every October it becomes important, no, *necessary*
to see the leaves turning, to be surrounded
by leaves turning: it's not just the symbolism,
to confront in the death of the year your death,
one blazing farewell appearance, though the irony
isn't lost on you that nature is most seductive
when it's about to die, flaunting the dazzle of its
incipient exit, an ending that at least so far
the effects of human progress (pollution, acid rain)
have not yet frightened you enough to make you believe
is real; that is, you know this ending is a deception
because of course nature is always renewing itself—
 the trees don't *die*, they just pretend,
 go out in style, and return in style: a new style.

2.

Is it deliberate how far they make you go
especially if you live in the city to get far
enough away from home to see not just trees
but only trees? The boring highways, roadsigns, high
speeds, 10-axle trucks passing you as if they were
in an even greater hurry than you to look at leaves:
so you drive in terror for literal hours and it looks

like rain, or *snow*, but it's probably just clouds
(too cloudy to see any color?) and you wonder,
given the poverty of your memory, which road had the
most color last year, but it doesn't matter since
you're probably too late anyway, or too early—
    whichever road you take will be the wrong one
    and you've probably come all this way for nothing.

3.

You'll be driving along depressed when suddenly
a cloud will move and the sun will muscle through
and ignite the hills. It may not last. Probably
won't last. But for a moment the whole world
comes to. Wakes up. Proves it lives. It lives—
red, yellow, orange, brown, russet, ocher, vermillion,
gold. Flame and rust. Flame and rust, the permutations
of burning. You're on fire. Your eyes are on fire.
It won't last, you don't want it to last. You
can't stand any more. But you don't want it to stop.
It's what you've come for. It's what you'll
come back for. It won't stay with you, but you'll
    remember that it felt like nothing else you've felt
    or something you've felt that also didn't last.

from *The New Republic*

Past Lives

◇ ◇ ◇

It's a habit: what we remember
in what moods or places. That night, I thought,
calmed by the food and wine, I could have walked
with you *until the twelfth of never*

or something like that. So we walked like that,
hours through the Marais studying
doors, vestibules, courtyards in the brimming
three-quarter moonlight. Pit-stopped, we sat

curbside, to listen at a music shop
where an unshaven minyan played lute
and mandolin. Well after they'd stopped
we realized they'd stopped.

Seated among strangers at a café
I thought of another café: I was nineteen,
before you, long-haired, somewhere in between
sexes, eleven stone, dull and shy.

The Germans at the next table brought me
the German woman I'd made, so made do
with. Four Brits brought Black & Tans, the dues
I'd paid without East End heroin, without Lori

with whom I'd done bad grades, bad years, nights
of looking for the bar I'd overheard one woman
mention to another one with some
gesture and chic I could never get right.

That's when I made records at Elephant
and Castle, smoked locked in the downstairs john
alone. Later, I sucked eggs, ate plankton
to undo what the pot did. I went

away. On New Year's Eve in Greece
a fist fight over feminism end-
ed in a pile-up when the other girl's girlfriend
panicked and called out the Greek police.

I ordered a second brandy for what I missed
and missed my father who funded my insolence.
We passed by the music store, the lights still on,
the instruments on pegs, the players gone.

from *Ploughshares*

DAVID SHAPIRO

The Seasons

◇ ◇ ◇

SUMMER

I saw the ruins of poetry,
Of a poetry
Of a parody and it was
Terraces and gardens
A mural bright as candy
With unconcealed light
The ceiling sprayed upon us
With a bit of the Atlantic
Fish leaping about a henotheism
That permits no friend
And leaves us happier
In the sand than in our room
You are not a little bird in the street
Protected by a stationary car
And protesting too little
Synthesize the aqueduct and
The tepidarium and the lion's pit
The sun stapled shut
The sun not a wandering error
Sunspots are hair
Sun from above or in the light's maw
The sun as a windshield and we drove to time's beach
The sun another snowman

A monkey for a child
Unkidnapped calm
Good day! good time! pulverized shore
At night, when everyone is writing
At night, when everyone is reading
Or learning to read in the dark
Time, with its patent pending
Half-eaten fruit of those
Who fear no lions
No weapons
No suspects, no motives
Walking down the beach on
Our heads: man and dog
Forced alike to swim in hurricanes
By the father, actually to dog paddle
Without a subject like a fireweed
Or a thistle
But the law we did not abide and carried by air
A single drop and I mean drop
Of a honeysuckle would satisfy me then
A cricket arises at the bottom of the lawn
Alone and vague it hesitates to mount the curb
A natural fire discovered in the grillework of these woods
The long column of summer days
Scornfully you lower all the eyelids
And we breathe together a long time

AUTUMN

A project and a lack of derealization
And a warehouse like a button
A facade in dark gray velvet
With strips of false marble lettering
Bending with the remover to remove
Absorbed into the sky like a gourd
My temporary window like a garden
And the stairwell split open

224

Into the interior view of a sieve
Of stairwells elaborate in cross section
And the axiometric of Charles Lindbergh
A mannikin feted in his aviator clothes
At the Salon of Autumn
With your hands full of women's
Accessories
And the President with his lips
In the frigidaires
And the tires rolling up at the annual
Automobile salon
Something enormous: the real estate
You did not buy
Sun spots bleeding beneath an oak
No floor
No young fate
The history of time-lapse photography
Is falling now
You cannot even take dictation like daughters
You have destroyed a little of everything
How dare you interrupt my house
Of empty pictures
Make music too loud to listen to
Want the bed too low
Don't want this to exist
Want me to become unconscious
Of too many colors

A house to sink
Violins without bridges
Pencils too heavy to be carried
Dictionaries stuck in the ground
And the violin lies on the long black piano and replies

WINTER

Hard winter
Unlivable house
Unlivable snow
It is true January
However
My son is smiling in his sleep
After death there are extremes
Of temperature
An automobile is attached to the planet
And it sails the ice like a caravel
It is a word without songs
And one stops on the highway
To observe the snow's perspective
As the executions are executed
With a technical precision
Like Ricci's spicatti
And the dead slide sidewise
While the moon moves outward
Failing to grip the roadway
Like a bed sliding under the frame
Of a cloudless sky
February has clumped and intimated
That I find you in these halls
Of powerlessness
The fields are messier each day
Freezing water throttles the sky
We are idle, like a pair
Of wild cars on the highway
O northern widowed word
Ice like a sidewalk on the river
A difficult year
And the head emits a hot kind of hope
The truth a novel highway going round
The suburbs and ultimately I
Become part of myself not you and a gulf and sea
Held at precise angles to forbid us

Crypto-opponents to join
In natural darkness
Whose tied feet the imaginary rat gnawed through
In comatose sleep I saw you last
No cemetery holds you nor a single
Fire that I could burn
I pretend to approach your metal mouth,
You put it close to me
Brush your lips with ice
In a key he rarely chose the F sharp minor
You used to say Oh you could say anything

SPRING

A boy who stayed awake
And what he saw
Very near as opposed to
To the west of everything
He kisses the bug
The charred blossoms of the dogwood
Family sculpture or
Family carving
My father would point to the
Anomalous forsythia
Because of this truthless
Encyclopedism
It is just as good to meet
A dog or a cat
What they left out: Anger
Sex and history
My grandfather died singing
Called the best death
As my father stayed at the music stand
Or the dancer wants to do
That new thing: dancing until the end
A construction site in sunlight
I had written: Superbia's loutish

Psychological best-of-horse show
Does your promise shine like a highway
Like an effaced green work on a wall
Singing and partly singing
I walked with my son a little way
I say good-bye but not enough
He whirls around I disappear
You need the shadow of a child
Like an avalanche
He was glad he had stayed awake
And he stayed awake to this day
You the chrysalis and I the traditional ancestor exploded like
    aluminum

DRAWING AFTER SUMMER

I saw the ruins of poetry, of a poetry
Of a parody and it was a late copy bright as candy.
I approach your metal mouth, you put it close to me.

By the long column of a summer's day
Like a pair of wild cars on the highway
I saw the ruins of poetry, of a poetry.

The doll within the doll might tell the story
Inside the store: the real estate you could not buy.
I approach your metal mouth, you put it close to me.

Violin lies on piano and makes reply.
Hunted words. Gathered sentences. Pencils too heavy to carry.
I saw the ruins of poetry, of a poetry.

The history of time-lapse photography
Is a student exercise. Throttle the sky.
I approach your metal mouth, you put it close to me.

The moon moves outward failing to grip the roadway.
I see you stuck in the ground like a dictionary.
I saw the ruins of poetry, of a poetry.
I approach your metal mouth, you put it close to me.

from *American Poetry Review*

Living Color

◇ ◇ ◇

At first there's greenish flesh until the knob's
turned farther to the right, and then the flesh turns paler, pink;
   the gray walls behind the silent faces
      shimmer, and next the sound's turned up,
the lips are moving, the hands, the voices, rising, moving—
      is this what fright is, these
pale interchangeable faces,
   is this the body of the world
     that can be seen but never touched,

    the faces floating there, the hands,
and all the broken things?
   The set casts its flickering light onto the walls
      as the ghost-bodies dressed in their momentary garments
bend to kiss
     the gleaming armor of the world.
They have given themselves over
   to quickness,
    to sound bites, to thirty- or sixty-

   second spots.
How slow we are against them
   who dream of change but rarely, finally, change.
     Now the man is walking toward the woman.
He sits down beside her on the bed,
    the walls pale gold;

the bedspread flowered, gold. On her dresser
    are many small bottles, delicate long-stemmed
        vials, perfume and makeup,

        and on the wall above it
a mirror that holds them from behind
    showing us what the man and woman cannot see
        of who they are; the man's broad back
in his striped suit, the woman barely covered by a negligee,
        her brown hair tumbling down.
As if they had no names. As if they had no
    faces, no address.
        But she lifts her face to him

        and her skin is smooth as the gold lamp light
falling in a calm closed circle on the carpet
    so that we are meant to think:
        it is important to know what happens
next. But how grotesque
        they appear when I turn off the sound,
trapped in a world where speech is ceaselessly
    required, in which mouths move and move
        but nothing can come out

        and still they must keep moving
the way neon pulses on and off, on and off
    against a wall. No stillness there. No rest.
        And no one can be left alone for long;
if the woman stands at her window
        it is clear soon enough someone will come knocking
on her door. There is no room
    for silence. I turn off the set.
        I watch the dark blank screen,

        how it holds only the merest shading of a face,
barely there but still it's there,
    no sound at all, no humming sound, no hushed

electric purr, just blank
like the door a child wakes to in the night,
                  the voices shimmering and slurring
on the other side, in darkness,
            but there is no screen to hold them, making them its ghosts,
            there is no way to shut them off.

from *Ploughshares*

CHARLES SIMIC

Country Fair

◊ ◊ ◊

If you didn't see the six-legged dog,
It doesn't matter.
We did, and he mostly lay in the corner.
As for the extra legs,

One got used to them quickly
And thought of other things.
Like, what a cold, dark night
To be out at the fair.

Then the keeper threw a stick
And the dog went after it
On four legs, the other two flapping behind,
Which made one girl shriek with laughter.

She was drunk and so was the man
Who kept kissing her neck.
The dog got the stick and looked back at us.
And that was the whole show.

from *The New Yorker*

The Wound

◊　◊　◊

1

The spear is his alone. Nobody else
can heft its ash shaft. His friend, Patroklos,
borrows the rest—and loses all but the spear.

His father's, it is his, his heritage,
a mortal weapon, a mortal's weapon. The gods
had nothing to do with this. The shield, the greaves,

all those layers of corselet and girdle
Hephaistos made, they make a pretty story.
But Achilles dies. It is his nature to die.

His actions, therefore, are serious, as the gods'
can never be who float on forever, their feet
not quite touching the dark earth, their blood

a colorless ichor. Death is the long shadow
Achilles casts. And Peleus' spear, his father's
ash-and-bronze weapon, is properly his,

as Thetis had to learn. It is hard for her not to
avert her eyes from the corner where it looms,
propped with his armor, its omen all too clearly

shining in sunlight and glinting in firelight.
As much as his heel is his, his spear is his,
stands for him, and means him like his name.

2

Those old men must have known
what they were saying, what they hinted:

to those who could understand, it was all
clear as water; to anyone else,

dark as water when wind blows
to ripple the surface slate and silver.

For Telephus' wound, the only cure
was a touch of the same spear that made it,

Achilles' spear. Poetic justice?
Yes, and perhaps lore from the old

healing arts from the age when spears
were pointed with iron—the rust would have been

curative in a wound. Still,
the specification of that spear,

Achilles' own—what were they saying?
A part of the plot, to make the killer

also the healer? An allopathic
remedy demonstrating the double-

nature of people and even of things?
Troy cannot fall unless a son

of Herakles help the Achaian host!
So had the Oracle warned them all,

and what other son of the hero is here?
No way around it then, unless

Achilles help his enemy, touch him,
heal with the spear that is his alone,

and therefore share between them a bond
they both feel, and the same shame.

3

Or
was the
spear nothing
in itself, but
an implement for
the production of pain?
Was it, perhaps, the same pain
in which the cure's magic
lay concealed like a
whole tree in an
acorn? The
balm was
tears!

4

We have all felt the liquid fire, burning and annealing,
the hot rush of our tears that are the anodyne
for the pain we feel. And any tears will produce,
at least for a moment, that wonderful ease, the release
of the spirit's suffering. Tragedy does it, the pity
and terror will turn the faucets on and perhaps prompt us

to remember our own lives' disasters, our unassuagable losses.
But a day later, or only an hour, and we are no better, no
different from what we were before the start of the evening's
entertainment.

But suppose for a moment those tears
you were shedding were not just any tears, not Lear's,
or Antigone's, or Aida's, or even Bambi's mother's,
but yours, the identical tears, provoked by the very same
pain that had first produced them. . . . The old scars
are not so insensitive. They seem tough, but they are only
hard on the surface; underneath there is a dull ache
that will not go away, that you have known so long
as to confuse it with the normal human condition,
or anyway yours, your nature being always to feel
that not-quite-disabling throb or twinge or frisson.
And then at that same occasion, the same production
of tears that turn out to be the right and only solvent
for that odd amber or exotic epoxy that had frozen
the disabling hurt into its place in the heart's
heart, the soul's most secret chambers.

The talking cure
Of Dr. Freud? What else is it but a reaching back
to the source of the pain, the source of the original
tears, or to speak in myths and parables, the touch
for Telephus of that spear? Achilles' spear
made the wound in the first place, goring his flesh
and tearing from him those tears; only a new
outpouring of those same tears will make him whole.

5

The issue of Herakles' rape of the princess Auge,
he was exposed newborn on the mountainside. . . .
But we are, let's admit it, all of us, children of lust
of which we are ashamed and afraid, and we are all
exposed newborn.

What else is it to come into this world? And the long
odds of our being saved by the mercies of a goat
(or was it a shepherd, or, in Pausanias' version,
an open boat tossed by the waves?) . . . The chances
are never good,

and we are right to feel rage as we blame those huge
monsters upon whom we depended for their betrayal,
even knowing how helpless they were, how they struggled
with forces greater than themselves—mountains or waves
that dwarfed them down

to a helplessness almost as abject as ours. We cannot
afford such generous understanding that tends to loosen
our grip on the single issue of life and death,
our own survival. Telephus is wounded
as all of us are

in the deepest part of his being, his infant's love
for his mother—who, of course, turns up again
in Mysia, where he arrives after many years
of vicissitude and adventure, to rout the foe
(Idas, the Argonaut,

but it hardly matters; there's always a foe and occasion
for battle) and he is rewarded, offered a bride,
the king's adopted daughter, and the rite is performed,
but just as they're ready to consummate their union,
a horrendous serpent

comes slithering in between them, for which thank heaven!
Because you and I have figured it out already,
our ears pricking up at that "adopted" business.
Auge, of course, is his mother. He is saved yet again,
but that doesn't help,

because sometimes, the thought is as good or bad as the deed.
And who has not had such thoughts? However deep
we bury them out of the light, they come in the nighttime
to worry our dreams, to suppurate and ooze
their poison like wounds

that won't heal. Which is why the almost incoherent legend,
not having been built up or reduced by some major
dramatist, persists, as a buzzing in the ear.
The certainty is that we have been hurt and deeply,
which is why we hope

for a cure, no matter how strange or from however unlikely
a source, even as strange as the rage of Achilles
which is our own rage, the mania we'd all assume
if only we had the heroic or brute strength
to impose our will

and exact the satisfaction to which we are
entitled. Lacking that, we must supplicate
the power, plead what has harmed us to be turned to our use
for justice's sake, or pity's, and kiss the rod.
Let the spear heal.

from *Boulevard*

The Woman as Figure

◇ ◇ ◇

Why, when I see the child
walking with the woman at a little distance
from the blowing trees, see the pale blue figures
of the fog, and the patches of light like just-opened
passages on the sea, does my mind veer
to violence, why then do I think something terrible
is about to happen, and why do I think the woman
has known this all along, and is waiting for it to begin,
the blows and the harsh breathing and the cries
of accusation and helplessness? I think
I am being used by something violent and merciless,
and I can't think of a way to make
this perception believable or pertinent, the way the woman
entering a church to get out of the rain
will shake the water from her hair
and look around her at the ornately extruded display,
the tons of bullion, to find a point of simplicity,
maybe the embroidered hem, maybe the soft curve
of a saint's elbow, maybe the single sliver of purple light
falling across the back of a grayed man knelt
praying, and take this into herself,
as one would take a small piece of treasure
offered in passing by a king, who himself,
worried and overcome by the problems of the state,
dreams of a garden, the one he knew as a child,

where he walked among the long hesitations of twilight,
planning battles and gaily painted ships
on fire and death sentences only he could rescind.

from *New American Writing*

The Haiku Master

◊ ◊ ◊

Master
Under the plum moon, he sits
like a frog on a lily pad,
waiting, waiting for what?

> *Pupil*
> I, too, am illuminated
> by the moon, enraptured
> by the frog's *Thrum! Thrum!*
> My heart beats loudly
> like a big bass drum.

> > *Master/Pupil*
> > He asks with a smile,
> > "What shall you seek, seeker?"
> > And I, the fool, answer,
> > "The stars! The plum moon! Love!"

Pupil
July, August, September . . .
Desire follows desire
these hot sleepless nights
of late summer.

Master
In the mirror: ego.
The I-maker looks out,
liking, disliking, what it sees.

    Pupil
    Great minimalist,
    there are too many words!
    How shall I choose among them?

Master
Paring the apple, he eats
it slowly, bit by bit.
Down to the nothing of it.

    Pupil
    October, November, December . . .
    Hidden, I watched you
    tear the last leaf
    from the calendar.

    Master
    Once I dreamed the snow
    fell all night,
    effacing the earth.
    And woke to what I dreamed.

Pupil
Once, as the snow fell,
I was at peace
with myself. No more.

    Master
    Black ink, white paper,
    the characters appear:
    a farewell party where
    I am both host and guest.

Pupil
I saw you to the ferry.
We waved. The pier
I stood on moved away.

Master
Spring. Now I'm a ghost
and you're my dream,
a flame of shadow
in a world of green.

Pupil
You're gone. A cricket
tunelessly sings,
That was a life!

Master
It's black and white here.
I don't care. No koto
plays, but I don't miss it.
Soon I'll be pure spirit.

Pupil
My canvas is ready,
small receding square.
My brush, one hair.
Now to paint what isn't there.

from *The New Criterion*

RUTH STONE

For Seven Women

◇ ◇ ◇

Gender loyalty, alien to the pits and ducts of ourselves;
how to unscrew this pattern?

Now here's another matter; the season of bagworms,
and yet the moths were so random, so azure.

One lives alone out of circumstance, until the face
in the multiple mirrors is sour dough, full of its own gas.

The ocean is near, swallowing everything—a little cup
of water moving along the galaxy.

In Morocco my child goes down to the beach toward evening.
She forgets her tormentor, the headmaster's wife.

The ocean takes her, the broth of itself flowing inside her.
She rests with her feet in the scallops of water.

I cannot consider Canna, Alice or Shoko without Verlaine
Basho or Connie Smith.

What is this pattern in the light of bagworms? Nevertheless,
the mornings here are a sweet shock to the blood.

The light as it falls on the louvered windows,
a pattern of slits; and above that, the balconies.

For a short time you are a stranger. Then the vision fades.
Then you become the door, opening and closing.

In the mountains, on my way home from the village, I would
pass my sister's grave. Embalming fluid is pink like antifreeze.

How red she looked in the casket. Next year her grave-site caved in.
She stood on her head in the box. The sexton dumped in more dirt.

Dirt, dirty, soil is so useful. We track it in. The white carpet grows
yellow. Down here in the south along highways and boulevards,
     crepe myrtle.

I am a stranger crossing the bone bridge to meet the other.
Our skulls shine like calligraphy in a longed-for language.

     from *Boulevard*

War Movie: Last Leave, 1944

◇ ◇ ◇

Then. No. Now.
A long silk scarf of voice, pulled through the loop of throat—
Jo Stafford singing on the radio.
He wants so much to hear a voice like that, and it exists,
as simply as creation, the way the world provides
an image for the feeling
that's richer than the feeling, so that part of the satisfaction
is possession, part the perfection of the longing.
The way you know through flowers what perfect human flesh is,
the way the wife perfects the dim maternity she somehow
    flowered from,
and you derive the gold circles on your hands
from the sun's blinding ultimate wedding band.

There's a hotel room with a key that fits the door,
and inside, drinking coffee, arguing
or sleeping, the two of them keep marrying.
The arch of every nine-to-five is Notre Dame
where, strangely, you don't need ever to have been.
On Lexington, walking with his arm around her,
out of the earshot of that mother-in-law, the war,
he sees a man lunching on a roll and a cold beer,
and he's so goddamned grateful that he has to swear.
Love is good work, but they stagger sometimes
like a pair of stevedores beneath all the thinking
that it takes to feel, and strange to know precisely

how young on Bleecker and who you are at three-fifteen is:
bronze and sculpture.
And they've got tickets left for the Lombard picture.

The quivering caged canaries of the houselights dim;
the audience, cashmered in theme and shadow, dreams
the accumulating story as it snows on them.
The pilot is at peace, living in the film,
but his young wife only watches him, an afterlife
of movie changing his right cheek. She's swept under fire,
sensing all alone the dark as inexhaustible.
She's in love and terror; and it's hers now, the world's parure,
the legendary suite of matched black jewels.
And she watches the angle of her husband's head
cresting from his shoulders, and she swears
that if it's asked of her, she'll care
for his death as tenderly as any child his body gives her.
The screen swastika flickers in his wire rims.
She strokes his hair, he turns; she takes the cross from him.
Their young night comes toward them outside like a daughter,
wearing city lights like white gardenias in her hair.
Effortlessly, unlike Christ's disciples, they stay awake
with her, the fifth of their five nights, the brunette girl
that history—older, experienced, irresistible—is about to take.

from *Ploughshares*

I Am a Finn

◇ ◇ ◇

I Am a Finn

I am standing in the post office, about
to mail a package back to Minnesota, to my family.
I am a Finn. My name is Kasteheimi (Dewdrop).

Mikael Agricola (1510–1557) created the Finnish language.
He knew Luther and translated the New Testament.
When I stop by the Classé Café for a cheeseburger

no one suspects that I am a Finn.
I gaze at the dimestore reproductions of Lautrec
on the greasy walls, at the punk lovers afraid

to show their quivery emotions, secure
in the knowledge that my grandparents really did
emigrate from Finland in 1910—why

is everybody leaving Finland, hundreds of
thousands to Michigan and Minnesota, and now Australia?
Eighty-six percent of Finnish men have blue

or gray eyes. Today is Charlie Chaplin's
one hundredth birthday, though he is not
Finnish or alive: "Thy blossom, in the bud

laid low." The commonest fur-bearing animals
are the red squirrel, musk-rat, pine-marten
and fox. There are about 35,000 elk.

But I should be studying for my exam.
I wonder if Dean will celebrate with me tonight,
assuming I pass. Finnish literature

really came alive in the 1860s.
Here, in Cambridge, Massachusetts,
no one cares that I am a Finn.

They've never even heard of Frans Eemil Sillanpää,
winner of the 1939 Nobel Prize in Literature.
As a Finn, this infuriates me.

I Am Still a Finn

I failed my exam, which is difficult
for me to understand because I am a Finn.
We are a bright, if slightly depressed, people.

Pertti Palmroth is the strongest name
in Finnish footwear design; his shoes and boots
are exported to seventeen countries.

Dean bought champagne to celebrate
my failure. He says I was just nervous.
Between 1908 and 1950, 33 volumes

of *The Ancient Poetry of the Finnish People*
were issued, the largest work of its kind
ever published in any language.

So why should I be nervous? Aren't I
a Finn, descendant of Johan Ludvig Runeberg
(1804–1877), Finnish national poet?

I know he wrote in Swedish, and this
depresses me still. Harvard Square
is never "empty." There is no chance

that I will ever be able to state honestly
that "Harvard Square is empty tonight."
A man from Nigeria will be opening

his umbrella, and a girl from Wyoming
will be closing hers. A Zulu warrior
is running to catch a bus and an over-

painted harlot from Buenos Aires will
be fainting on schedule. And I, a Finn,
will long for the dwarf birches of the north

I have never seen. For 73 days the sun
never sinks below the horizon. O
darkness, mine! I shall always be a Finn.

from *The Iowa Review*

MOLLY TENENBAUM

Reminiscence Forward

◇ ◇ ◇

We were starving. We had nothing.
But we had bread.
There was nothing to eat.
But there were plenty of tomatoes.
We put the tomatoes on the bread.
We had nothing, but we had garlic.
We would put garlic on the tomatoes and bread.
We were starving, but we put olive oil
on the garlic and tomatoes and bread.
There were plenty of tomatoes
and we ate them on the hillsides
with the garlic and oil and bread.

We were starving. We had nothing.
But we had a cup.
The cup was white inside.
It was pink outside.
The pink was a vine of roses.
There was nothing.
But there was white and pink.
And there were leaves.
The leaves were gold paint
in the pink roses outside
the white cup. Oh we had nothing.
The white in the cup, and the pink,
and the gold leaves.

It was empty. There was nothing.
But we had a window.
There were some lines
outside the window, and they were made of wood.
The lines were rails outside the window
and the rails were of a porch.
And there were stairs
down that led to fences, and on the fencetops
cats walked with their tails,
passing back and forth.
We were starving. There was nothing.
But we had railings, a window, steps and a view
of fencetops.

Truly we had nothing. Empty, starving, cold.
There was a pond.
We had nothing, truly.
The pond was small.
We couldn't see.
There might have been something.
But it was small and dark.
We really couldn't see, but there were grasses
at the edge: we saw them move,
the water darken.
We had nothing. We were so close
to nothing. From our railings
over our fencetops, while we held
our cup and ate
our oil and tomatoes and bread,
we looked into the pond.
We couldn't see, we had nothing, but it seemed
the blue pond was a thought
that could undo itself
and swim away.

We couldn't see. We were starving.
There was nothing. It was empty.
It was oil and bread.

It was a white cup.
It was railings and fencetops.
It was bluer and bluer.

from *Fine Madness*

Reruns

◇   ◇   ◇

SPLASH!

Like a rock, Elly
May's cake sank to the bottom
of the "ceement" pond.

*

IN OUTER SPACE

Judy Jetson spins
a disc and does the Orbit
to "Comet Of Love."

*

WITH A LITTLE GRIN

Morticia snipped off
the rose and placed the stem in
the tombstone-shaped vase.

*

PATTY TO CATHY

"While you study as
me, I'll leave as you, then go
as me on my date!"

*

HOUSEWORK

Samantha looked at
the dirty dishes. "Just this
once," she thought, and twitched.

*

NEW YEAR'S EVE

The cork popped off the
bottle and, effervescent,
Jeannie overflowed.

*

HONEY IN THE FLESH

She knew how to use
her high-voltage curves like an
unconcealed weapon.

*

BATMAN AND ROBIN

hang by threads above
a bubbling vat of acid.
To be continued . . .

MODEL CHILDREN

Kitten told the truth.
Princess set aside her pride.
Bud made right his wrong.

*

ISLAND GIRLS

Mary Ann dons one
of Ginger's dresses, but it
falls flat on her chest.

*

GOSSIP

Gidget and Larue
knock heads as they press their ears
to the princess phone.

*

FRED'S BREAKFAST

With a club, Wilma
cracked open the three-minute
pterodactyl egg.

*

PUBERTY

Wally pounds on the
bathroom door. "C'mon, Beav! You've
been in there for hours!"

FRACTURED FAIRY TALE

This kissing princess
was such a dog that the frog
she smacked simply croaked.

GREEN ACRES

The smoke from Lisa's
burnt pancakes slowly blackens
the fresh country air.

THE MOD SQUAD

Julie, Pete and Linc
bust some thugs, then head back to
their pad to turn on.

LIKE BIRD OR BALLOON

Sister Bertrille fades
to a speck in the blue sky
above San Tanco.

from *Brooklyn Review*

Revenge

◇　◇　◇

He was standing on the hotel balcony
when I awoke, watching the late afternoon

sluice down green-gold
over the fronds of the royal palms.

Palms in wind make a sound
like knives being sharpened,

languorous in my dispersing sleep,
slice-slicing against themselves.

He was watching the melon-colored light
run over the slow swells,

and the pleasure boats trailing
their long white creamy wakes,

their engines shuddering.
My waking thought was that

I was waking *inside a century*,
a cage bigger than our lives,

and that the freedom to roam around in it
was an illusion we both had, or an irony

we'd once abided by but had forgotten,
walking in the drifting dunes of light,

the snows of Perdido, snows of crushed coral,
on the edge of the trespassing sea.

The sheets were imprinted on my skin.
The cool air fingered each crease

and the fresh grass matting felt
pleasingly harsh and raw underfoot.

No one could see me
there in the palm shadows, naked

and dappled by the sun's warm camouflage.
The passing seconds were almost visible,

a faintly glamorous stream of light
that flowed over the moving boats,

brightened the frictional leaves.
He put his arm around my shoulders,

the smell of the day in his shirt,
so that his thumb not quite touched

my nipple, which shriveled,
and with the other hand slowly

unbuttoned and unzipped himself,
all the while watching the pleasure boats

glide past us trailing bits of broken mirror,
their engines pulsing steadily,

fueled by what's left of the future.

from *Antæus*

Omeros

◇   ◇   ◇

Seven Seas rose in the half-dark to make coffee.
Sunrise was heating the ring of the horizon
and clouds were warming like loaves. By the heat of the

glowing iron rose he slid the saucepan's base on—
to the ring and anchored it there. The saucepan shook
from the weight of water in it, then it settled.

His kettle leaked. He groped for the tin chair and took
his place near the saucepan to hear when it bubbled.
It would boil but not scream like a bosun's whistle

to let him know it was ready. He heard the dog's
morning whine under the boards of the house, its tail
thudding to be let in, but he envied the pirogues

already miles out at sea. Then he heard the first breeze
washing the sea-almond's plates; last night there had been
a full moon white as his eyes. He saw with his ears.

He imagined roofs as the sun began to climb.
Since the disease had obliterated vision,
when the sunset shook the sea's hand for the last time—

and an inward darkness grew where the moon and sun
indistinctly altered, he moved by a sixth sense,
like a clock without an hour or second hand,

wiped clean as the plate that he now began to rinse
while the saucepan bubbled; blindness was not the end.
It was not a palm tree's dial on the noon sand.

So his mind sailed like the plate through black thunderheads
even in broad daylight, with no present or past,
like the moon that rose from the basin's foaming suds,

making dinner at dawn, and, at supper, breakfast.
He slept in Egypt and woke in Benin. Galleys
beat their oars to his fingers. He turned off the ring

of the stove and sensed its warm iris, like his eyes
as the flames turned blue, then rose, suddenly fading
with his sight. The coffee made his nostrils widen.

The dog scratched at the kitchen door for him to open
but he made it wait. He drummed the kitchen table
with his hand. Blackbirds were quarrelling for breakfast.

Except for one hand he sat as still as marble,
with his egg white eyes, his spoon repeating the past
of another sea, measured by stroking hammers.

O open this day with the conch's moan, Omeros,
as they did in my boyhood, when I was a noun
gently exhaled from the palate of the sunrise.

A lizard on the seawall darted its question
at the waking sea, and a net of golden moss
brightened the reef, which the sails of their far canoes

avoided. Only in you, across centuries
of the sea's parchment atlas, can I catch the noise
of the surf lines wandering like the shambling fleece

of the lighthouse's flock, that Cyclops whose blind eye
shut from the sunlight. Then the canoes were galleys
over which a frigate sawed its scythed wings slowly.

In you the grey seeds of almonds guessed a tree's shape,
and the grape leaves rusted like serrated islands,
and the blind lighthouse, sensing the edge of a cape,

paused like a giant, a cloud held high in its hands,
to hurl a boulder that splashed into phosphorous
stars, then a black fisherman, his stubbled chin coarse

as a dry sea-urchin's, hoisted his flour-sack
sail on its bamboo spar, and scanned the opening line
of our epic horizon; writing I look back

to rocks that see their own feet when light nets the waves,
as the long dugouts set out with their carved captains,
since it was your name that startled the sunlit wharves

when schooners swayed, idly moored to their cold capstans,
and wind turned the harbor's pages back to the voice
that hummed in the vase of a girl's throat: "Omeros."

from *Partisan Review*

Song

◇   ◇   ◇

A yellow coverlet
    in the greenwood:
spread the corners wide to the dim, stoop-shouldered pines.
    Let blank sky
    be your canopy.
Fringe the bedspread with the wall of lapsing stones.
    Here faith has cut
    in upright granite
"Meet me in Heaven" at the grave of each child
    lost the same year,
    three, buried here
a century ago. Roots and mosses hold
    in the same bed
    mother, daughter, dead
together, in one day. "Lord, remember the poor"
    their crumbling letters pray.
    I turn away.
I shall meet you nowhere, in no transfigured hour.
    On soft, matted soil
    blueberry bushes crawl,
each separate berry a small, hot globe of tinctured sun.
    Crushed on the tongue
    it releases a pang

of flesh. Tender flesh, slipped from its skin,
  preserves its blue heat
  down my throat.

from *The Atlantic Monthly*

Lasting Influence

◇　◇　◇

This is the repugnant part, where now
you covet the loss which a moment before
brought you the severed torso in the dream.
Since your friends are feasting, you must act quickly.
The child's carriage careens on the stair.

Dancing a rondo on the lacustrine tile,
you look up suddenly to a bevelled undoing.
This is no respite or reward.

For so many years you have cast out, learning to
search (you think of roses), and now it is clear
that the driveway which borders this undulant lawn
is the twilight escape route of robbers. In another life,
they catch the children at the critical moment
and bundle the bodies from the cold.

The imagined wit, you think, is never worth the bargaining.

Then the plane takes off, and the woman with the poodle
snuffs your cigar and takes a brick from her purse
and lifts a train of somnolence from the seat.
You are drifting; she has bent your ear, singing;
you are under the wing of an implacable monster.
Grace is elephantine, it does not mean reward.

So you undid something unexpected, and in your delight
you forgot to inquire whether it was something reasoned
or only a precarious dish on a shelf. Possession become
indistinguishable, fireflies raffling on a screen,
a route of departures crossed like wires through which,
during hideous nights, voices make divisions of lives.
Each day you have locked a door and turned out a lamp
that brought only the sorriest comfort while lit.
Now the whole rift derives clearly.

She calls to say, she is ready to depart, is there anything
you need? Then it is you recognize the precipice
for what it is, then you see that out there, on the
dawning bridge of a fallacious jump, a cowboy is
coming after you, calmly askew, promising breath.

from *The Paris Review*

Reading Lao Tzu Again in the New Year

◇   ◇   ◇

Snub end of a dismal year,
$\qquad\qquad$ deep in the dwarf orchard,
The sky with its undercoat of blackwash and point stars,
I stand in the dark and answer to
My life, this shirt I want to take off,
$\qquad\qquad$ which is on fire . . .

Old year, new year, old song, new song,
$\qquad\qquad$ nothing will change hands
Each time we change heart, each time
Like a hard cloud that has drifted all day through the sky
Toward the night's shrugged shoulder
$\qquad\qquad$ with its epaulet of stars.

———————

Prosodies rise and fall.
$\qquad\qquad$ Structures rise in the mind and fall.
Failure reseeds the old ground.
Does the grass, with its inches in two worlds, love the dirt?
Does the snowflake the raindrop?

I've heard that those who know will never tell us,
$\qquad\qquad$ and heard

That those who tell us will never know.
Words are wrong.
Structures are wrong.
                    Even the questions are compromise.

Desire discriminates and language discriminates:
They form no part of the essence of all things:
                                    each word
Is a failure, each object
We name and place
                    leads us another step away from the light.

Loss is its own gain.
                    Its secret is emptiness.

Our images lie in the flat pools of their dark selves
Like bodies of water the tide moves.
They move as the tide moves.
                        Its secret is emptiness.

————————

Four days into January,
                        the grass grows tiny, tiny
Under the peach trees.
Wind from the Blue Ridge tumbles the hat
Of daylight farther and farther
                            into the eastern counties.

Sunlight spray on the ash limbs.
                            Two birds
Whistle at something unseen, one black note and one interval.
We're placed between now and not-now,
                            held by affection,
Large rock balanced upon a small rock.

from *Poetry*

CONTRIBUTORS' NOTES AND COMMENTS

JONATHAN AARON was born in Northampton, Massachusetts, in 1941. His first book, *Second Sight* (Harper & Row, 1982), won a National Poetry Series open competition. His second book is due from Wesleyan in 1992. He teaches writing at Emerson College in Boston. He has won a National Endowment for the Arts award and two grants from the Massachusetts Council on the Arts. He and his wife and stepson live part of the year in France. He is a great admirer of dogs. He looks forward to his first reading of *Don Quixote*. At least once a day a line of Donald Justice's passes through his mind: "Time has little meaning in Tibet."

Of "The Voice from Paxos," Aaron writes: "This poem retells an anecdote in Plutarch's *On the Cessation of Oracles*. Why retell it —and in a poem? I can't answer, but maybe the following will make sense. First, studying history is for me a helpful way of reading the present (insofar as the present can be read at all). When you read someone like Plutarch, for instance, you're in fact scrutinizing, albeit indirectly, your own time. By way of a refraction process of sorts, the indirect view often allows a clearer picture of the present than the direct view does. Second, Plutarch's story, based on fact or not, tells the truth about what it's like to experience, suddenly, the conviction that something irrevocable is happening to the world. You can't really understand or judge such a moment because you're too much a part of it to comprehend it, and besides, the consequences take time to develop. But your awareness is sharp and abiding—knowledge existing on the level of instinct, maybe, with its own weird identity and force. At any rate, this is how my thinking runs a week after the start of the war in the Persian Gulf. . . ."

AI was born in the Southwest in 1947. In 1990 she was the Morton Professor at the University of Louisville. She has won two grants from the National Endowment for the Arts and a Guggenheim Fellowship. She has published four books: *Cruelty* (1973), *Killing Floor* (1979), *Sin* (1986), and *Fate* (1991), all from Houghton Mifflin. *Killing Floor* was the Lamont Poetry Selection for 1979.

Of "Evidence: From a Reporter's Notebook," Ai writes: "This poem is only loosely based on the Tawana Brawley incident. It was really inspired by a film I saw called *The Big Carnival* by Billy Wilder. It's about a reporter whose career is in decline and who has been exiled to New Mexico from New York. One day he's on the scene when there's a cave-in at a mine where a guy's been digging for artifacts. The reporter decides this is his big chance and decides to take the story as far as he can. After a while it all spirals out of control and ends on a profoundly dark note. I loved it. Kirk Douglas is a great bastard in this film, and as I often deal with similar characters, I think I was even more inspired than usual. I thought it would be great to write a poem about a TV reporter who in essence does the same thing. She rides her horse, her story, until it stumbles under her, then she shoots it and moves on without remorse. But it's more than that, too, and I like to think it actually has a lot more dimension than the film. Anyway, rent the video or see it on cable. Let me emphasize that the poem does not have the same story line or even finally the same idea as the movie, but they are based on similar characters and occupations, and what is really the cliché of the reporter who single-mindedly goes after a story, whether today or in the 1950s. Maybe all existence is just a few cast changes after all."

DICK ALLEN was born in Troy, New York, in 1939. He is director of creative writing at the University of Bridgeport, where he holds the Charles A. Dana Endowed Professorship of English. He has received grants from the National Endowment for the Arts and the Ingram Merrill Foundation. His four books of poetry include *Flight and Pursuit* (1987) and *Overnight in the Guest House of the Mystic* (1984), both from Louisiana State University Press. The latter was nominated for the National Book Critics Circle Award in poetry.

Allen writes: " 'Talking with Poets' presents a seemingly romantic picture of the poet. But any life, considered at its essence, can be seen as romantic. I wished to write of how the poet's daily struggle with subject is as harrowing as the struggle of any other worker. My cop friend Greg Iacovetti is in the poem, as are Sylvia Plath and Pasternak and a boring shoptalk party of poets.

"The poem's initial inspiration came from my standing beside Kurt Vonnegut as he bent to a door lock, straightened, announced that the door lock was made in Indianapolis, then launched into a brief history of Indiana manufacturing. I found myself wishing I'd hear poets speak with equal fascination and passion, outside their poems, of things they knew well. . . . When I came home from that poets' party years later, I had to take my friends' books from the bookcases—and my own books as well—to find out who we *really* were.

"From inception to completion, the poem took me ten years to write. In the last few months I went through many revisions trying for the discursive (yet still roughly iambic and trochaic) rhythm I wanted, and for webbings of alliteration, assonance, and imagery. 'Blue Sailors' are chicory. The word *gossip*, with its perfectly descriptive second syllable, initiated the poem's pattern of sounds."

JULIA ALVAREZ has published a book of poems, *Homecoming* (Grove Press, 1984), and a collection of short stories, *How the Garcia Girls Lost Their Accents* (Algonquin Books, 1991). Born in New York City, she spent her early childhood in the Dominican Republic, the homeland of both her parents, returning to New York at the age of ten. Such shuttling between countries taught her that, as the poet Czeslaw Milosz has said, "language is the only homeland." She has taught at Phillips Andover Academy, the University of Vermont, and the University of Illinois, and has been a staff member at the Breadloaf Writers' Conference. In 1984–85 she held the Jenny McKean Moore Writing Fellowship at George Washington University. She has won a General Electric Younger Writers' Award, a National Endowment for the Arts fellowship, and an Ingram Merrill Foundation grant. She teaches creative writing and literature at Middlebury College.

Alvarez writes: " 'Bookmaking' is one in a series of ten love poems written to a bookmaker, who loves books as much as I do but in a different way. I had thought of a book not as a physical object but as a container of words. Then, through my bookmaking lover, I discovered books, the actual physical objects in my hands—the paper, the covers, the print. On a trip to New York I went to the Pierpont Morgan Library, a museum that celebrates the physical book as well as its contents. It was a form of love-making to involve myself with the display at the museum on the making of books. Through our love affair, the bookmaker had also, of course, reminded me of the forgotten body. And before those grand cases in the museum it seemed that all of our passionate loving—as lovers, writers, bookmakers—would not be enough to cover all the world in the time left.

"This, too, about 'Bookmaking' and the other poems in the series: I had been ashamed for many years as a properly brought up Catholic Hispanic woman to make mention of desire in a poem unless it was coming from a man's body. I dared with this series to express deep, sweet woman's passion, the body's passion at its ripening and deepening in middle age. I wanted to write love poems in the tradition of the spiritual writers. However, unlike John of the Cross, I didn't want the body to be a metaphor for the spirit but vice-versa: the word to become flesh, love's body its own communion. I did not know how to do this. At the time I was writing these poems, I was reading Rumi's luminous poems to his beloved guide and spiritual leader. Rumi led me by providing an epigraph to each poem. I felt intoxicated writing these poems. By the time I was done with them, the love affair was over, but these hungry, passionate poems were written."

JOHN ASH was born in Manchester, England, in 1948, and was educated at the University of Birmingham. Since 1985 he has lived in New York City. He has won grants and awards from the Ingram Merrill Foundation, the Whiting Foundation, and the Anne and Erlo Van Waveren Foundation. He has written reviews for the *New York Times Book Review*, the *Washington Post Book World*, the *Village Voice*, and *Art in America*. His books include *The Goodbyes* (1982), *The Branching Stairs* (1984), and *Disbelief* (1987), all from Carcanet. *The Burnt Pages*, a new collection of poems, will be published by Random House in 1991.

Of "Cigarettes," Ash writes: "The poem is so self-explanatory that I can't think of anything to say about it other than that it is self-explanatory, an essay-poem."

JOHN ASHBERY was born in Rochester, New York, in 1927. He is the author of thirteen books of poetry, including *Flow Chart* (Knopf, 1991), and a volume of art criticism, *Reported Sightings* (Knopf, 1989). His *Self-Portrait in a Convex Mirror* (Viking, 1975) received the Pulitzer Prize for poetry as well as the National Book Critics Circle Award and the National Book Award. He has been named a Guggenheim Fellow and a MacArthur Fellow, and is a chancellor of the Academy of American Poets. In 1989–90 he delivered the Charles Eliot Norton lectures at Harvard. He is currently Charles P. Stevenson, Jr. Professor of Literature at Bard College. He was guest editor of *The Best American Poetry 1988*.

GEORGE BRADLEY was born in Roslyn, New York, in 1953. The hospital has since been razed. He is the author of two books of poetry: *Terms to Be Met* (Yale University Press, 1986) and *Of the Knowledge of Good and Evil* (Knopf, 1991). Bradley works now and then as a freelance writer, which is why he is very grateful to have recently received a grant from the National Endowment for the Arts. He is trying hard not to compose anything obscene for at least twelve months.

Bradley writes: " 'Great Stone Face,' as the title is intended to imply, is a poem gotten by Wallace Stevens upon Buster Keaton. I suppose I had in mind, in considering the inscrutability of human experience, both the comic's famous deadpan and the 'face of slate' that figures in 'Notes Toward a Supreme Fiction.' For all the allusion to comedy, however, I'm afraid this is a relentlessly abstract poem (though I hope that is part of the point), which is one reason why I worked in the bit about the crocus and forsythia and flowering leaves. The splashes of color are meant to reward anybody who gets that far, perhaps surprising the determined reader as much as they astonish the dogged speaker of the verse."

JOSEPH BRODSKY was born in Leningrad in 1940 and came to the United States in 1972, an involuntary exile from the Soviet Union.

His books of poetry available in English include *A Part of Speech* (1980) and *To Urania* (1988), both from Farrar, Straus & Giroux. His book of essays, *Less Than One* (Farrar, Straus & Giroux, 1986), won the National Book Critics Circle Award for criticism. In 1987 Joseph Brodsky was awarded the Nobel Prize for literature. He is currently Andrew Mellon Professor of Literature at Mount Holyoke College. His recent play, *Democracy!*, has been performed in several European cities.

GERALD BURNS was born in Detroit in 1940. At present he teaches upper-level English at Kirby Hall School in Austin, Texas. In 1985 he won a National Endowment for the Arts fellowship for poetry. His most recent book is *A Thing About Language*, published in 1989 by Southern Illinois University Press. He is at work on a XII-book long poem, *The Myth of Accidence*. The first eight sections have been published, mostly in *Temblor*. An earlier book of verse theory, *Toward a Phenomenology of Written Art*, is available from McPherson & Co.

Of "Double Sonnet for Mickey," Burns writes: "I was surprised when I saw *Kiss Me Deadly* at the Brattle Theater how much poetry is tucked away in it, and touched at how vulnerable the Mickey Spillane characters seemed with Harvard right across the street. So this poem really is written for Spillane, to answer in a way the questions the film pretends to raise. Since Ogden Nash it's certainly possible to write long lines that rhyme. I wrote a long poem on Law, 'Fretting an Upscale Themis,' that's 111 slant-rhymed couplets. You could write a book on the reinvention of rhyme, chapters on Creeley, Snodgrass, maybe Ginsberg's blues period. Rap's an odd thing, to see rhyme so brutal like fluorescent shoelaces. Rhyme looks intended. Do you read poetry? Do you rhyme the world somehow into sense? Is rhyme permitted at all, even as eavesdropper, in film noir? Rhyme now is impudent, and not powerless. Choosing to rhyme may mean you have that margin."

AMY CLAMPITT was born in New Providence, Iowa, in 1920, graduated from Grinnell College in 1941, and has since lived mainly in New York City. She has been the recipient of a Guggenheim Fellowship and of awards from the American Academy and Institute of Arts and Letters, the Academy of American Poets and, most recently, the Lila Wallace–Reader's Digest Fund. Her books include *The Kingfisher* (1983), *What the Light Was Like* (1985), *Archaic Figure* (1987), and *Westward* (1990), all from Knopf. *Predecessors, Et Cetera*, a collection of essays in the University of Michigan's Poets on Poetry series, is scheduled for publication in 1991. She is currently at work on a play about the life of Dorothy Wordsworth.

Of "A Whippoorwill in the Woods," Clampitt writes: "The recollection-of-a-recollection with which the poem ends is one that, off and on, I'd been trying to write about for years. Hearing about, and then hearing, the call of a whippoorwill during a stay in the country brought the subject into focus once again, and this time a stanza form appeared or evolved, I'm not sure which."

MARC COHEN was born in Brooklyn, New York, in 1951. He is the author of *On Maplewood Time* (Groundwater Press, 1989). Since 1986 he has been co-director of the Intuflo Reading Series, and is an editor of Intuflo Editions, a series of limited-edition poetry chapbooks. He lives in New York City and is the production manager for Datability, a computer software firm in Chelsea.

Of "Blue Lonely Dreams," Cohen writes: "I wrote this poem in January 1989, shortly after moving downtown to Greenwich Village. The coincidences mentioned in the poem had been on my mind since the previous February, and Roy Orbison's death somehow brought the poem to fruition. Like Bellow's Herzog, I decided to write directly to the dead. While working on this poem I suffered from acute displacement. Outside, there were odd sounds, and most of the Village streets had names instead of numbers, so we were constantly getting lost while taking walks or running errands. Inside, the paintings were still not hung, the stereo wasn't sounding quite right, and there were still plenty of boxes to be unpacked. The walls of the new apartment were painted eggshell white, and the new wall-to-wall carpeting was light blue."

ALFRED CORN was born in Georgia in 1943. He has published five books of poems with Viking Penguin. A recipient of the Guggenheim, National Endowment for the Arts, and Ingram Merrill fellowships, he was also named for an Award in Literature from the

American Academy and Institute of Arts and Letters and made a fellow by the Academy of American Poets. He has taught at Yale, Connecticut College, the City University of New York, UCLA, and Columbia. Last year he was the George Elliston Professor of Poetry at the University of Cincinnati, and this year he is teaching at the New School. He lives in New York City.

Of "Infernal Regions and the Invisible Girl," Corn writes: "I've written a few poems in the voice and consciousness of figures from literary tradition, but this is my first dramatic monologue, with the convention of actual speech and an implied audience. It's an odd form, rather like hearing one half of a telephone conversation and guessing at the responses at the other end, solely on the basis of what is heard (or, here, recorded on the page). The great delight for the person adopting a previous voice is to use a set of speech conventions not available to contemporary American poets, who are under an ironclad injunction to 'write in their own natural voice.' As we know, when you put limits on how poetry is written, with the same stroke you put limits on possible new content. In that sense poems in dramatic voice are subversive to the exclusionary conventions of contemporary American poetry.

"I stole several phrases from Mrs. Trollope's *Domestic Manners of the Americans* as a sort of pump-priming to catch the texture of her voice. Once on the track, transcription came with an ease and, well, naturalness that took me by surprise. Mrs. Trollope is a very amusing writer and in herself amusing. The important things she has to say are blended with observations and turns of phrase that make us laugh. It's a quality she shares with Jane Austen. Writing this poem was a long-shot effort to approach as near as I could a style of mind and discourse mine only in the sense that we are revealed by what we admire."

STEPHEN DOBYNS was born in Orange, New Jersey, in 1941. He has published seven books of poems and thirteen novels. His most recent book of poems is *Body Traffic* (Viking, 1990). His most recent novel is *After Shocks/Near Escapes* (Viking, 1991). He is professor of English at Syracuse University.

Of "Desire," Dobyns writes: "Although I don't write many autobiographical poems, this one began just as the first stanza relates. I like poems that are aggressive and full of surprise, and the sound and content are sculpted to that end. This poem I think of as an aggressive meditation. I also feel that the increased sensitivity to gender issues has tended to make men feel overly apologetic, timorous and hypocritical. As the poem says, 'What good does it do to deny desire?' The poem argues that it is better to embrace and analyze our natures than to deny them. Nietzsche writes someplace, 'A more complete human being is a human being who is more completely bestial.' The truth of that sentence needs to be celebrated and understood, not whined about."

STEPHEN DUNN was born in Forest Hills, New York, in 1939. He is professor of creative writing at Stockton State College in New Jersey and has received fellowships from the Guggenheim Foundation and the National Endowment for the Arts. He has won *Poetry* magazine's Levinson Prize and Oscar Blumenthal Prize and *Poetry Northwest*'s Theodore Roethke Prize. The most recent of his eight collections of poetry is *Landscape at the End of the Century* (Norton, 1991). "Bringing It Down" is included in that volume. His essays have appeared widely over the last several years.

Dunn writes: "I got a draft of 'Bringing It Down' in one sitting, though it wasn't until some two years later that the poem felt complete, which occurred when I added, 'There weren't enough/ rewards in this world,/ he felt, for the things/ he imagined,/ but didn't do.' That might be interesting to someone who's engaged by the poem. Other than that, I can say I hoped the man in the poem would be perverse enough to be recognizable, true."

CAROLYN FORCHÉ was born in Detroit in 1950. She has worked as a journalist in El Salvador for Amnesty International and as the Beirut correspondent for "All Things Considered" on National Public Radio. *Gathering the Tribes*, her first collection, appeared in the Yale Series of Younger Poets in 1976. *The Country Between Us* (Harper & Row, 1982) was chosen as the Lamont Selection of the Academy of American Poets. She has translated Salvadoran poet and novelist Claribel Alegría's *Flores del Volcan* and has written the text for *El Salvador: Work of Thirty Photographers*. In collaboration with William Kulik, she has translated Robert Desnos's *Selected*

Poems (The Ecco Press, 1991). In 1992, Norton will publish her anthology of twentieth-century "poetry of witness." She is now a member of the writing faculty of George Mason University and an associate fellow at the Institute for Policy Studies in Washington, D.C. In 1990 she received a Lannan Foundation Fellowship.

Of "The Recording Angel," Forché writes: "The title refers to the Metatron, the prince of the Seraphim charged with the welfare and sustenance of human life. This sequence is part of a work-in-progress, a book-length poem on the subject of the twentieth century and memory, tentatively titled *The Angel of History*."

ALICE FULTON was born in Troy, New York, in 1952. Her books include *Powers of Congress* (David R. Godine, 1990), *Palladium* (University of Illinois Press, 1986), and *Dance Script with Electric Ballerina* (University of Pennsylvania Press, 1983). She has received fellowships from the Guggenheim Foundation and the Ingram Merrill Foundation. Her work was included in the 1988 and 1989 editions of *The Best American Poetry*. Currently she is an associate professor of English at the University of Michigan, Ann Arbor.

Of "The Fractal Lanes," Fulton writes: "The mathematician Benoit Mandelbrot coined the word 'fractal' to describe certain structures of nature previously thought to be amorphous or chaotic. There are two types of fractals: random and geometric. The geometric type is self-similar. A self-similar mechanism is, formally speaking, a kind of cascade, with each stage creating details smaller than those of the preceding stages. The bark patterns on oak, mud cracks in a dry riverbed, and a broccoli spear are examples of fractal forms previously regarded as formless or chaotic. Now scientists are able to find a deep logic in those circumspect structures and in phenomena such as the distribution of galaxies or the flooding of the Nile: They have become irregular structures with enough regularity to map. I think of them as nature's 'free verse.'

" 'The Fractal Lanes' describes the process of perception and self-similar fractals. Formally, it contains a nesting of design within design: a cascade in the form of an acrostic. I'm intrigued by the acrostic's ability to hide an opposing vertical within the poem's horizontal sweep. Its contrary motion can unhinge the poem's dominant content. I like its leftness, its aesthetic gaucherie. Acrostics are inherently secretive. I prefer mine to be subversive: distaff spindles, creating dissent as they descend. This subversion takes the form of humor in 'The Fractal Lanes.'

"Before I tried writing acrostics, I didn't have much respect for the form. I thought it would be easy to manage. But writing the kind of acrostic I envisioned proved surprisingly difficult. The challenge was to keep the line intact while hitting the mark on every turn. The acrostic, as I used it, also presented a readymade stanzaic form. The question then became how to sculpt arbitrary stanzas into necessary ones; how to maximize the force of lengthy stanzas and showcase the brevity of tercets. The poem has more dashes than most. I think dashes aerate—visually, aurally, and syntactically—dense lines. And they foster some useful ambiguity.

"Readers seldom find acrostics unless they're pointed out. And what's the point of building an invisible structure? 'The Fractal Lanes' was written to make evident the other acrostics in my book, *Powers of Congress*, as well as to be self-reflexive. By the time readers arrive at this poem, they've read the book's other acrostics, probably without noticing the cascading phrase. I hoped that readers, having focused on the poems' rhymes, meter, etc., while remaining oblivious to the acrostic dimension, would grasp a larger point about perception, marginality, and invisibility. The acrostics enact an underlying concern of my poetry: the notion that we see what we've been trained to see or what we've seen before. Surely there are infinite patterns, meanings, and people rendered invisible by our unintentional disregard. We fail to see them (or some aspect of them) either because we're unaccustomed to their presence or because we've been taught to 'read' existence in a certain limiting fashion."

LOUISE GLÜCK was born in New York City in 1943. She has received grants from the Guggenheim Foundation and the National Endowment for the Arts, as well as an award in literature from the American Academy and Institute of Arts and Letters. Her fourth book, *The Triumph of Achilles*, received the National Book Critics Circle Award for poetry, the Boston Globe Literary Press Award for poetry, and the Poetry Society of America's Melville Cane Award. "Celestial Music" was delivered as the Phi Beta Kappa Poem at

Poem at Harvard University in 1990. She teaches at Williams College and lives in Vermont. Her most recent collection, *Ararat*, was published in 1990 by Ecco Press.

Of "Celesial Music," Glück writes: "Of all fantasies, the dream of being out of the reach of time has always been, for me, the most persistently seductive. At the same time it seems impossible to deny the resemblance between unchanging and inert: Art that aspires to be immutable, perfected music may unfortunately prove lifeless. 'Celestial Music' was an experiment, an attempt to find a more casual language, to use a more common occasion—I hoped these changes of manner would disrupt old patterns of thought. What's continuous is the obsession; what's changed is its function. Hunger for the eternal is present here as thematic issue rather than embodied aesthetic. I hope the debate feels unresolved; the poem, in any case, seemed a great adventure to write."

JORIE GRAHAM was born in New York City in 1950. She grew up in Italy, studied in French schools, attended the Sorbonne, New York University, Columbia University, and the University of Iowa. She has been awarded a number of grants including, most recently, the John D. and Catherine T. MacArthur Foundation Fellowship. Her publications include four books of poetry: *Hybrids of Plants and of Ghosts* (1980) and *Erosion* (1983), from Princeton University Press, and *The End of Beauty* (1987) and *Region of Unlikeness* (1991), from the Ecco Press. She lives in Iowa City and teaches at the Writers' Workshop. She was guest editor of *The Best American Poetry 1990*.

Of "The Phase After History," Graham writes: "The poem evolved, as many of my poems do, through a process of waiting. First Stuart died, an event I couldn't 'understand.' Then one day, a year or more later, I was terrified by the birds—caught in the extinguished wood stove—that came flying out, when I opened the little door, completely coated with ashes. I spent most of the day trying to find the second one, sitting and listening, as the poem says. I had been reading *Macbeth*. I was alone in the house and the poem found the birds, *Macbeth*, and Stuart in its one field."

MELISSA GREEN was born in Boston in 1954. *The Squanicook Eclogues*, published by Norton in 1987, was awarded the Norma Farber First

Book Award from the Poetry Society of America. She also received the Lavan Award from the Academy of American Poets. She is currently at work on a book of prose and a book-length poem about twelfth-century France.

Green writes: "At the time I wrote 'The Consolation of Boethius,' I had in mind a friend who suffered grievously in prison for being at odds with the state. Ill health plagued him as well, and I thought of Boethius whose muse dictated one final book and, in it, consolation for all future struggles. I imagined then what one last visit from the Muse would mean for a poet and how there could be no possible consolation for putting down one's pen for the last time."

DEBORA GREGER was born in Walsenburg, Colorado, in 1949. She is the author of three books of poetry published by Princeton University Press: *Movable Islands* (1980), *And* (1986), and *The 1002nd Night* (1990). Her work was included in the 1988 and 1989 editions of *The Best American Poetry*. She teaches in the creative writing program at the University of Florida at Gainesville.

LINDA GREGERSON was born in Illinois in 1950 and holds degrees from Oberlin College, the Iowa Writers' Workshop, and Stanford University. She is the author of *Fire in the Conservatory* (Dragon Gate, 1982), a book of poems. She has received awards from the Ingram Merrill Foundation and the National Endowment for the Arts. For six years she was an editor at *The Atlantic*. She currently teaches Renaissance literature at the University of Michigan and is completing a book about erotic constructions of subjectivity in *The Faerie Queene* and *Paradise Lost*.

Of "Safe," Gregerson writes: "As to the verse form: I've taken to using these tercets in an effort to vary the pacing of the poem on the page. When the block stanzas I used in earlier poems began to seem airless and static, overcompressed, I tried a new template: two longer lines (usually four or five feet) divided by a one- or two-foot pivot line. Syntax is probably the closest thing I've got to a habit of mind, or voice, and I needed some means of rendering the tension between lineation and syntax, the syncopated tug of war between unfolding argument and the argument latent in syntactical form.

"The poem's larger argument is with loss. I'm not sure it's possible to write an elegy, or to talk about one, without wronging the dead. Grief is shamefully self-absorbed. And grief-in-verse has a thousand ways of turning exploitative, especially when death has been accompanied by violence. Elegy tries to console us with a failed rescue attempt. The paradox is a stark one, it seems to me, even when people can agree to believe in an afterlife. 'Safe' was written for my friend Karin Strand, who died in Rochester, New York, just before Christmas 1986."

ALLEN GROSSMAN was born in Minneapolis in 1932. He has been for many years professor of poetry and general education at Brandeis University. From 1991 he will be professor of English at Johns Hopkins University. He is currently a MacArthur Fellow. "The Ether Dome (An Entertainment)" will be the title poem of his forthcoming *New and Selected Poems* to be published by New Directions in 1991.

Of "The Ether Dome (An Entertainment)," Grossman writes: "The poem called 'The Ether Dome' is a world-originating (a cosmogonic) poem—therefore, a 'long' poem. Such a poem is always 'An Entertainment' because the world composes itself, the person is healed, in the leisure of the God or the person. A 'long' poem may be a poem of a half-million lines (such as the *Mahabharata*) or twenty thousand lines (such as the *Iliad*) or six hundred lines (such as *The Wasteland*) or seventy-five lines (such as 'Un Coup de dés') or four lines (such as 'Westron Wind') or one word (*Aum*). The shorter the material text, the larger the action. 'The Ether Dome' exfoliates a long moment (a few mortal seconds) of love—a man sees a woman ('Asenath') at a party.

"Composition is explanation, as Gertrude Stein says; and explanation in a poem presents 'the meaning of the world' (the significant relationships of the facts of the world) as the accomplishment of articulate combination, or 'composition' (Poe). In this poem, 'The Ether Dome (An Entertainment),' some of the principles of composition are the reproduction of the material logic of the world (e.g., in Winter the sun goes South); the mediation of antithetical signs (e.g., the Apollo Belvedere and the Egyptian mummy—still to be seen in the 'Ether Dome' of history, Massachusetts General

Hospital, Boston, Massachusetts); the totalization of levels of style (e.g., epic sublime, lyric transcendental subjectivity, Mac-Gonagalian doggerel); the foregrounding of fundamentally 'anti-thetical' practices (e.g., healing/wounding, insight/delusion, sanctity/absurdity, sex/love, etc.); the simultaneous inscription of stories of separate origination, and the otherwise uncommunicating voices they situate. Artistic composition of fundamental terms in poetry is a possible order (probable in the degree the poem is 'good') of the world—constituted, as the 'world' is, of the same fundamental terms.

"The many sentences and lines of 'The Ether Dome (An Enter-tainment)' are designed ('What *does* love intend?') to authorize a single 'kerygmatic' imperative—one valid rule possible to keep, in the light of the compositional exploit of the poem: 'And then, my dear, you must know everything.' "

THOM GUNN was born in England in 1929. Since 1954 he has lived in California, mostly in San Francisco. He teaches one semester a year at the University of California, Berkeley. His last book was *The Passages of Joy* (Farrar, Straus, & Giroux, 1982). His next book, *The Man with Night Sweats*, will appear in 1992.

Of "The Beautician," Gunn writes: "My friend Bob Bair told me this story once, about his mother, who at one time was a hairdresser in Mansfield, Ohio. But he used the word *beautician*, and it seemed to me a necessary part of the story, as was his phrase *not kind*, of the men's treatment of the corpse. I wrote the poem in 1981, half-lost it, and dug it up again to publish it at the end of the decade."

DONALD HALL was born in Connecticut in 1928. He lives in New Hampshire where he makes his living as a freelance writer. In 1990 he published *Anecdotes of Modern Art* with Oxford University Press, and with Ticknor & Fields a book of essays called *Here at Eagle Pond*, and *Old and New Poems*.

Hall writes: "Once I found the five-syllable line for 'Tubes,' it came on rather quickly. I had fiddled with the material for several years without getting anywhere. Then in *The Best American Poetry 1989*, which I edited, I read George Starbuck's comment on his poem, which ended: 'So I stole a form from altogether elsewhere. From Donald Hall as a matter of fact, who suddenly did 5-by syllabics in about 1960, to great effect.' Reading Mr. Starbuck, I had the thought: I haven't tried anything in five-syllable syllabics for thirty years. 'Tubes' found its line and finished itself in a few months, Hall to Starbuck to Hall."

BROOKS HAXTON was born in Greenville, Mississippi, in 1950. His two book-length narrative poems are *The Lay of Eleanor and Irene* (Countryman Press, 1985) and *Dead Reckoning* (Story Line Press, 1989). His two collections of poems are *Dominion* (Knopf, 1985) and *Traveling Company* (Knopf, 1989). A recipient of grants from the Ingram Merrill Foundation, the National Endowment for the Arts, the New York Foundation for the Arts, and the Washington, D.C., Council for the Arts, he has been teaching at Sarah Lawrence College since 1985. He lives with his wife and son in White Plains, New York.

Haxton writes: "A few months before I wrote 'Garden,' I finished nine months' work on a fairy tale in pentameter couplets. The fairy tale was less than five hundred lines, but the writing went very slowly. When that was done, I wrote shorter, more improvisational poems, which tended to be very different from one to the next. Ranging among many kinds of shorter lyrics still appeals to me, and I have kept working this way for the last two years."

DANIEL HOFFMAN was born in New York City in 1923. A former consultant in poetry of the Library of Congress, he is poet in residence at the University of Pennsylvania. *An Armada of Thirty Whales*, the first of his ten books of verse, won the Yale Series of Younger Poets Award in 1954; his most recent volume, *Hang-Gliding from Helicon: New and Selected Poems 1948–1988* (Louisiana State University Press), was given the Paterson Poetry Prize for 1989. He is the author also of *Brotherly Love* (Random House, 1981) and of several books of criticism, including *Poe Poe Poe Poe Poe Poe Poe* (Paragon House, 1990). He has received grants from the Ingram Merrill and Guggenheim foundations and from the American Academy and Institute of Arts and Letters.

JOHN HOLLANDER was born in New York City in 1929. He has published fifteen books of poetry here and abroad, the most recent being *Harp Lake* (Knopf, 1988), and several books of criticism and theory, including *Melodious Guile* (Yale University Press, 1988). Among other awards he has received the Bollingen Prize, the Levinson Prize and, most recently, a MacArthur Fellowship. He is A. Bartlett Giamatti Professor of English at Yale.

Of "The See-Saw," Hollander writes: "This 'mad song' grew out of two germs. The first was the note of Hegel's now preserved in the epigraph, which seemed to me the silliest thing I'd read in months. I'd jotted it down, together with a reminder of the old nursery rhyme 'See-saw,/Margery Daw,/Jack shall have a new master,' etc. The idea of confounding it with an idée fixe of see-sawing itself seemed inevitable. The other was the *dah-di-di-dah* rhythm of the words 'Margery Daw,' which I'd scrawled right under Hegel's note; being that of a sort of sapphic-stanza short line (with the final unstressed syllable missing), it seemed to belong at the end of a stanza of three longer lines. But I started out with it in 'Margery Daw,' and then it wandered crazily through subsequent stanzas, even as the name metamorphosed. I hadn't planned for the speaker to break out into German, but he suddenly did, perhaps because of Hegel, perhpas because I was remembering the voices of German refugee nannies in Central Park playgrounds in my early childhood."

PAUL HOOVER was born in Harrisonburg, Virginia, in 1946. He has been poet-in-residence at Columbia College (Chicago) since 1974. With Maxine Chernoff, he is an editor of the literary magazine *New American Writing*. He is a winner of the General Electric Foundation Award for Younger Writers (1984) and a National Endowment for the Arts fellowship in poetry (1980). His most recent book of poetry is the book-length poem, *The Novel*, published by New Directions in 1990. His four other books include *Idea* (The Figures, 1987) and *Nervous Songs* (L'Epervier Press, 1986). In 1988, Vintage Contemporaries published his novel *Saigon, Illinois*, a chapter of which appeared in *The New Yorker*.

Hoover writes: "Like many of my recent poems, 'Desire' examines the uncertainties of authorship, especially the rift between language and experience. Caught in the trap of received poetic convention ('It is this stale language, closed by the immense pressure of all the men who do not speak it, that he must continue to use'), as well as the terrifying possibility that his is an original discourse that can neither be spoken nor understood by others, the poet struggles to interpret the world as he finds it. Unavoidably *there*, snow falls five inches from his eyes, but it's also the size of a sentence, so that letters of the alphabet, as well as snowflakes, implicitly fall. The friction of metaphor creates light and the momentary appearance of clarity, but inevitably 'the light king fades,' leaving the corpse of poetry on the sofa, like a guest who died mid-celebration. The affectionate poet always desires to embrace objects, 'making distance rare,' but there is also the fear that language, self-sufficient to the point of effeteness, doesn't really care. Containing words and other clutter, the body packed in lime beneath the author's house is probably the poem-as-technique, yet another victim of his egotistical desires. (John Wayne Gacy, Chicago's famous serial murderer of young men, comes to mind.) There is merit in the urge to make the world cohere, but unity lies in scatter as well as in the usual synthesis of two elements that comprises metaphor. Rupture loves difference the way metaphor loves unity in diversity. This is another way of saying that the ideology of deconstruction lies in its *reduction* of language to the monadic ideal of dissemination, or scatter. As intellectual imperialism, it 'comes on like trucks,' aggressively invading a territory.

"Like desire, language seeks to connect with experience. However, there is a variety of strategies with which to connect, the preferred model being 'both/and' rather than 'either/or.' Meanwhile, political events such as the 1989 killings at Beijing's Tiananmen Square present themselves as unavoidably as snow. At the point of the announcement, 'I can touch/you now/in sequences/of light,' the poem argues for a directness and intimacy that is also complex in development. History as a train (active linearity) also *sways* like a train, containing numerous ironies, burnings, and derailments. The shadows of tyrants appear on the train's windows as a flickering rogues' gallery. Because they fear 'accident's practical connotations'—uncertainty and ambiguity—they want to hit poetry on the nose. Among these tyrants I would include poets who want to reduce poetry to only one interpretation, the point at which desire becomes rapacity. The night that is blind with tyrants is obviously opposed to the world of snow and windows. What meaning 'shits on' earlier in the poem is the urge to reduce it to either synthesis or scatter, as meaning changes its character with its context. The context in which the poem was written was the beginning of cold weather following the summer of Tiananmen Square, as it became apparent that the students would be unable to overcome their brutal suppression."

RON HORNING was born in Akron, Ohio, in 1947. He lives and works in Los Angeles. He has published a broadside of prose vignettes, *What Time Must Be Like* (Nimbus Books, 1987). Parts of *The Unexamined Life*, a book of poems written in collaboration with David Lehman, have appeared in *Pequod, Shiny International*, and *Boulevard*.

Horning writes: " 'Second Nature' was the last of eighteen sonnets written in the late spring and early summer of 1990 for a sequence of twenty-one poems that includes a translation of a sonnet by Laforgue and an adaptation of a poem in four quatrains by Nerval. Thanks to Annette, life was simple enough then. Weekdays I woke up at four in the morning to write for three hours before going to my job at a bookshop in West Hollywood. After the bus ride home, I ate, read, and went to sleep early. Weekends I worked on poems all day long. The last line of the poem was the first one I wrote—rather, it was all I had left at the end of one three-hour morning. How I wished I had been able to write more! But I knew already that the line was the end of a poem as well as a beginning, and the following morning I wrote the first thirteen lines in less time, perhaps, than the last line had taken. Then Simon, a year and a half old and ready for anything, pushed open the door with a shout to see what his father was doing."

RICHARD HOWARD was born in Cleveland in 1929, and educated at Columbia University and the Sorbonne. He is the author of nine books of poetry, of which the third, *Untitled Subjects*, was given the Pulitzer Prize in 1970. The translator of some 150 works from the French, he has received the P.E.N. translation medal, the National Book Award (for his complete translation of Baudelaire's *Flowers of Evil*) in 1983, and the Order of Merit from the French government. He is the author of two works of criticism, *Alone with America* (Atheneum, 1970; enlarged edition 1980) and *Preferences* (Viking, 1974). President of American P.E.N. in 1978–79, he is a member of the American Institute of Arts and Letters and was a Guggenheim Fellow in 1966–67.

Of "What Word Did the Greeks Have For It?" Howard writes: "Rarely does the editorial fit come upon me, though on the occasions when it does, some external incident must prod me into such action as words can take. As Elizabeth Bishop once observed, an oracle often speaks to us from the pages of the daily paper, and my Pythia appears to have been the agony columns, appropriately enough."

JOSEPHINE JACOBSEN was born in Coburg, Canada, of American parents in 1908. She served as poetry consultant to the Library of Congress for two terms (1971–73) and for four years on the literature panel of the National Endowment for the Arts (1980–84). In recent years she has received an award in literature from the American Academy and Institute of Arts and Letters (1982), an honorary fellowship from the Academy of American Poets (1986), and the Lenore Marshall Award for her book *The Sisters* (1987). She has had seven appearances in the *O. Henry Prize Stories* anthologies. She lives in Maryland.

Of "The Woods," Jacobsen writes: "I prefer to feel that any poem of mine should speak for itself, since indeed 'there is no dictionary word' to describe its essence. I can say that 'The Woods' uses, first, factual experience, and then the woods as a metaphor for the darkness—mental, physical, emotional—into which human beings move, some emerging changed, some never really emerging; but that leaves unexamined many implications that lie within the privacy between reader and poem."

DONALD JUSTICE was born in Miami, Florida, in 1925. He is on the faculty of the University of Florida. In 1980 he received the Pulitzer Prize for his *Selected Poems* (Atheneum, 1979). His most recent book was *The Sunset Maker* (Atheneum, 1988). He has edited *The Col-*

lected Poems of Weldon Kees (University of Nebraska Press, 1962) and is co-editor of Henri Coulette's *Collected Poems* (University of Arkansas Press, 1990).

Of "Body and Soul," Justice writes: "I would like to live in the big city but can't afford to: This poem comes out of my feeling for the city. I have forgotten what mews it was that Crane so ornamented (I swear that I only this moment noticed the pun on *mews*), but there must have been one, perhaps more. Probably more. As for the title, I must have been thinking of Coleman Hawkins."

VICKIE KARP was born in New York City in 1953. Her poems have appeared in *The New Yorker, The New York Review of Books*, and the 1989 edition of *The Best American Poetry*. In 1988 her documentary film, *Marianne Moore: In Her Own Image*, ran as part of the "Voices and Visions" series on PBS, and her play, *Driving to the Interior*, was staged at the Symphony Space Theatre in New York and at the Annenberg Theatre in Philadelphia.

Of "Elegy," Karp writes: " 'Elegy' is an attempt to hold on to someone I love who died. It is a reconstruction, in language, of the first stages of grief."

ROBERT KELLY was born in New York City in 1935. He is currently Asher B. Edelman Professor of Literature at Bard College, and director of the writing program at the Avery Graduate School of the Arts. The poem in this anthology appears in his forthcoming book, *A Strange Market* (Black Sparrow Press). Recent collections of fiction are *Cat Scratch Fever* (1991) and *Doctor of Silence* (1988), both from McPherson and Co. Recent collections of poems are *The Flowers of Unceasing Coincidence* (Station Hill Press, 1988) and *Not This Island Music* (Black Sparrow, 1987).

Of "A Flower for the New Year," Kelly writes: "In the cold spring of 1987 Mary Goodlett and I were traveling in England and stopped in to see her old friends Kate and Sidney Smith on St. Barnabas Road in Cambridge. All over the dooryard purple clematis flourished in the chill rain, purple as the magic flower that, snatched, sent Persephone to the underworld. A winter or two later I, not much of a knower of flowers, was on my way to see my parents, who lived on Long Island, so I had to pass through densely crowded Penn Station. I found myself trying to remember the name of that flower, now that I was passing through this terrible wintry underworld, thousands of gray-faced homeless people alienated from the busy pink-faced holiday travelers as if they were another species, wingless pigeons, shabbier than rats. And alienated, worse, from one another. That's what hurt, seeing the homeless unconnected even with each other, as if beyond even the wish for common ground. And all I could do was try to remember the name of a flower. The poem tells all this evasion of mine clearly enough. And now Sidney Smith, that old Darwin scholar, who offered us some 1798 Madeira he had just decanted and showed us an unsuspected William Blake engraving in Erasmus Darwin's text, is dead. And my mother and father died a month apart this year. And my dear Mary died in the next New Year, she who tended the poor little clematis that managed even this past summer of 1990 to be alive enough still to fling one exiguous but gorgeous blossom on the gray porch wall.''

JANE KENYON was born in Ann Arbor, Michigan, in 1947. She has received fellowship grants from the National Endowment for the Arts and the New Hamsphire State Council on the Arts. "Let Evening Come" is the title poem of her third book of poetry (Graywolf Press, 1990). She lives and writes in Wilmot, New Hampshire.

Of "Let Evening Come," Kenyon writes: "This poem was virtually given to me at a time when a dear friend was dying of cancer, and I could see nothing but darkness ahead. I struggled with the end a little, but the rest was finished from the beginning.''

KARL KIRCHWEY was born in Boston in 1956 and has lived in the United States, Canada, England, and Switzerland. His poems have appeared in *Antæus, Boulevard, Grand Street, The Nation, The New Republic, The New Yorker, The Paris Review, Prairie Schooner, Southwest Review, The Yale Review*, and elsewhere. His first collection of poems, *A Wandering Island*, was published in the Princeton Series of Contemporary Poets in 1990. He is currently director of the Poetry Center of the 92nd Street YM-YWHA in New York City.

Of "The Diva's First Song," Kirchwey writes: "The incidental details of this poem were supplied by a brief stay some years ago in a London hotel of unaccustomed opulence. I was there with my wife, who is a singer. I was intrigued by the lengths to which luxury goes in order to make one thing look like another, rather than itself. And it occurred to me that the disguise or elimination of self (in any overtly autobiographical sense) is one of the first tasks of art, though paradoxically it often requires a purgatorial act of self-absorption and self-discipline. The way was then clear for me to imagine the diva's voice, resonant in such luxurious trompe l'oeil surroundings, even while she herself is profoundly alone, passing the time, waiting for her evening performance. The figure of the Italian glassblower asserts that he and the diva can breathe life into nearly perfect art; the question that remains is what sacrifices of self or of experience are required to accomplish this. The diva is alone; is she also lonely?

"The poem has as its companion piece 'The Diva's Second Song,' both titles inspired by the late Yeats lyrics of chambermaids and ladies, their wisdom altered by time and experience. In this second poem, the pure self-absorption of the diva begins to dissipate through recollection of a loss she has suffered in the real world, beyond the myriad roles she has truly felt but only temporarily assumed. The door to her hotel suite is opened, and she is no longer alone."

CAROLYN KIZER was born in Spokane, Washington, in 1925. She received the Pulitzer Prize in 1985 for her book *Yin: New Poems* (Boa Editions, 1984). Her subsequent volumes include *The Nearness of You* (Copper Canyon, 1986), which received the Theodore Roethke Prize, and *Carrying Over* (Copper Canyon, 1988), a book of translations from the Chinese, French, Macedonian, and other languages. The Poetry Society of America awarded her its Frost Medal in 1988.

Kizer writes: " 'Marriage Song' was written after studying a Chou dynasty poem translated by both Arthur Waley and Ezra Pound. The original poem seems to be anonymous; therefore, one may readily speculate that it was written by a woman. This may account for the opacity of the translations by both men and the wide difference in their interpretations. It occurred to me that it would be fun to incorporate a pseudo-scholarly commentary on the poem and its translators and interpreters within a poem of my own. I think and hope I have invented a genre! I'd love to quote both Pound and Waley in their entirety—the Pound version being three stanzas long, the Waley five stanzas. One of the few passages on which these poets agree refers to 'tossing and turning,' although in Waley it is the man who tosses and turns, while in Pound it *seems* as if it is the woman!"

KENNETH KOCH was born in Cincinnati, Ohio, in 1925. He lives in New York City and teaches at Columbia University. His most recent books are *One Thousand Avant-Garde Plays* (Knopf, 1988), *Seasons on Earth* (Viking, 1987), *On the Edge* (Viking, 1986), and *Selected Poems* (Random House, 1985). A British (and larger edition) of his *Selected Poems* will be published by Carcanet in 1991. An operatic version of his play, "The Construction of Boston," with music by Scott Wheeler, was produced in Boston in 1989 and 1990. Koch has received grants and awards from the Guggenheim Foundation, the Ingram Merrill Foundation, and the American Academy and Institute of Arts and Letters.

Of "A Time Zone," Koch writes: "The poem is named for Apollinaire's poem 'Zone,' which influenced its line lengths, rhymes, and music and tone in general. Being in New York in the fifties and early sixties with my friends seemed to me then, and seems now at a distance of thirty and more years, exciting, irreplaceable, interesting, and worth writing about. The chronology of 'A Time Zone' is irregular: The poem starts with a production of 'The Construction of Boston' in 1962, then goes back to the fifties, and so on. Everything in the poem, as far as I know, is true."

JOHN KOETHE was born in San Diego in 1945. His books of poetry include *Blue Vents* (Audit/Poetry, 1969), *Domes* (Columbia University Press, 1973), and *The Late Wisconsin Spring* (Princeton University Press, 1984). He has received the Frank O'Hara Award for Poetry, the Bernard F. Conners Award from *The Paris Review*, and a Guggenheim Fellowship for 1987–88. He is professor of philosophy at the University of Wisconsin in Milwaukee.

Koethe writes: " 'Morning in America' was intended to be a political poem that could also be read as a projection of an individual state of mind. Around the time I wrote it I was experimenting with writing poems 'backwards,' beginning with the last line and ending with the first (I had just finished writing a poem a bit over two hundred lines long in this way). One felt as though one were discovering or uncovering a poem that had been there all along, rather than creating it *ex nihilo*—or better, one felt both the passive pleasure of watching an unknown process unfold and the active pleasure of bringing it about."

MARK LEVINE was born in Flushing, New York, in 1965, was raised in Toronto, and received degrees from Brown University and the University of Iowa. His poems have appeared in *The New Yorker, Black Warrior Review, Ploughshares, The Paris Review, Threepenny Review*, and other magazines.

Levine writes: " 'Work Song' was my first published poem, and thus might conveniently serve as a kind of introduction, a provisional statement of intent. Walking home on a bitterly cold night in late 1989, I began to repeat to myself the words 'My name is Henri': In this sense, I suppose the literal and metaphoric occasions for the poem's composition were the same. When one's glasses are fogged, when one's head is concealed in a ridiculous hood and the sidewalks are icy and one can't hear or see the oncoming traffic— at such literal/metaphoric moments of banal experience, the distinctions between 'real' and 'surreal,' 'action' and 'thought,' 'emotion' and 'politics,' 'work' and 'dream' appear deceptive and irrelevant. As they are."

LAURENCE LIEBERMAN was born in Detroit in 1935. He is the author of six collections of poetry, including *The Creole Mephistopheles* (Scribners, 1989; Collier paperback, 1990), *The Mural of Wakeful Sleep* (1985), and *Eros at the World Kite Pageant* (1983), both published by Macmillan. He is the author of two books of criticism, *The Achievement of James Dickey* (Scott, Foresman) and *Unassigned Frequencies: American Poetry in Review* (University of Illinois Press, 1978). His awards include a grant from the National Endowment for the Arts and a Jerome Shestack Prize from *American Poetry Review* (1986). He teaches creative writing at the University of Illinois in Urbana and is the poetry editor of the University of Illinois Press.

Lieberman writes: " 'Dark Songs: Slave House and Synagogue' is the title poem of my next collection. As indicated in other parts of the book, Admiral Rodney launched his attack on Statia mainly to punish the island for secretly providing the thirteen American colonies with food and arms during their Revolutionary War with England. Though the events portrayed in my poem occurred in 1781, the story drew fire from a sequence I've been writing about the U.S.-led invasion of Grenada in 1983.

" 'Dark Songs' is a poem of mourning. When I visited the ruins of the synagogue and slave house, I was struck by the identical thin yellow bricks and other similarities of architecture. The poem's *vision* began when I stood alone at the top of the staircase, oddly intact, between the shattered walls of the synagogue. Grief came upon me so fast, I was sobbing heavily before I knew I'd begun to cry. I wept first for my mother, who had died a few years before, and soon the pain spread to the fate of Statian Jews and blacks and beyond.

"I am deeply indebted to Josser Daniel, the 'oral historian' named in the poem, whose remarkable tales of Statia's past so powerfully evoked for me the spirit of two-hundred-year-old events that they seemed to be happening today."

ELIZABETH MACKLIN was born in Poughkeepsie, New York, in 1952. She works as a copy editor in New York and has been poetry editor of *Wigwag* magazine since its inception in 1988. In 1990 she received an Ingram Merrill award. Her work has appeared in *Lyra, The New Yorker, The Paris Review, Southwest Review*, and other periodicals. A book of her poems is forthcoming from Norton.

Of "At the Classics Teacher's," Macklin writes: "The facts in this poem were picked up over ten years or so, beginning with a classics student's mentioning that *phlox* in Ancient Greek meant 'fire.' The Simone Weil thought is from Weil's essay 'The Iliad, or The Poem of Force' (translated by Mary McCarthy; Pendle Hill, 1956) and from various other places in her work. Hecuba says *oimoi* in Euripides' 'Trojan Women.' (*Oimoi* means 'woe.')

"The poem itself was written in the spring of 1989, a month or two after an incident in Central Park during which a well-off white woman was attacked by a group of teenagers from a poor black neighborhood nearby."

J. D. MCCLATCHY was born in Pennsylvania in 1945 and now lives in New York City. He has taught at Yale, Princeton, UCLA, and other universities, and for many years served as poetry editor of *The Yale Review*. The author of three collections of poems, *Scenes from Another Life* (Braziller, 1981), *Stars Principal* (Macmillan, 1986), and *The Rest of the Way* (Knopf, 1990), he has also written opera libretti, edited several books, and gathered his essays in *White Paper* (Columbia University Press, 1989). His honors include an award from the American Academy and Institute of Arts and Letters, and fellowships from the Guggenheim Foundation and the National Endowment for the Arts.

Of "An Essay on Friendship," McClatchy writes: "I had wanted to take a break from the knotty lyric and write a poem in a more relaxed, discursive style, so I assumed an Augustan model and settled on a French film as my lead-in. Renoir's *Règle du jeu*, always my favorite, is a Mozartian drawing-room tragedy about adultery, about romantic love and practical loyalties. (A few sections of the poem depend on a reader's remembering bits of the film. No one who has seen the film is likely to have forgotten them, and the reader who *hasn't* seen it—well, I envy him that first magical encounter!) The purpose of my own poem is to explore differences between love and friendship, the former viewed as half farce, half soulwork, the latter as compromised, life-saving, and enduring. Throughout, I've wanted to make my points as much by little fictions as by larger generalizations; and my format is rather strict, to inhibit any drift toward merely loose talk."

JAMES MCMANUS was born in the Bronx, New York, in 1951. His poems have appeared in *American Poetry Review, New Directions, TXT* (Paris), *Honest Ulsterman* (Belfast and London), *The Glasgow Herald, Mots de Passe* (Brussels), *TriQuarterly*, and *New American Writing*. He has received prizes and fellowships from the Ford Foundation, Arts International, the Shifting Foundation, and two from the National Endowment for the Arts. His novels include *Out of the Blue* (Crown, 1983), *Chin Music* (Crown, 1985), and *Ghost Waves* (Grove-Weidenfeld, 1988). He teaches at the School of the Art Institute of Chicago.

Of "Smash and Scatteration," McManus writes: "I wrote the poem in the spring of 1989 while listening to the soundtrack of the movie *Performance*, Glenn Gould's version of *The Well-Tempered Clavier*, and Bill Frisell and Vernon Reid's *Smash and Scatteration*; I also was getting divorced after thirteen years of marriage. Whence the poem's formal dimensions, I think. The Tiananmen Square and Q.T. motifs were suggested to me by the photographer Jennifer Arra; the thumbs-forward hands, the 'love of the game' clause, and the phrasing of the final stanza were suggested by Michael Jordan."

JAMES MERRILL was born in New York City in 1926. He received his B.A. from Amherst College in 1947 and published his *First Poems* in 1951 (Knopf). His books have received two National Book awards, the Pulitzer Prize, and the Bollingen Prize. The epic poem begun in *Divine Comedies* (Atheneum, 1976) and extended in two subsequent volumes was published in its entirety as *The Changing Light at Sandover* (Atheneum, 1983), which won the National Book Critics Circle Award. His most recent books are *Late Settings* (Atheneum, 1985) and *The Inner Room* (Knopf, 1988). He divides his time between Stonington, Connecticut, and Key West, Florida.

On four consecutive weekday evenings in May 1990, the Metropolitan Opera in New York City staged the four operas that constitute "The 'Ring' Cycle," thus providing the occasion for James Merrill's poem in this anthology.

SUSAN MITCHELL grew up in New York City and now lives in Boca Raton, Florida, where she teaches at Florida Atlantic University. She is a graduate of Wellesley College and holds a master's degree from Georgetown University. *The Water Inside the Water*, a collection of poems, was published by Wesleyan University Press in 1983. She has been a fellow of the Fine Arts Work Center in Provincetown, Massachusetts, and has received grants from the National Endowment for the Arts and from the state arts councils of Massachusetts, Illinois, Vermont, and this year, Florida. Her essay "Dreaming in Public: A Provincetown Memoir" appeared in *The*

Best American Essays 1988, and her "Sibyls, Shards, and Other Semi-Precious Litter" was awarded the 1990 Terrence Des Pres Prize by *Parnassus: Poetry in Review.* Her work was included in the 1990 edition of *The Best American Poetry.*

Of "Sky of Clouds," Mitchell writes: "The poem came very fast, interrupting a university report I had been working on, but the shift from one kind of thinking to another was surprisingly smooth—easy as changing channels on TV. I've never been able to explain how I know a poem is coming, only that I suddenly feel restless and unable to concentrate on what seconds before I was deeply immersed in. What I felt as I wrote 'Sky of Clouds' was diffuse excitement unrelated to the poem's content; that excitement had to do with the speed at which I was interweaving and swerving. The swerves begin almost immediately, one occurring when the narrator switches point of view to talk about herself, another when she breaks away from the opening anecdote of the dance and rejects the strategy of continuous narrative. 'Sky of Clouds' is one swerve after another all the way to the end. Because of the many split-second decisions I had to make on my narrator's behalf, I felt as if I were steering a motorboat through a waterway filled with cyprus stumps and floating mangroves and at the same time the water-skier hanging on for the ride: I had to be super alert, but I also wanted to luxuriate in the scenery.

"Even if the poem feels more whizzed than written, it nonetheless records my daily fascination with the way the natural world of Florida always seems artificial. Florida comes naturally rouged, so the whole idea of natural versus unnatural doesn't hold up here where the voluptuous strangler fig looks like soft sculpture and the leaf stalks of the pygmy date palm appear as carefully woven as baskets. In its combinations of the natural and the artificial, Florida reminds me of Spenser's Bower of Bliss, but where Spenser found such mixtures insidious, the same commingling makes me want to fashion a language equally hybrid—an androgynous or amphibious language. That's why the word *ferriferous* comes into the poem. *Ferriferous* feels soft and malleable in my mouth—cloudlike. But because it's an unusual word, it also feels made—like those shadows palm fronds cast on walls: a wrought iron, art deco version of the living tree."

GARY MITCHNER was born in Middletown, Ohio, in 1946. He is a professor of English at Sinclair Community College, Dayton, where he directs the annual writers' conference. In addition, he teaches at Wilmington College (where he did his undergraduate work) and has taught at the University of Cincinnati and at Hampshire College in Amherst. He did his graduate work at the University of Michigan and at the University of Cincinnati, where he won the Elliston Poetry Prize. Richard Howard has published his poetry in *The New Republic, Shenandoah*, and the *Western Humanities Review*.

Of "Benedick's Complaints: *Much Ado About Nothing*," Mitchner writes: "This poem is a part of a series that I am writing based upon various stage productions I have seen of Shakespeare's plays; the series began with a poem about Steven Berkoff's *Coriolanus*. This one arose from a production at Cincinnati's Playhouse-in-the-Park, and a companion piece called 'Beatrice's Protests' was written from a Stratford-upon-Avon production I saw last summer when I was taking a Shakespeare course at Cambridge. I have written or am in the process of writing poems from Peter Hall's *Merchant of Venice*, the Kline *Hamlet*, and Mabou Mines' *Lear*. I have published a similar series called 'Shaw Poems' in *Shenandoah*. The end-stopped lines are not typical of these series, but Beatrice and Benedick spoke to me that way. The poems are extreme variations on the cento form (passages from works of the past), since I have attempted only to capture the quality of the diction of the piece."

A. F. MORITZ, born in Niles, Ohio, in 1947, is a 1990–91 Guggenheim Fellow in poetry. His books of poems include *The Tradition* (Princeton University Press, 1986); others have been published in Canada, where he has lived since 1974. He is co-author (with Theresa Moritz) of *The Oxford Literary Guide to Canada* (1987) and *Stephen Leacock: A Biography* (Stoddart, 1985), and has translated books of poems by Ludwig Zeller and Benjamin Peret. From 1986 to 1990 he was assistant professor of English at the University of Toronto. He has received Ingram Merrill and Canada Council fellowships in poetry.

Moritz writes: "I feel it's important for a poem's form to be its main expressive agency and in a sense its only one, the one into which all others are resolved. In 'Protracted Episode' the interior four stanzas record a voice that starts strongly for affirmation and then, succumbing to its own thoughts, reforms its original impulse into a vision of perpetual sameness and defeat. But what it had set out to contradict, what had seemed horror, is now put to itself in beautiful and consoling terms. This is a characteristic movement of human culture I'm often concerned to satirize, without being able to remove myself from it. The two frame stanzas show the effect of the voice on a traveler, analogous himself to the voice, whose journey presumably was meant to reach the same contra- diction of human self-thwarting the voice orginally had proclaimed. The parallel between the two speakers resembles the way in which Dante often represents himself as tending toward the sinners he meets in hell, so that Virgil has to reprimand him; here, obviously, the traveler follows his own will and takes a different course. I think the use of the frame to suggest the form of the poet's and the readers' involvement in what is told comes from my love of 'The Rime of the Ancient Mariner.' Here the frame speaker resem- bles, in a way, the Mariner, but his reaction as listener is opposite to that of the Wedding Guest, as the tale itself is different; he succumbs to a gravity it is hard to resist.''

THYLIAS MOSS was born in Cleveland in 1954. She teaches at Phillips Academy in Andover, Massachusetts. *Pyramid of Bone* (University of Virginia Press, 1989), her second book of poems, was nominated for the National Book Critics Circle Award. She has since published two new collections: *At Redbones* (Cleveland State University Press, 1990) and *Rainbow Remnants in Rock Bottom Ghetto Sky*, which Charles Simic selected for the National Poetry Series (Persea Books, 1991). She has received a poetry fellowship from the National Endowment for the Arts. Her work was included in the 1989 and 1990 editions of *The Best American Poetry*.

Moss writes: "Why 'Lunchcounter Freedom'? Because I wasn't there, in the snack shops and cafeterias of Alabama, Mississippi, et al. And because I wasn't there, I have a kind of advantage over those who can rely on memory; I can reconstruct, reinvent history, perhaps arriving at other truths. 'Lunchcounter Freedom' also reflects the idea that at least part of what is commonly held to be Southern racial tension results from attempts at denying the attraction to, sometimes even preference for, the opposite race."

JOYCE CAROL OATES was born in Lockport, New York, in 1938. She is the Roger S. Berlind Distinguished Professor in the Humanities at Princeton University and has been a recipient of the National Book Award for her novel *them*. Everyone comments on her "productivity" while, for her, the effort of writing, rewriting, re-rewriting a poem like the one included in this anthology is daunting. If only one could know beforehand that such effort will seem, in someone else's eyes, to have been worth it!—what a relief, and an encouragement. Her most recent books are *The Time Traveler*, a book of poems (Dutton, 1989), *Because It Is Bitter, and Because It Is My Heart*, a novel (Dutton, 1990), and *I Lock My Door Upon Myself*, a novella (The Ecco Press, 1990).

Of "Edward Hopper's *Nighthawks*, 1942," Oates writes: "The poem grew out of my long fascination with Hopper and with this painting in particular. Why it is so mesmerizing, I don't know, but others respond to it similarly. The stark lighting, the stiff angularity of the human figures, the dreamlike or nightmarelike atmosphere: all are riveting, and to one in love with storytelling like myself, the temptation to invent a narrative for the interior of the work was very strong. It is especially gratifying that Mark Strand, who has written so beautifully about art—and is, I've heard, doing a book on Hopper—should respond positively to this poem."

BOB PERELMAN was born in Youngstown, Ohio, in 1947. He now lives in Philadelphia where he teaches at the University of Pennsylvania. His books include *Captive Audience* (The Figures, 1988), *Face Value* (Roof, 1988), *The First World* (The Figures, 1986), *To the Reader* (Tuumba, 1984), and *Primer* (This, 1981); he is the editor of *Writing/Talks* (Southern Illinois University Press, 1985).

Perelman writes: " 'Chronic Meanings' was written on hearing that a friend had AIDS; it is an attempt on my part to see what happened to meaning as it was interrupted. If one expects a poem to be more or less narrative, focusing sharply or softly on spots of time, 'Chronic Meanings' might feel evasive. But in fact I was trying to be direct; the sentences came as matter-of-factly from my experience and imagination as I could manage. At the same time I knew I would be writing down only the first five words of each sentence, so there was a great pressure for some sort of concision, though I certainly wasn't after a haiku-like or 'poetic' compression: I wanted to feel what real life, conventional articulation felt like when it was halted in the middle. I did work on (edited) the results to avoid habit and redundancy. As opposed to the classical received sense of poetry outbraving time, 'Chronic Meanings' seems to me to face the other way and to try to register time's evanescence."

ROBERT POLITO was born in Boston in 1951. He was educated at Boston College and Harvard University and has taught literature and film at Wellesley College. He is now assistant director of the graduate program in creative writing at New York University. He has written studies of Byron and James Merrill and is co-editor of *Fireworks: The Lost Writings of Jim Thompson* (Mysterious Press, 1989). His biography of Thompson will be published by Knopf.

Of "Evidence," Polito writes: "When I was in graduate school in the late 1970s the Fogg Museum assembled some police photographs into an exhibition designated *Evidence*. These weren't sensational Weegee/Warhol evocations of death and disaster, but the starker, more enigmatic images developed by investigators in routine pursuit (as Sergeant Friday might say) of a crime or accident. Arriving late to the scene the police photograpers had to intimate the anterior transgression from the surviving detritis: skidmarks leading . . . nowhere; bullet shells, blood on a wall . . . no body. As with many famous 'Dutch Interiors,' a photograph made sense only after the viewer teased an antecedent story from it. Such implied or tacit narratives eventually helped determine the *shape* of the poem, though I carried the title around for more than a decade before I was able to use it.

"While working on 'Evidence' I was reading and beginning to write about the novels of Jim Thompson—hence, perhaps, the italics that disrupt the poem, as lurid hallucination, or as a documentary descent into rock 'n' roll hell, or as a displaced stub of insight. The multiple voices and skidding diction of the poem plot the stresses between what might be called a sophisticated lyric tradition and a sense of the world that is virtually its opposite."

KATHA POLLITT was born in New York City in 1949. She is the author of *Antarctic Traveller* (Knopf, 1982), which won the National Book Critics Circle Award. Her grants and prizes include fellowships from the National Endowment for the Arts and the Guggenheim Foundation, a Peter I. B. Lavan Younger Poets Award, and a Fulbright to Yugoslavia. In 1991 she taught at Barnard College and the Poetry Center of the 92nd Street YM-YWHA. Her book reviews and essays on literary and political subjects have appeared in many publications, including *The Nation*, of which she is a contributing editor.

Of "Night Subway," Pollitt writes: "For years I wanted to write a poem about the subway, but I didn't. And for almost as long, I wanted to make some literary use of Herodotus' wonderful anecdote about Xerxes weeping as he reviewed his troops, but I didn't do that either. Then one day I suddenly put the two clusters of ideas and associations together, and 'Night Subway' practically wrote itself."

SUSAN PROSPERE was born in Oak Ridge, Tennessee, and has lived most of her life in the South. She works as a legal assistant at Vinson and Elkins law firm and as a part-time instructor at the University of Houston. She has received a *Nation*/Discovery Award, a P.E.N. Southwest Houston Discovery Award, and an Ingram Merrill grant. She received a J.D. from Tulane Law School and an M.A. from the University of Houston. Her poems have appeared in *The New Yorker, Antæus, Field, Poetry, The Nation*, and *The American Scholar*. A collection of her poems, *Sub Rosa*, is scheduled for publication by Norton.

Of "Into the Open," Prospere writes: "Because the dramatis personae and the plot were essentially provided by Hans Christian Andersen, I saw my task in writing this poem as one of appropriation rather than transformation. It was with trepidation, a little guilt, and mounting excitement that I stood outside the tale—much as a voyeur might stand outside a window, peering in at an experience that is titillating yet secondary. Clearly, I had to find an entrance, a way to experience the drama firsthand, and ultimately I attempted to achieve this end by marking my own territory— intensifying selected objects, for example, the deer, the ladder, the dark heart of the stove, with metaphoric value—and by assuming various guises (all female)—appearing first as the woman, then as the shepherdess, and finally as the 'I.' It occurs to me in retrospect that the progression is not merely a change in costume but a slow undressing, a movement from secrecy to exposure, from contemplation to action, from caution to risk. In order to avoid closure and the dictates of Andersen's narrative, I chose to end the poem here—with longing, with aspiration for the open, for the final, ultimate act. Nonetheless, as most of us know, the shepherdess, overcome by the enormity of the wide world and weighted by the countervailing gravity of domestic safety, returns with the sweep to her place on the shelf. It is my hope that the shadow life of the fairy tale and of our own fears lends poignancy to the imploring, seductive voice at the end of the poem. It is my sorrow that Death appears at either end of the journey—as the provocative rake smiling down on us from the opening of the chimney or as a familiar, as an oppressive companion sharing our tiny space, swallowing all the air."

JACK ROBERTS was born in Morristown, New Jersey, in 1960. He graduated with a degree in chemistry from the University of Chicago and currently teaches literature and writing at Rutgers University. He is working on a doctorate in English renaissance lyric as well as a first collection of poems, *River Blindness*. In 1989 he cofounded and now directs the Delaware & Raritan Canal Poetry Series.

Of "The New Reforms," Roberts writes: "I've never lived very far from the big cities, and their monuments and railway terminals, their libraries and arenas have always been a source of great fascination for me. I don't know why I'm particularly drawn to these structures; I suppose I'm intrigued by their silences, by the mysteries of their design. Some of this excitement comes through in 'The New Reforms,' though the city in the poem is not one I've visited. What happens toward the end seems to me now, quite unaccountably, as much informed by *The Pilgrim's Progress* and *National*

Geographic as by the 'B' horror flicks of my childhood. I don't know what business I had casting this poem in an unrhymed terza, but I'm not unhappy that the lines fell out this way or that the longer form guided me through some interesting situations and emotions."

DAVID ST. JOHN was born in Fresno, California, in 1949. He is the author of four collections of poetry, *Hush* (1976), *The Shore* (1980), *No Heaven* (1985), all from Houghton Mifflin, and *Terraces of Rain* (Recursos Books, 1991), as well as three limited edition books, *The Olive Grove* (1980), *The Orange Piano* (1987), and *The Unsayable, the Unknowable, and You* (1991). He has received grants and fellowships from the John Simon Guggenheim Memorial Foundation, the National Endowment for the Arts (twice), the Ingram Merrill Foundation, and the Maryland Arts Council. *Hush* was awarded the Great Lakes College Association Prize as the best first book of poetry of 1976; *The Shore* was awarded the James D. Phelan Prize from the San Francisco Foundation. In 1984, he received the Prix de Rome Fellowship in Literature awarded by the American Academy and Institute of Arts and Letters. He is poetry editor of the *Antioch Review* and professor of English at the University of Southern California.

Of "Merlin," St. John writes: "During 1984–85, while living at the American Academy in Rome, I was fortunate enough to get to know the great Italian writer Italo Calvino and his wife, Chichita. Their kindness, warmth, and generosity to me touched me deeply, and my conversations with Italo allowed me to learn about twentieth-century Italian fiction and poetry with a dimension that only he could provide. Italo and Chichita were planning to come to the States in the fall of 1985, where he would give the Norton lectures at Harvard; during one of my last visits in the late spring, Italo showed me the just-completed first lecture, *Lightness*. I left Rome early that summer with the consoling knowledge that I'd be able to see Italo and Chichita just a few months later in Cambridge. Then, a week after my return, sitting in my apartment in Baltimore one day, I was suddenly overcome with a sense of horror and dread. I know it sounds melodramatic, but it happened. I went around the corner to a drugstore and, not really knowing why, bought a copy of the daily *New York Times*; in it was Italo's obituary. It felt as if all the magic in the world, certainly in the world of literature, had quite suddenly been taken away. If our time has had a Magus, it was Italo Calvino."

SHEROD SANTOS was born in Greenville, South Carolina, in 1948, and raised in the South Pacific, France, and various parts of the United States. He has received the Delmore Schwartz Memorial Award, the Oscar Blumenthal Prize from *Poetry* magazine, and grants from the National Endowment for the Arts and from the Guggenheim and Ingram Merrill foundations. He is currently director of the program in writing at the University of Missouri. His two books of poetry are *Accidental Weather* (Doubleday, 1982) and *The Southern Reaches* (Wesleyan University Press, 1989).

Of "Two Poems," Santos writes: "These two poems form the portrait segments of a longer sequence, in alternating sections of verse and prose, which deals with the dissolution of a marriage. Love never ends the way we expect. It's no more imaginable than the way we'll die. And so, at the end, couples enter a phase where language—that boundless potential new lovers feel will carry them into the future—seems not only disempowered but strangely traitorous as well: as though whatever one said turned back on oneself. Perhaps the silence we find them burdened with here suggests that sharp reversal; perhaps it suggests some 'shared' misfortune, the very link their silence mourns. In any case, despite the somewhat elegiac tone I've adopted in these poems, I also hope that taken together the sections compose a kind of homage: to the couple's determined if futile efforts to persist in that state outside of words."

LLOYD SCHWARTZ was born in Brooklyn, New York, in 1941. He teaches at the University of Massachusetts in Boston, where he alternates as director of the creative writing program, and is also classical music editor of the *Boston Phoenix* and classical music critic on *Fresh Air* (National Public Radio). He is the author of *These People* (Wesleyan Poetry Series, 1981), *"That Sense of Constant Readjustment": Elizabeth Bishop's* North & South (Garland, 1987), and co-editor of *Elizabeth Bishop and Her Art* (University of Michigan Press, 1983). He has received a National Endowment for the Arts creative writing fellowship grant for his poetry and three ASCAP–Deems Taylor Awards for his music criticism. *Goodnight, Gracie*, his new book of poems, will be published by the University of Chicago Press in 1992.

Schwartz writes: "I'm not a nature poet. Of course, when Isaiah says 'All flesh is grass,' when George Herbert writes 'we are but flowers that glide,' or when Shakespeare begins Sonnet 73 with 'That time of year thou mayst in me behold / When yellow leaves, or none, or few do hang / Upon those boughs which shake against the cold / Bare ruin'd choirs where late the sweet birds sang,' these archetypal metaphors for the transience and brevity of life (including a writer's writing life) are unutterably stirring. I've also been deeply and mysteriously moved by certain aspects of nature itself, and in the case of the miraculous transformation of green leaves into fall foliage, even obsessed. 'Leaves' makes up a triptych of what Gail Mazur has called 'American sonnets': fourteen-line verse paragraphs—like Robert Lowell's—that offer the writer the shape and 'feel' of a sonnet without encouraging the chunkiness of Shakespearean or Petrarchan rhyme schemes. It seemed an appropriately ambiguous form for what was both a sincere attempt at a traditional nature poem and an ironic, not entirely reluctant 'deconstruction' of one."

ROBYN SELMAN was born in New York City in 1959. She earned an M.F.A. from Sarah Lawrence College in 1984. In 1985 she was awarded an emerging poets prize from The Writer's Community. Her poems have appeared in publications such as *Ploughshares, Conditions*, and *Puerto Del Sol*; her criticism has appeared in *The Village Voice Literary Supplement* and *The Nation*. She lives in Greenwich Village where she directs the Judith's Room Bookstore Emerging Talent Competition.

Selman writes: " 'Past Lives' is one of those good things that can come out of anxiety. I wrote the poem when I was twenty-five, visiting Paris with my lover. I was feeling very displaced and frightened that night—experiencing the kind of fear that causes everything you see to become hyper-real. I was keeping grief locked down inside, feeling guiltily one way while, I imagined, the world and my lover were feeling different. The next day I wrote the poem in one swoop, in the late afternoon, lying on a sofa looking out on an ancient street. I was surrounded by loss and the passage of time; the poem's details soothed me as they conjured people and places I would no longer see. The more in tune with the details I became, the more they gave way to one another. I calmed down; imagination became a voice of perspective to rely on in tough times."

DAVID SHAPIRO was born in Newark, New Jersey, in 1947. He graduated from Columbia College in 1968, studied at Cambridge University on a Kellett Fellowship, and received a doctorate at Columbia in 1973. His books of poetry include *January* (Holt, Rinehart and Winston, 1965); *Poems from Deal* (Dutton, 1969); *A Man Holding an Acoustic Panel* (Dutton, 1971); *The Page Turner* (Liveright, 1973); *Lateness* (Overlook Press, 1977); *To an Idea* (Overlook, 1984); *House (Blown Apart)* (Overlook, 1988), and the forthcoming *After a Lost Original* (Solo Press). He is the author of critical books on John Ashbery, Jim Dine, Jasper Johns, and Piet Mondrian. Currently a tenured art historian at William Paterson College in Wayne, New Jersey, he has taught at Columbia, Princeton, Brooklyn College, and Cooper Union.

Of "The Seasons," Shapiro writes: "Jasper Johns asked to trace my son for a panel of his 'Seasons.' My son was about three and wouldn't sit still during the attempt at tracing his shadow. The painter asked, 'I wonder when a child becomes interested in his shadow.' Later he used an older child, but the image of my son comically crayonning over Jasper Johns's tracing—an attempt at forcing his concentration—remains with me, and my admiration for the whole synoptic painting remains. (I used to paint rabbit-ducks for Jasper and urged him to use the pun in one of his paintings, and one does indeed hang over the child in 'The Seasons,' though I am not sure whether the artist was thinking of Wittgenstein's use, Gombrich's famous commentary, and/or my suggestion, but I wrote a poem about it called 'Realism.') I wrote 'The Seasons' in five parts in part as an homage to this careful master, whose every season has been called autumnal. Because I admire his use of 'recycled' older imagery, I went through unpublished poems searching for 'bits and pieces' of seasonal material. I had once dreamed of sending John Cage a book of my poems in random permutations, and this poem was an attempt to achieve a certain aleatoric music, though my preference for unity in multeity would probably repel the composer. In 'Winter,' a few lines parody Tu Fu in the Hung translations. The man who stops on the highway to observe perspective is Johns himself and comes from an anecdote he recounted. My grandfather was Berele Chagy, one of the 'golden *chazzanim*,' and he died *davvening* if not singing in 1954. I recently found an early interview with him (from the 1930s) eerily headlined: 'I Will Die Singing.' The villanelle is an attempt to mimic Johns's aristocratic ink details 'after' his own painting. I tried to think of a way in which a poem could be a tracing of a few details. In my poem, the villanelle functions as an envoi, not really an independent section. The poem of course must live by itself and not be excused by any morbid dependency on the great, melancholy work that inspired it.''

LAURIE SHECK was born in New York City in 1953. She is the author of two books of poetry, *Io at Night* (Knopf, 1990) and *Amaranth* (University of Georgia Press, 1981). She has been the recipient of fellowships from the Ingram Merrill Foundation and the National Endowment for the Arts, and currently teaches at Rutgers University.

Of "Living Color," Sheck writes: "In her essay on the *Iliad*, Simone Weil wrote of how, under certain circumstances, people are turned, by force and degradation, into 'things.' It was Weil's warning to us. I am interested in the various ways the soul is degraded, violated, debased; in what environments the soul flourishes and in what environments it is treated, as Weil said, as a 'thing' stripped of all complexity and beauty and terror. The odd modern experience of 'watching,' of 'reality' transmitted onto screens so that images appear on them as embodied yet strangely disembodied, close yet oddly distant, catches this freezing of the soul, and its violation, from another angle.''

CHARLES SIMIC was born in Belgrade, Yugoslavia, in 1938, came to the United States at the age of sixteen, went to high school in Oak Park, Illinois, and attended New York University. He received the Pulitzer Prize in 1990 for his thirteenth book of poems, *The World*

Doesn't End. His new collection is titled *The Book of Gods and Devils* (1990). Both books are published by Harcourt Brace Jovanovich. Awarded a MacArthur Fellowship in 1984, he teaches at the University of New Hampshire.

Of "Country Fair," Simic writes: "I witnessed this scene in the mid-1970s at the nearby fair in Deerfield, New Hampshire. What a life, I thought at the time. It's not enough to have six legs, they want you to do tricks, too.

"Then it occurred to me. That's what a poet is: a six-legged dog."

DAVID R. SLAVITT was born in White Plains, New York, in 1935. He went to Yale, took a graduate degree at Columbia, worked at *Newsweek* from 1958 to 1965, and has been on his own, writing, ever since. He has published forty-five books, and the forty-sixth will be *Virgil*, a critical study that Yale University Press will bring out in 1991; the forty-seventh will be *Short Stories Are Not Real Life*, a collection of short fiction to appear in 1991 from Louisiana State University Press; and the forty-eighth will be *Four Plays of Seneca*, which Johns Hopkins University Press will publish late in 1991. "The Wound" appeared in *Eight Longer Poems* (Louisiana State University Press, 1990). He has had a National Endowment for the Arts grant in translation, Pennsylvania Council on the Arts grants in fiction and poetry, and an award from the American Academy and Institute of Arts and Letters.

Of "The Wound," Slavitt writes: "It is difficult to remember now exactly what prompted the thought, but I can recall that I made a connection between the Telephus myth and the processes of psychotherapy, the simplest A-is-like-B sort of assertion. What made that particularly interesting to me was that my daughter had just decided to do a residence in psychiatry. There were other promptings as well. Among these there was the thought I'd already had of a collection of longer poems, pieces of such scale as to defy most magazine editors and, therefore, unfashionable (and, therefore, appealing). Many of the poems in this collection are suites, a form that Robert Penn Warren used often. He was one of my teachers at Yale, so there was a kind of nod in his direction, too— I'd heard he was ill. Most of this, obviously, is gossip, and it may confuse as much as it helps, but I risk it because I am fond enough of the piece to suppose it is relatively clear in its meaning, and a lofty silence, which would be correct, would be pretentious."

CHARLIE SMITH was born in Moultrie, Georgia, in 1947, and attended schools and colleges in Georgia, North Carolina, New Hampshire, and Iowa. He is the author of the poetry books *Red Roads* (Dutton, 1987) and *Indistinguishable from the Darkness* (Norton, 1990). His fiction includes the novels *The Lives of the Dead* (Linden Press/ Simon & Schuster, 1990), *Shine Hawk* (Paris Review Press/Simon & Schuster, 1988), and *Canaan* (Simon & Schuster, 1985) as well as a book of novellas, *Miss Infinity and Her Boys* (Simon & Schuster, 1991). He lives in New York City.

Of "The Woman as Figure," Smith writes: "My poems tend to come from images and sounds that have been so hacked about and put upon that I don't recognize whatever antecedents they might have. A tree on this New York street becomes a tree on a river in south Georgia, in a time and place I haven't experienced, where softly and insistently a man strange to me is leaning down out of leaves to tell a story about carrying a foil-wrapped package of cheese up the crumbling stairs of a Veronese house to his lover. This particular figment expresses in some way my perception of the violence that ambles around behind the scenes spitting and waiting its turn, and the sadness and hopelessness of power, and of any adventure dedicated to explaining and mastering the world—or it doesn't."

ELIZABETH SPIRES was born in Lancaster, Ohio, in 1952 and grew up in nearby Circleville. Her books of poems are *Annonciade* (Viking Penguin, 1989), *Swan's Island* (Holt, Rinehart and Winston, 1985), and *Globe* (Wesleyan, 1981). Currently she lives in Baltimore and is writer-in-residence at Goucher College and an adjunct visiting associate professor in the Writing Seminars at Johns Hopkins. In 1990 she received the Sara Teasdale Poetry Prize from Wellesley College for *Annonciade*. Her work was included in the 1989 and 1990 editions of *The Best American Poetry* and will be included in *New American Poets of the 90s* (David Godine, 1991).

Of "The Haiku Master," Spires writes: "For a long time I associated the writing of 'haiku' (a term I use loosely) with elderly versifiers and antique poetry societies. I myself had been forced to write haiku by a high school English teacher in a dreary 'Introduction to Poetry' course and, as a result, had sidestepped the form for twenty years. But a year or two ago, to my surprise, I found myself writing haiku-like fragments that, when linked together, formed a kind of elliptical narrative (haiku with a plot!). Haiku is taken so seriously by its devotees that I decided to make my poem as self-conscious and self-referential as possible: I incorporated conventional seasonal motifs and used as many 'poetical' images as I could think of (the frog on the lily pad, etc.) as I constructed a dialogue between a haiku master and an overeager student, an impassioned novice prone to outbursts of emotion and sentimentality. If I were to psychoanalyze my unconscious motivation for writing 'The Haiku Master,' I might say now it was a cathartic release from being forced, as the teacher of too many poetry workshops, to be the arbiter of 'good' and 'bad' poetry. The ultimate form that my poem took was certainly influenced by William Heyen's wonderful book *Lord Dragonfly* (Vanguard, 1981), which showed me that the Westernized haiku sequence is still viable and need not be treated as lightly or as tongue-in-cheek as I have done in my poem."

RUTH STONE is a professor in the English department at the State University of New York in Binghamton. She received a Whiting Writer's Award in 1986. Her collection of poems, *Second Hand Coat*, was published by David Godine in 1987. A new book, *Who Is the Widow's Muse*, illustrated by Phoebe Stone, will be published in 1991 by Yellow Moon Press in Cambridge, Massachusetts.

Stone writes: " 'For Eight Women' is a poem of moments of perception in loosely connected couplets. I was thinking of some of the women who have been important in my life. The local background of Norfolk, Virginia, where I was teaching at Old Dominion University, appears in the poem. I personally like the couplet that describes the ocean (and the world) as a little cup of water moving along the galaxy. Thinking of the longing for a language that can bridge the abyss that lies between all things infinitely small, infinitely large, and the dilemma of the divided human being, led me to memories of Canna Maeda, who translated the poetry of Basho while she was at the Bunting Institute at Harvard, along with Shoko Akea, who was there as the first Japanese woman to receive a Fulbright, and Constance Smith, the first director of the Bunting (when it was called the Radcliffe Institute for Independent Study). Also, Alice MacIntyre, who has translated so brilliantly the poems of Paul Verlaine."

PATRICIA STORACE was born in Chicago and grew up in Mobile, Alabama. Her book of poems, *Heredity*, was the winner of the first Barnard New Women Poets Prize and was published by Beacon Press in 1987. Her essays appear in *The New York Review of Books* and other publications. She is poetry editor of *The Paris Review*.

Storace writes: " 'War Movie' started with hearing for the first time a record of songs by a famous singer of the 1940s, Jo Stafford. That pop songs could sustain this level of anxiety and answering heroism was a revelation; this was pop music about love and death. I tried to get something of the same effect in 'War Movie,' to show an ordinary couple at a moment when circumstance changes them both into heroes. It is a theme natural to movies because of how movies represent human physical proportions, and I tried here to find a way to get close-ups of great detail and intensity of emotions instead of bodies."

JAMES TATE was born in Kansas City, Missouri, in 1943. He was awarded the Yale Younger Poets Prize in 1966. His most recent books of poetry are *Constant Defender* (Ecco Press, 1983), *Reckoner* (Wesleyan University Press, 1986), and *Distance from Loved Ones* (Wesleyan/University Press of New England, 1990). He teaches at the University of Massachusetts.

Tate writes: "In Paris I gave a reading a week ago (January 1991). A woman in the audience asked why French poetry at the moment is so bad and why American poetry is so good. I said French poetry has peaked while in America we're starving for it. We need a poet for every Burger King. We're dying for it. We need it more than anybody."

MOLLY TENENBAUM was born in Los Angeles in 1957. She received an M.F.A. from the University of Washington and currently teaches composition at community colleges in the Seattle area. She also plays old-time banjo for local dances. Her poetry has appeared in *Fine Madness, Poet Lore, Poetry Northwest, The Seattle Review*, and other magazines.

Tenenbaum writes: "The first stanza in 'Reminiscence Forward' is adapted from a scene in Les Blank's film *Garlic Is as Good as Ten Mothers*. An Italian man who hid in the hills during the war insists there was nothing to eat then, nothing at all; but as the interviewer presses, the man has to admit that, well, there were a few things to eat after all. When I started to work with that scene, I discovered that when I placed two contradictory statements next to each other, they wouldn't cancel each other out. In fact, each seemed stronger for being immediately opposed. I started playing with varying the weights of the various statements, making them stern in tone or tender in imagery. It seemed that no matter how adamantly I unsaid what I'd said, I still had something left, and the bonds between the statements were always stronger than before. It was impossible to come up with nothing, no matter what I did. Perhaps that's why the man survived. My nickname for this poem is 'The Nothing Poem.' "

DAVID TRINIDAD was born in Los Angeles in 1953. His books include *Monday, Monday* (Cold Calm Press, 1985), *November* (Hanuman Books, 1987), and *Hand Over Heart: Poems 1981–1988* (Amethyst Press, 1991). He currently lives in New York City, where he teaches poetry workshops at the Writer's Voice at the 63rd Street YMCA. He is the poetry editor of *OutWeek* magazine.

Trinidad writes: " 'Reruns' was inspired by Amy Gerstler's many haiku, which I've always liked very much. A while back she encouraged me to try some of my own. I wrote one about Nancy Sinatra's boots and it got a lot of laughs at readings, so I decided to do more. I wrote one about Barbie and one about Marilyn Monroe paper dolls, but neither worked. Then I wrote one about a TV show from my childhood and was off and running. I wrote them everywhere: on napkins at restaurants, on message pads at work, and on the inside of matchbooks as I sat in traffic jams obsessively tapping out syllables on the steering wheel of my car. Some were better than others; I threw a lot away. A few shows just wouldn't fit into the form. (I remember writing at least twenty about *That Girl*, for instance, and failing every time.) Again taking my cue from Amy Gerstler, I aimed at keeping seventeen I liked, one for each syllable in a haiku.

"A lot of people have asked me which show 'Honey in the Flesh' is based on. It's *Honey West* (1965–66), in which Anne Francis (the one with the mole) played a 'girl private eye.' Honey had all sorts of great gadgets (such as a radio transmitter in her makeup compact) and a pet ocelot named Bruce."

CHASE TWICHELL was born in New Haven, Connecticut, in 1950. She has published three books of poetry: *Northern Spy* (1981) and *The Odds* (1986), both with the University of Pittsburgh Press, and *Perdido* (Farrar, Straus & Giroux, 1991). Currently a lecturer in the creative writing program at Princeton, she has also taught at Hampshire College and the University of Alabama. Recent grants include fellowships from the National Endowment for the Arts and the John Simon Guggenheim Memorial Foundation.

Of "Revenge," Twichell writes: "I wrote this poem toward the end of a book with an obsessive subject (*Perdido*). Because it became clear to me early on that each poem was to be part of a larger enterprise, I found myself writing *in reference to* poems that would appear earlier and *in anticipation of* those that would follow it. This was both liberating and intimidating. How could a poem have both hindsight and prescience? The subject was the relation between sex and death. 'Revenge' is meant to illuminate one fulcrum point, where knowledge of mortality tips into an intensification of pleasure in the present moment. Once the connection between the two is made conscious, intimacy with one betrays intimacy with the other."

DEREK WALCOTT was born in Saint Lucia, the West Indies, in 1930. His books of poems include *Another Life* (1973), *The Star-Apple Kingdom* (1979), *The Fortunate Traveller* (1982), *Midsummer* (1984), and *The Arkansas Testament* (1987), all from Farrar, Straus & Giroux. The same publisher has issued four books of his plays; *Dream on Monkey Mountain* won an Obie Award in 1971. *Collected Poems: 1948–1984* received the Los Angeles Times Book Prize for poetry in 1986. "Omeros" is an excerpt from the epic poem of that title, which Farrar, Straus & Giroux published in 1990. The recipient of a MacArthur Fellowship in 1981, Walcott divides his time between Boston, where he teaches at Boston University, and Trinidad.

ROSANNA WARREN was born in Connecticut in 1953. She is at present assistant professor in the University Professors program and in the departments of English and modern foreign languages at Boston University. She is also a contributing editor of *Partisan Review*. She has received a *Nation*/Discovery award, a grant from the Ingram Merrill Foundation, a Guggenheim Fellowship, and an American Council of Learned Societies Fellowship. She has published two books of poems: *Snow Day* (Palaemon Press, 1981) and *Each Leaf Shines Separate* (Norton, 1984). She is the editor of *The Art of Translation: Voices from the Field* (Northeastern University Press, 1989).

Of "Song," Warren writes: "In this poem the alternating line lengths, the off rhymes, the conventional pastoral allusions try to provide a home for the unspeakable. Grief is unoriginal; it is also in each case savagely private and felt to be unique. By invoking poetic conventions of mourning and the community of loss evinced in a small country graveyard, I tried to approach, obliquely, the primitive shock of loss, the primitive and ritual urge toward preservation of the lost."

SUSAN WHEELER was born in Pittsburgh in 1955. A press officer at New York University, she has received the Grolier Prize and the Roberts Award, and her poems have appeared in *O.blēk, Sulfur, New American Writing, Witness, Massachusetts Review, Helicon Nine, Rowohlt Literaturmagazin*, and *The Best American Poetry 1988*.

Wheeler writes: " 'Lasting Influence' was written at a hard time for me, and I needed to be hard on the idea of loss without giving over to it. Any kind of schemed resolution had to get debunked, as did what remains as a cornball notion of rescue. What gave me the most pleasure was the aptness of my favorite two-part nonsense joke as a kid—about a bricklayer, a poodle owner, and a cigar smoker—as each of the losses in the joke turns up in a new guise. It seemed a perfect example of completely prescribed, if wingo, language making over what's otherwise just another grief."

CHARLES WRIGHT was born in Pickwick Dam, Tennessee, in 1935. He lives in Charlottesville, Virginia, and teaches in the English department of the University of Virginia. His most recent book of poems is *The World of the Ten Thousand Things: Poems 1980–1990* (Farrar, Straus & Giroux, 1990). He was co-recipient in 1983 of the National Book Award in poetry for *Country Music/Selected Early Poems* (Wesleyan University Press). In 1988 he published *Halflife* (University of Michigan Press), a book of prose improvisations and interviews, as well as *Zone Journals* (Farrar, Straus & Giroux), a book of poems.

Wright writes: " 'Reading Lao Tzu Again in the New Year' is from the first section of a new manuscript I am working on that has the working title of *Chickamauga*. Many of the poems in the section are tripartite in structure, as is 'Lao Tzu . . . ,' three different ways of looking at the same thing—or the same subject matter said three different ways. Structural formations and transformations are of continuing interest for me, and *Chickamauga* is a field for that interest."

MAGAZINES WHERE THE POEMS
WERE FIRST PUBLISHED

American Poetry Review, eds. Stephen Berg, David Bonanno, and Arthur Vogelsang. 1704 Walnut Street, Philadelphia, Pa. 19103.

Antæus, ed. Daniel Halpern. The Ecco Press, 26 West 17th Street, New York, N.Y. 10011.

The Atlantic Monthly, poetry ed. Peter Davison. 8 Arlington Street, Boston, Mass. 02116.

Boulevard, ed. Richard Burgin. 2400 Chestnut Street, #3301, Philadelphia, Pa. 19103.

Brooklyn Review, eds. Ronna J. Levy and David Trinidad. English Department, Brooklyn College, Brooklyn, N.Y. 11210.

Fine Madness, eds. Sean Bentley, Louis Bergsagel, Christine Deavel, John Malek, and John Marshall. P.O. Box 31138, Seattle, Wash. 98103.

Gargoyle, eds. Richard Peabody and Peggy Pfeiffer. Paycock Press, P.O. Box 30906, Bethesda, Md. 20824.

The Georgia Review, ed. Stanley Lindberg. University of Georgia, Athens, Ga. 30602.

Grand Street, ed. Jean Stein. 135 Central Park West, New York, N.Y. 10023.

Green Mountains Review, poetry ed. Neal Shepard. Johnson State College, Department of English, Johnson, Vt. 05656.

Harvard Magazine, poetry ed. Donald Hall. 7 Ware Street, Cambridge, Mass. 02138.

The Hudson Review, eds. Paula Deitz and Frederick Morgan. 684 Park Avenue, New York, N.Y. 10021.

The Iowa Review, ed. David Hamilton. 308 EPB, University of Iowa, Iowa City, Iowa 52242.

Mudfish, ed. Jill Hoffman. Box Turtle Press/Attitude Art Inc. 184 Franklin Street, New York, N.Y. 10013.

New American Writing, eds. Maxine Chernoff and Paul Hoover. 2920 West Pratt, Chicago, Ill. 60645.

The New Criterion, poetry ed. Robert Richman. 850 Seventh Avenue, New York, N.Y. 10019.

New Letters, ed. James McKinley. 109 Scofield Hall, University of Missouri/Kansas City, 5100 Rockhill Road, Kansas City, Mo. 64110.

The New Republic, poetry ed. Richard Howard. 1220 19th Street, NW, Washington, D.C. 20036.

The New York Review of Books, eds. Barbara Epstein and Robert Silvers. 250 West 57th Street, New York, N.Y. 10107.

The New Yorker, poetry ed. Alice Quinn. 20 West 43rd Street, New York, N.Y. 10036.

O.blēk, eds. Peter Gizzi and Connell McGrath. Box 836, Stockbridge, Mass. 01262.

The Paris Review, poetry ed. Patricia Storace. 541 East 72nd Street, New York, N.Y. 10021.

Partisan Review, poetry ed. Rosanna Warren. Boston University, 141 Bay State Road, Boston, Mass. 02215.

Pequod, ed. Mark Rudman. Department of English, Room 200, New York University, 19 University Place, New York, N.Y. 10003.

Ploughshares, associate poetry ed. Joyce Peseroff; rotating guest editors (including, in 1990, Marilyn Hacker, Rita Dove, and Fred Viebahn). Emerson College, 100 Beacon Street, Boston, Mass. 02116.

Poetry, ed. Joseph Parisi. 60 West Walton Street, Chicago, Ill. 60610.

Provincetown Arts, ed. Christopher Busa. P.O. Box 35, 650 Commercial Street, Provincetown, Mass. 02657.

Sites, ed. Dennis L. Dollens. 446 West 20th Street, New York, N.Y. 10011.

Southwest Review, ed. Willard Spiegelman. 6410 Airline Road, Southern Methodist University, Dallas, Tex. 75275.

Temblor, ed. Leland Hickman. 4624 Cahuenga Blvd., #307, North Hollywood, Calif. 91602.

The Threepenny Review, ed. Wendy Lesser. P.O. Box 9131, Berkeley, Calif. 94709.

Western Humanities Review, poetry ed. Richard Howard. 341 Orson Spenser Hall, University of Utah, Salt Lake City, Utah 84112.

The Yale Review, poetry ed. J. D. McClatchy. P.O. Box 1902A Yale Station, New Haven, Conn. 06520.

ACKNOWLEDGMENTS

Grateful acknowledgment is made to the publications from which the poems in this volume were chosen. Unless specifically noted otherwise, copyright of the poems is held by the individual poets.

Jonathan Aaron: "The Voice from Paxos" appeared in *The New York Review of Books*, August 16, 1990. Reprinted by permission of the poet.

Ai: "Evidence: From a Reporter's Notebook" from *Fate* by Ai. Copyright © 1991 by Ai. Reprinted by permission of Houghton Mifflin Co.

Dick Allen: "Talking with Poets" appeared in *The Hudson Review*. Reprinted by permission of the poet and the editors of *The Hudson Review*.

Julia Alvarez: "Bookmaking" appeared in *Green Mountains Review*. Reprinted by permission of the poet.

John Ash: "Cigarettes" appeared in *Mudfish*. Reprinted by permission of the poet.

John Ashbery: "Of Dreams and Dreaming" appeared in *Grand Street*. Reprinted by permission of the poet.

George Bradley: "Great Stone Face" appeared in *Partisan Review*. Reprinted by permission.

Joseph Brodsky: "In Memory of My Father: Australia" appeared originally in *The New Yorker*, March 5, 1990. Reprinted by permission; copyright © 1990 by Joseph Brodsky.

Gerald Burns: "Double Sonnet for Mickey" appeared in *Temblor*. Reprinted by permission of the poet.

Amy Clampitt: "A Whippoorwill in the Woods" from *Westward* by Amy Clampitt. Copyright © 1990 by Amy Clampitt. Reprinted by permission of the poet and Alfred A. Knopf, Inc. The poem appeared in *Boulevard*.

Marc Cohen: "Blue Lonely Dreams" appeared originally in *The Paris Review*. Reprinted by permission of the poet.

Alfred Corn: "Infernal Regions and the Invisible Girl" appeared